Also by Jean Hewitt:

THE NEW YORK TIMES LARGE TYPE COOKBOOK,
new revised edition
THE NEW YORK TIMES MAIN DISH COOKBOOK
THE NEW YORK TIMES NATURAL FOODS COOKBOOK
THE NEW YORK TIMES HERITAGE COOKBOOK
THE NEW YORK TIMES WEEKEND COOKBOOK
E NEW YORK TIMES SOUTHERN HERITAGE COOKBOOK
NEW YORK TIMES NEW ENGLAND HERITAGE COOKBOOK

Family
Circle

Quick Menu
Cookbook

TH

Family Circle
Quick Menu
Cookbook

JEAN HEWITT

Times
BOOKS

Designed by Beth Tondreau
Illustrations by A. Peschcke

Library of Congress Cataloging in Publication Data

Hewitt, Jean.
    Family circle quick menu cookbook.

    Includes index.
    1. Menus.   2. Cookery.   I. Family circle.
II. Title.   III. Title: Quick menu cookbook.
TX728.H48 1978   641.5′55   77-87826
ISBN 0-8129-0750-7

Contents

75 QUICK AND DELICIOUS MENUS

(Complete with triple-tested recipes, shopping lists, work plans and the approximate time each menu takes to prepare.)

This book is designed to help you when you arrive home exhausted after a day at the office, doing volunteer work or playing two sets of doubles and there's still dinner to fix. By choosing a menu from inside these pages you will find it easy instead of a hassle. Key your choice of menu to the season—the book is divided into four sections to make it easier—and match the amount of time you are willing to spend to the estimated preparation time given for each menu. No two people work at the same speed so times given are approximate. There are menus to serve two, four and six or more to meet all situations and lifestyles.

Use the detailed work plans to eliminate any worry about where to start and how to proceed, and to assure that everything will be ready on time. Shopping a problem? No time to make a list? This book has a market list with each menu. The lists assume that you are cooking in a kitchen stocked with basic supplies, and a description of a well-stocked refrigerator-larder is on page 3. None of the staples are on the market lists. None of the menus are outrageously expensive and the most economical of all are marked.

Once in a while you might be willing to spend some time the night before, or early on the day, for preparation to cut the last minute time in the kitchen to a minimum. Many of the menus in the book call for ten to thirty minutes of work ahead. Look for tips like washing salad greens, spinning dry and storing in plastic bags that can save valuable minutes just prior to the dinner hour. There are alternate suggestions of ways to cope with cooking the main meal of the day as quickly and efficiently as possible without sacrificing good-looking, tasty results. The book concentrates on from-scratch cooking and few highly processed foods are called for.

As you follow the work plans you'll figure out more shortcuts and you should make mental notes of what takes the most time. Maybe repositioning the pans and cooking utensils you use most often will help or washing fruits and vegetables when they are brought from the store. And always choose the best utensil or appliance to do each job most efficiently. Entertaining at home has become a fun, relaxed way to visit with friends and the menu does not have to start with eggs en gelee and go on through interminable courses. Make a pot of Balkan Sausage Ragout to serve with carrot salad and pumpernickel bread and have easy Espresso Parfait Pie for dessert, which is one of the menus in the book, and you'll have happy guests and family. And last, but not least, assign, cajole or expect someone else to pick up and do the dishes after family meals and help after guests leave.

JEAN HEWITT
Westerly, Rhode Island

Family Circle
Quick Menu
Cookbook

BASIC SUPPLIES
FOR A WELL-STOCKED KITCHEN

2 sticks butter or margarine
Parmesan cheese
6 eggs

6 yellow onions
1 bulb garlic

All-purpose unbleached white
  flour
Granulated sugar
Confectioners' sugar
Light brown sugar
Cornstarch
Baking powder
Baking soda
Cream of tartar
Cornmeal
Long-grain rice
Unflavored gelatin

Shortening
Vegetable oil
Olive oil
Honey
Soy sauce
Worcestershire sauce
Tabasco or liquid red pepper
  seasoning
A-1 sauce
Catsup

Cider vinegar
Wine vinegar
Maple syrup

Dijon-style mustard
Mayonnaise
Frozen chopped chives
Canned chicken broth
Canned beef broth
Tomato sauce
Tomato paste

Sesame seeds
Raisins

Salt
Black peppercorns and mill
Seasoned salt
Seasoned pepper
Cayenne pepper
Paprika
Italian seasoning mix
Garlic powder
Garlic salt
Dry mustard
Onion flakes
Parsley flakes
Celery salt
Chili powder
Crushed red peppers
Curry powder
Dried sage

3

Dried thyme
Dried tarragon
Dried mint
Dried marjoram
Dried oregano
Dried basil
Bay leaves
Italian herb mixture
Dried rosemary

Vanilla
Almond extract

Ground nutmeg
Ground ginger
Ground cinnamon
Ground allspice
Ground coriander
Ground cumin
Ground cardamom
Caraway seeds
Cinnamon sticks
Whole cloves

Spring

SOPHISTICATED BUT SWIFT TO FIX

Chicken Livers and Mushrooms
Noodles • Sautéed Zucchini
Radish and Alfalfa Sprout Salad
Pears in Kirsch with Raspberry Puree

TOTAL TIME
About 30 minutes

Chicken livers are among the quickest cooking meats I know. They can be bought in small quantities or saved from whole chickens until you have enough for a meal. This elegant little meal can be put together in 30 minutes.

MARKET LIST

½ pound chicken livers
1 egg
 Parmesan cheese
¼ cup plain yogurt
2 shallots or green onions
½ cup sliced mushrooms
2 small zucchini
 Parsley
1 green onion
1 bag radishes

 Lettuce leaves
½ cup alfalfa sprouts
2 ripe pears
 Lemon
⅓ cup sherry, brandy or chicken broth
⅓ cup Kirsch or Cointreau
1 package (10 ounces) frozen
 raspberries in syrup
¼ pound fine noodles

WORK PLAN

1. Hard cook the egg; chill in ice water.
2. Make the dessert; chill.
3. Cook noodles according to package directions; drain; toss with table-spoon butter.
4. Cook chicken livers. Put on water for zucchini. Cook zucchini.
5. Finish salad; serve.

7

CHICKEN LIVERS AND MUSHROOMS
Makes 2 servings

½ pound chicken livers
3 tablespoons butter or margarine
¼ cup finely chopped shallot or green onion
½ cup sliced mushrooms

Flour
⅓ cup sherry, brandy, or chicken broth
¼ teaspoon crumbled sage
¼ teaspoon salt
⅛ teaspoon pepper

1. Sauté the livers in the butter until browned outside but still pink in the middle. Remove with a slotted spoon to a bowl.
2. Add the shallot and mushrooms and cook 5 minutes. Sprinkle with 1 tablespoon flour; stir in the sherry, brandy or broth.
3. Add sage, salt, pepper and chicken livers. Reheat.

SAUTÉED ZUCCHINI
Makes 2 servings

2 small zucchini, sliced in ¼-inch slices
2 tablespoons butter
¼ teaspoon salt

⅛ teaspoon pepper
2 tablespoons grated Parmesan cheese
2 tablespoons chopped parsley

Cook the zucchini in boiling salted water to cover 5 minutes; drain well and return to pan. Add remaining ingredients and toss.

RADISH AND ALFALFA SPROUT SALAD
Makes 2 servings

1 hard-cooked egg
¼ cup plain yogurt
2 teaspoons finely chopped green onions
1½ cups sliced radishes

⅛ teaspoon salt
Pinch pepper
Lettuce leaves
½ cup alfalfa sprouts

1. Sieve the egg yolk into a small bowl. Stir in the yogurt, finely chopped white of egg, green onions, radishes, salt and pepper.
2. Toss and arrange in lettuce leaves. Top with sprouts.

PEARS IN KIRSCH WITH RASPBERRY PUREE
Makes 2 servings

2 large ripe pears
Lemon juice
⅓ cup Kirsch or Cointreau

1 package (10 ounces) frozen
raspberries in syrup, partially
thawed

Halve, peel and core the pears. Toss in lemon juice, place in bowl with Kirsch or Cointreau, toss to coat, cover and chill, turning once in a while if possible. Puree the raspberries in an electric blender. Serve 2 halves of pear in dessert dish; spoon puree over.

MENU
Serves 2

RED CHECKERED TABLECLOTH SPECIAL

Scallops en Brochette with Vegetables
Rice (see page 137)
Greek Salad
Warm Danish Spice Cookies or Bought Cake
Topped with Ice Cream or Plain Yogurt

TOTAL TIME
45 minutes

Fish is one of the quickest and easiest foods to cook and these colorful skewers of scallops and vegetables are no exception. And there are no leftovers except for the cookies which will freeze well for another meal, lunch boxes or a picnic.

MARKET LIST

½ to ¾ pound fresh or frozen sea
   scallops
8 strips bacon
2 tablespoons feta cheese or blue
   cheese
½ cup sour cream
1 egg
½ pint vanilla ice cream or 1 container
   (8 ounces) plain yogurt

8 mushroom caps
1 large green pepper
3 medium-size tomatoes
1 head Bibb or Boston Lettuce
   Lemon
1 cup chopped dates
½ cup chopped walnuts
8 Greek olives

WORK PLAN

1. Preheat the oven to 350°. Make cookies; bake.
2. Arrange the salads on plates; chill. Make dressing; chill.
3. Prepare brochettes; refrigerate until 15 minutes before serving; cook.
4. 20 minutes before serving, put rice on to cook.

SCALLOPS EN BROCHETTE WITH VEGETABLES
Makes 2 servings

½ to ¾ pound fresh or frozen sea scallops
8 strips bacon, cut in half
8 mushroom caps
1 large green pepper, cored, seeded and cut into eighths
2 medium-size tomatoes, quartered
Oil and vinegar dressing

1. Wrap each scallop in a piece of bacon and thread onto 2 skewers.
2. On 2 more skewers alternate mushroom caps, green pepper pieces and tomato wedges. Brush scallops and vegetables with oil and vinegar dressing.
3. Broil 4 inches from the source of heat, turning all 4 skewers several times and brushing with the dressing until the bacon is crisp and the vegetables are crisp tender.

GREEK SALAD
Makes 2 servings

1 head Bibb or Boston lettuce
1 medium-size tomato cut into wedges
8 Greek olives
2 tablespoons feta cheese
¼ cup olive oil
1 tablespoon lemon juice
⅛ teaspoon salt
Pinch pepper
⅛ teaspoon oregano

Wash and dry lettuce and arrange on 2 plates. Garnish with tomato and olives; sprinkle with the feta cheese. Combine the remaining ingredients; shake or beat to mix and pour over salads just before serving.

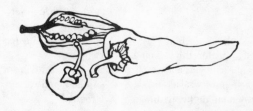

DANISH SPICE COOKIES
Bake at 350° for 30 minutes
Makes about 2 dozen
Chock full of dates and nuts, these cookies can be eaten right away or stored in a cooky jar to mellow.

2 cups sifted all-purpose flour	1 cup firmly packed light brown sugar
½ teaspoon salt	½ cup dairy sour cream
¼ teaspoon baking soda	1 egg
1 teaspoon ground cinnamon	1 teaspoon vanilla
¼ teaspoon ground cloves	1 cup chopped dates
½ cup (1 stick) butter or margarine	½ cup finely chopped walnuts

1. Sift, flour, salt, baking soda, cinnamon and cloves onto wax paper.
2. Melt butter in a medium-size saucepan over moderate heat. Remove from heat. Add sugar and beat with a wooden spoon until combined. Beat in sour cream, egg and vanilla until smooth.
3. Stir in flour mixture until thoroughly combined; stir in dates and nuts. Spread evenly into a greased 15-by-10-by-1-inch pan.
4. Bake in a moderate oven (350°) for 30 minutes or until top springs back when lightly touched with fingertip. Cool in pan on wire rack. Cut into oblongs.

MENU
Serves 2
* *Inexpensive*

CHICKEN STUFFED ON THE OUTSIDE

Fantastic Baked Chicken
Baked Squash • Spinach with Sour Cream
Lettuce Wedges with Blue Cheese Dressing
Cantaloupe with Anisette

TOTAL TIME
About 1¼ hours

The actual fixing time for this menu is close to 30 minutes, half of that at the beginning to get the chicken and squash into the oven and 15 minutes at the end to cook the spinach and fix salad and dessert. Bet you can think of umpteen things to do with the precious moments in between.

MARKET LIST

1 small broiler-fryer (about 2½ pounds), cut up
Parmesan cheese
1 small acorn or butternut squash
1 cantaloupe
½ head iceberg lettuce

1½ cups poultry stuffing mix
Anisette
Bottled blue cheese dressing
1 package (10 ounces) frozen chopped spinach

WORK PLAN

1. Preheat the oven to 350°. Fix chicken and bake. Prepare squash as directed and place in oven with chicken.
2. Scoop melon balls and put in individual serving dishes. Sprinkle with anisette to taste.
3. 10 minutes before chicken and squash are due to be ready cook the spinach.
4. Arrange ¼ head lettuce on two plates and spoon over blue cheese dressing.

FANTASTIC BAKED CHICKEN
Bake at 350° for 1 hour
Makes 2 servings

1½ cups poultry stuffing mix
2 tablespoons grated Parmesan cheese
½ clove garlic, crushed

¼ cup (½ stick) butter or margarine
1 small broiler-fryer (about 2½ pounds), cut up

1. Whirl the stuffing mix in an electric blender; turn onto wax paper and mix with cheese.
2. Add garlic to butter in a small saucepan and melt.
3. Dip chicken pieces in butter and then in crumbs. Place ½ inch apart in a baking dish. Bake in a moderate oven (350°) for 1 hour or until browned and done.

BAKED SQUASH
Bake at 350° for 1 hour
Makes 2 servings

---

1 small acorn or butternut squash
2 tablespoons butter or margarine
½ teaspoon salt

¼ teaspoon freshly ground black pepper
¼ teaspoon ground ginger

1. Halve the squash and remove seeds and fibers. Divide the remaining ingredients between the cavities in the 2 halves.
2. Place in a small baking dish. Pour in ½ cup boiling or hot water into dish. Cover tightly with aluminum foil or cover. Bake in a moderate oven (350°) while chicken is baking for about 1 hour or until tender.

SPINACH WITH SOUR CREAM
Makes 2 servings

1 package (10 ounces) frozen chopped spinach
1 tablespoon butter or margarine
1 small onion, chopped

1 clove garlic, finely chopped
⅓ cup sour cream
⅛ teaspoon nutmeg
½ teaspoon seasoned salt

1. Cook the spinach according to package directions; drain very well squeezing out as much liquid as possible.
2. Meanwhile, melt the butter in a small saucepan and sauté the onion and garlic until tender but not browned. Stir in the sour cream, nutmeg, seasoned salt and spinach. Heat, but do not allow to boil.

MENU
Serves 2

BURGERS WITHOUT BUNS

Nutty Burgers
Scalloped Potatoes
Cauliflower Salad
Fresh Strawberries Topped with Raspberry Yogurt

TOTAL TIME
About 1¼ hours

I have chosen to omit the buns from these walnut-flavored burgers and add scalloped potatoes that bubble away in the oven while you fix the rest of the meal and maybe have time to relax for 15 minutes before serving.

MARKET LIST

1 pound ground round or chuck
1 egg
¼ cup sour cream
1¾ cups milk
1 container raspberry-flavored yogurt
4 green onions
Lettuce leaves
1 pint fresh strawberries

3 medium-size potatoes
Cucumber
Lettuce leaves
1 package (10 ounces) frozen
   cauliflower
¼ cup sliced ripe olives (optional)
¾ cup chopped walnuts

WORK PLAN

1. Prepare the cauliflower salad; chill. Preheat oven to 350° and if you use a toaster oven it will use less energy.
2. Fix scalloped potatoes and start baking.
3. Make hamburger patties and refrigerate until 10 minutes before serving. Wash and hull strawberries and arrange in two dessert dishes.
4. 15 minutes before potatoes have finished cooking, finish salad, cook burgers. Spoon yogurt over berries just before serving.

Note: The cauliflower salad can be made early in the day; allow 15 minutes. Or start 1¼ hours before serving.

NUTTY BURGERS
Makes 2 servings

1 pound ground round or chuck
½ cup plus 1 tablespoon finely
   chopped walnuts
2 tablespoons finely chopped green
   onion
1 egg, lightly beaten

2 tablespoons soy sauce
¼ teaspoon salt
¼ teaspoon pepper
1 tablespoon oil
Cucumber slices
¼ cup sour cream

1. Lightly mix the beef, ½ cup walnuts, green onion, egg, soy sauce, salt and pepper. Shape into 4 patties.
2. Heat oil in skillet and pan-fry burgers over medium heat 4 minutes on each side or until done as you like them, or broil or grill 5 to 6 inches from heat, turning once.
3. Garnish with cucumber slices, a dollop of sour cream and chopped walnuts.

SCALLOPED POTATOES
Bake at 350° for 45 minutes
Makes 2 servings

3 medium-size potatoes, pared and thinly sliced
1¾ cups milk (approximately)
2 tablespoons butter or margarine
2 tablespoons flour
1 teaspoon salt
⅛ teaspoon pepper
2 tablespoons finely chopped onion
1 tablespoon butter

1. Place potatoes and milk in a medium-size saucepan, bring to boiling. Watch so that mixture does not boil over. Reduce heat and simmer 10 minutes. Drain potatoes and measure milk in 2-cup measure (there should be about 1½ cups).
2. Melt the butter, stir in the flour, salt and pepper; cook 1 minute. Remove from heat and stir in 1½ cups reserved milk to make a smooth mixture. Heat, stirring, until mixture bubbles.
3. In a small casserole layer half the potatoes, sprinkle with onion, and pour over half the sauce. Repeat with remaining potatoes and sauce. Dot with butter. Cover and bake 20 minutes. Uncover and bake 20 to 25 minutes longer or until potatoes are tender and lightly browned.

CAULIFLOWER SALAD
Makes 2 servings

1 package (10 ounces) frozen cauliflower
¼ cup oil
1 tablespoon wine vinegar
¼ teaspoon salt
⅛ teaspoon pepper
¼ teaspoon oregano
2 tablespoons chopped red or green onion
¼ cup sliced ripe olives (optional)
Lettuce leaves

1. Cook the cauliflower according to package directions until barely crisp-tender; drain; place in bowl.
2. In a small bowl beat together the oil, vinegar, salt, pepper and oregano. Pour over hot cauliflower; cover and chill.
3. When cold add onion and olives, toss and serve in lettuce cups.

MENU
Serves 4
*Inexpensive

ELEGANT AND CONTINENTAL

Minestrone
Fettuccine with Ham and Peas
Chicory and Romaine Salad
Cherries Jubilee

TOTAL TIME
About 1 hour

Getting away from the meat and potatoes syndrome doesn't necessarily mean going vegetarian but a combination of a little meat with protein-rich dairy foods such as cheese can make a pleasant compromise. Great for the budget too. A spectacular dessert that takes little effort will send everyone away to their next activity with a happy, satisfied feeling.

MARKET LIST

2 cups julienne strips cooked ham
1 cup heavy cream
  Parmesan cheese
½ head chicory
½ head romaine
½ cup green beans
½ pound spinach
1 small Idaho potato
1 medium-size carrot
1 stalk celery
½ cup shredded green cabbage
1 small green pepper
1 orange
1 small zucchini
1 ripe tomato or 1 can (8 ounces)
  tomato sauce
  Creamy garlic dressing or bottled
  dressing of your choice

2 cans (13¾ ounces each) beef broth
1 can (10½ ounces) cannelini beans
¼ cup shell macaroni
1 package (1 pound) fettuccini noodles
  or egg noodles
1 package (10 ounces) frozen green
  peas or chopped broccoli
⅔ cup raspberry or red currant jelly
3 tablespoons cherry-flavored liqueur
  (optional)
3 tablespoons orange-flavored liqueur
  (optional)
1 container (9 ounces) frozen cherries
  with juice
⅓ cup brandy
1 frozen pound cake (about 1 pound)
1 quart vanilla ice cream

WORK PLAN

1. Prepare soup through step 1. Prepare the dessert through step 1.
2. Continue with soup directions. Wash, drain, chill salad ingredients.
3. Make the sauce for the dessert which can be flamed ahead or flamed at the table just before serving.
4. Cook the noodles for the main dish and proceed as directed in the recipe.

MINESTRONE
Makes 4 servings

2 cans (13¾ ounces each) beef broth (3½ cups)
1 can (10½ ounces) cannelini beans
1 small Idaho potato, pared and diced (about ¾ cup)
1 medium-size carrot, pared and sliced (½ cup)
1 stalk celery, sliced (¾ cup)
½ cup shredded green cabbage (⅛ medium-size head)
1 small onion, chopped (¼ cup)
1 clove garlic, minced
¼ cup chopped green pepper

1 tablespoon vegetable oil
2 small zucchini, cubed (1 cup)
½ cup green beans, sliced into 2-inch lengths
¼ pound spinach, chopped (1 cup)
1 ripe tomato, chopped or half an 8-ounce can tomato sauce
¼ cup small shell macaroni
¼ teaspoon leaf oregano, rosemary or basil, crumbled
½ teaspoon salt
¼ teaspoon pepper
Grated Parmesan cheese

1. Bring beef broth to boiling in a large kettle or Dutch oven. Add cannelini beans, potato, carrot, celery and cabbage. Lower heat; simmer 15 minutes.
2. Sauté onion, garlic and green pepper in the oil in a small skillet until soft; add to kettle. Continue cooking for 15 minutes; add zucchini, green beans, spinach, tomato and macaroni. Turn up heat and cook for 20 minutes longer. Add herb of your choice, salt and pepper. Serve with Parmesan cheese to sprinkle over top.

FETTUCCINE WITH HAM AND PEAS
Makes 4 servings
Ham, peas and Parmesan cheese enhance the creamy noodles in this dish.

1 package (1 pound) fettucine or egg
  noodles
6 tablespoons butter or margarine
1 small onion, chopped (¼ cup)
2 cups julienne-cut cooked ham
1 package (10 ounces) frozen green
  peas or chopped broccoli, partially
  thawed

2 tablespoons flour
1 cup heavy cream
  Salt
  Pepper
½ cup grated Parmesan cheese

1. Cook fettucine, following label directions, just until barely tender.
2. While pasta is cooking, heat butter in a large skillet; sauté onion in butter until tender. Stir in ham and vegetables. Stir in flour; cook 3 minutes or until vegetables are tender but crisp. Stir in cream gradually. Bring to boiling. Taste; add salt and pepper, if needed.
3. Drain pasta; return to pan. Pour hot sauce over the fettucine. Sprinkle with cheese. Toss and serve immediately.

CHERRIES JUBILEE
Makes 4 to 6 servings
A classic and fabulous dessert, it's quick and easy because all the main ingredients are ready in the freezer.

⅔ cup raspberry or red currant jelly
3 tablespoons cherry-flavored liqueur
  (optional)
3 tablespoons orange-flavored liqueur
  (optional)
1 container (9 ounces) frozen cherries
  with juice slightly thawed

1 3-inch-piece orange rind (optional)
1 tablespoon cornstarch
2 tablespoons water
⅓ cup brandy
1 frozen pound cake (about 1 pound)
1 quart vanilla ice cream

1. Beat jelly, cherry liqueur and orange liqueur in a medium-size bowl with a wire whip. Add frozen cherries with juice and orange rind. Cover; let stand 1 hour at room temperature.
2. Combine the cornstarch with the water in a cup.
3. Pour cherry mixture into a medium-size skillet; stir in cornstarch mixture. Heat just until mixture bubbles and thickens slightly. In another saucepan, warm brandy. Pour brandy over the warm fruit mixture and ignite.
4. To serve: Serve the sauce over pound cake slices topped with ice cream.

MENU
Serves 4
Inexpensive

A TASTY CULTURE MIX

Walnut Chicken with Broccoli
Rice (see page 137) • Sliced Onion and Cucumber Salad
Honeyed Orange Chiffon Pie or Banana Split

TOTAL TIME
30 minutes ahead for chiffon pie, plus 30 minutes before serving

Main dishes with an oriental influence go together fast but they do not always have to be a part of an authentic Chinese or Japanese menu. In this instance I'm suggesting a crunchy Western-style salad and a light fruit-based dessert instead of umpteen courses and fortune cookies.

MARKET LIST

2 whole chicken breasts, skinned and boned or 1 pound boneless chicken breasts
5 eggs
¾ cup milk
½ cup heavy cream
½ bunch broccoli (1 pound)
½ bunch green onions
Fresh ginger
1 large sweet onion
3 cucumbers

1 cup walnut halves or pieces
Dry sherry
Bottled Italian dressing
12 2½-inch oatmeal cookies
2 tablespoons wheat germ (optional)
1 envelope unflavored gelatin
Honey
1 can (6 ounces) frozen orange juice concentrate
Rice

WORK PLAN

1. Night before or early on the day make the Honeyed Orange Chiffon Pie; chill.
2. 30 minutes before serving, put the rice on to cook. Prepare the salad; chill.
3. Assemble the ingredients for the Walnut Chicken; cook.

WALNUT CHICKEN WITH BROCCOLI
Makes 4 servings

2 whole chicken breasts, skinned and
boned or 1 pound boneless chicken
breasts
1 egg white
1 tablespoon cornstarch
½ teaspoon salt
½ teaspoon sugar
½ bunch broccoli (1 pound)
½ bunch green onions

8 tablespoons vegetable oil
¼ cup chicken broth or water
1 cup walnut halves or pieces
2 cloves garlic, crushed
3 slices fresh ginger or ¼ teaspoon
ground ginger
1 tablespoon soy sauce
1 tablespoon dry sherry

1. Cut chicken into 1-inch cubes. Place in bowl; add egg white, corn-starch, salt and sugar; toss until mixed.
2. Pare off tough outer layer of broccoli stalks; cut each stalk crosswise in half. Separate top half into flowerettes; cut lower half into ½-inch strips. Cut green onions into 1-inch lengths.
3. Heat large deep skillet, Dutch oven or wok over high heat. Add 2 ta-blespoons of the oil; swirl to coat bottom and side. Add broccoli and onions; stir-fry with slotted spoon until coated with oil. Add broth or water; cover; cook 2 minutes or until broccoli is tender-crisp. Remove to medium-size bowl.
4. Reheat pan. Add remaining oil. Add walnuts; stir-fry until lightly browned; remove to paper toweling to drain. Remove all but about 2 tablespoons oil from pan. Add garlic and ginger; fry until browned to flavor the oil and then discard. Add chicken; stir-fry until golden brown. Stir in vegetables, soy sauce and sherry. Taste for salt; add if needed. Spoon mixture onto warm platter; sprinkle with walnuts. Serve with hot fluffy rice, if you wish.

SLICED ONION AND CUCUMBER SALAD
Makes 4 servings

1 large sweet onion, peeled and thinly
sliced and separated into rings
3 cucumbers, peeled, halved, seeded
and cut into ¼-inch slices

¼ teaspoon salt
⅛ teaspoon pepper
Bottled Italian dressing

Place onion rings and cucumber slices in a bowl. Sprinkle with salt and pepper. Sprinkle with Italian dressing, toss and refrigerate for short time.

HONEYED ORANGE CHIFFON PIE
Makes one 9-inch pie

10 to 12 (2½-inch) oatmeal cookies
4 tablespoons (½ stick) butter or
  margarine
2 tablespoons wheat germ (optional)
1 envelope unflavored gelatin
½ cup sugar

4 eggs, separated
2 tablespoons honey
¾ cup milk
1 can (6 ounces) frozen orange juice
  concentrate
½ cup heavy cream, whipped

1. Crush cookies in a plastic bag with rolling pin (see note). You will have about 1¼ cups. Melt butter in medium-size heavy skillet; stir in cooky crumbs and wheat germ; stir over medium heat 1 minute. Press crumb mixture against side and bottom of a 9-inch pie plate. Chill while preparing filling.
2. Mix gelatin and ¼ cup of the sugar in medium-size saucepan; add egg yolks and honey; beat with a wooden spoon until well blended; gradually stir in milk.
3. Cook, stirring constantly, over medium heat 8 to 10 minutes or until gelatin is completely dissolved and mixture is slightly thickened and coats a spoon. Remove from heat. Stir in orange juice concentrate. Place pan in bowl of ice water to speed setting; chill, stirring often, until mixture starts to thicken and mounds when spooned.
4. While orange mixture chills, beat egg whites in medium-size bowl until foamy white; gradually beat in remaining ¼ cup sugar until meringue stands in soft peaks.
5. Fold whipped cream, then meringue, into gelatin mixture until no streaks of white remain. Spoon into chilled pie crust mounding high. Chill 4 hours or until firm.

Note: Cookies may be whirled in blender, but the crumbs will be much finer and the crust different in texture.

MENU
Serves 4

A COLD COLLATION

Asparagus Appetizer
Shrimp and Vegetable Medley • *Cold Rice Salad*
Whole Grain Muffins
Easy Orange Freeze or Orange Sherbet

TOTAL TIME
About 25 minutes ahead plus 35 minutes before serving

Surprises are always fun and here's a menu that offers the first spears of tender asparagus in a hot appetizer to be followed by a chilled main course counterbalanced with muffins hot from the oven. If you plan your time it all goes together with no effort.

MARKET LIST

1½ pounds cooked fresh shrimp or 1
    pound frozen cooked shrimp
 1 cup milk
1½ pounds asparagus
    Lettuce
    Parsley
 2 tiny white onions
¼ cauliflower or 1 10-ounce package
    frozen cauliflower
 2 large carrots
 2 green peppers or 1 green pepper
    and 1 red pepper

½ to 1 pound small mushrooms
 1 bunch green onions
 3 large juice oranges
 2 lemons
 1 stalk celery
 2 cups whole wheat flour
 1 cup whole bran cereal
¼ cup instant nonfat dry milk solids
    Honey
 2 cups cooked long-grain rice
¼ cup sliced ripe olives
    Dijon-style mustard

WORK PLAN

1. Night before or early in the day cook the rice for the salad. Cook shrimp and vegetables and put in marinade; chill. Fix orange dessert; freeze.
2. 35 minutes before serving finish rice salad; chill.
3. Preheat oven to 400°. Start preparing asparagus appetizer.
4. Make and bake muffins. Beat orange freeze and put back in freezer.

ASPARAGUS APPETIZER
Makes 4 servings
Tender green spears over a bed of shredded lettuce.

1½ pounds fresh asparagus
1½ tablespoons butter or margarine
 2 cups shredded lettuce
 3 sprigs parsley
1½ teaspoons sugar
 ¾ teaspoon salt

2 tiny white onions, sliced and
 separated into rings
½ teaspoon flour
1½ teaspoons butter or margarine,
 softened

1. Pare asparagus stalks thinly with a vegetable parer. Wash stalks well. Break off tough ends. Cut spears into 3- or 4-inch lengths.
2. Melt 1½ tablespoons butter in large skillet. Add lettuce, parsley, sugar and salt. Arrange asparagus on top, keeping stalks parallel to each other. Top with onion rings. Bring to boiling; lower heat; cover. Simmer 10 minutes or until asparagus is just tender. Discard parsley.
3. Blend flour and butter to a paste; add to liquid in bottom of pan. Cook until sauce is thickened, stirring carefully so that asparagus is not tossed. Lift lettuce, then asparagus and onion rings with tongs to small serving plates. Spoon pan juices on top.

SHRIMP AND VEGETABLE MEDLEY
Makes 4 servings

 2 cups cauliflowerettes or 1 package
  (10 ounces) frozen cauliflower
 2 large carrots, sliced ½-inch thick
1½ pounds cooked fresh shrimp,
  peeled and deveined, with tails left
  on or 1 pound frozen cooked,
  peeled and deveined shrimp
 1 green pepper, cut in 1-inch pieces
 ½ to 1 pound small mushrooms
 4 to 6 green onions, cut in 1-inch
  pieces

¼ cup lemon juice
⅓ cup cider or white wine vinegar
 2 teaspoons Dijon-style mustard
 2 teaspoons sugar
 1 teaspoon salt
 ⅛ teaspoon cayenne pepper
 2 tablespoons finely chopped parsley
 ½ cup olive or vegetable oil
  Lettuce leaves

1. Parboil cauliflowerettes and carrot slices in boiling salted water 5 minutes; drain if using frozen cauliflower; cook according to package directions and undercook slightly. Combine with shrimp, green pepper, mushrooms and onions in a large bowl.
2. Combine lemon juice, vinegar, mustard, sugar, salt, cayenne, parsley and oil in a jar with tight-fitting lid; cover; shake to mix well.
3. Pour marinade over shrimp and vegetables; toss to coat well. Cover; refrigerate several hours or overnight, tossing occasionally.
4. To serve, lift shrimp and vegetables out of marinade, arrange on lettuce-lined plates. Garnish with cherry tomatoes, if you wish.

RICE SALAD
Makes 4 servings

---

2 cups cooked long grain rice, chilled
¼ cup chopped green onion
1 small green or red sweet pepper, diced
¼ cup diced celery
¼ cup sliced ripe olives, drained

¼ cup oil
1½ tablespoons wine vinegar
½ teaspoon Dijon-style mustard
Salt and freshly ground black pepper to taste

In a small bowl combine the rice, green onion, pepper, celery and olives. Beat the oil with the vinegar and mustard and pour over rice mixture. Toss well, season to taste with salt and pepper and chill.

WHOLE GRAIN MUFFINS
Bake at 400° for 12 minutes
Makes about 1½ dozen muffins

---

2 cups whole wheat flour
1 cup whole bran cereal
¼ cup instant nonfat dry milk
3 tablespoons baking powder

¼ teaspoon salt
1 cup milk
⅓ cup honey
¼ cup vegetable oil

1. Combine flour, bran, dry milk, baking powder and salt in a large bowl; make a well in center of mixture.
2. Combine milk, honey and oil in a 2-cup measure; pour into well; mix just until dry ingredients are moistened.
3. Fill well-greased 2½-inch muffin-pan ⅔ full.
4. Bake in a hot oven (400°) for 12 minutes or until lightly browned. Remove to wire rack and turn out to cool.

Note: Leftover muffins freeze well.

EASY ORANGE FREEZE
Makes 4 to 6 servings
Kids and adults will love this orange-flavored ice for a snack or dessert.

3 cups water	2 cups fresh orange juice
2 cups sugar	¼ cup fresh lemon juice
1 tablespoon grated orange rind	

1. Combine water and sugar in a heavy saucepan. Bring to boiling; cover; simmer 5 to 8 minutes. Remove from heat; cool.
2. Grate 1 tablespoon rind from the oranges before squeezing; reserve. Stir orange and lemon juices and grated orange rind into sugar mixture; mix thoroughly; pour into a 9-by-9-by-2-inch pan. Place in freezer until frozen to a mush, about 5 hours. Serve as is, or turn mixture into a large mixing bowl. Beat until almost smooth. Return to pan and freeze until almost solid. (This makes a smoother mixture.) Serve in individual sherbet glasses. Garnish with additional orange sections rolled in toasted coconut, if you wish.

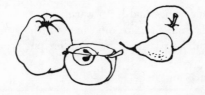

MENU
Serves 4

SOPHISTICATED FINISH FOR LEFTOVERS

Ham Croquettes with Mornay Sauce
Sweet and Sour Brussels Sprouts
Hot Biscuits • Red Cabbage Slaw
Bananas Baked with Pineapple and Honey

TOTAL TIME
About 15 minutes ahead plus 1 hour before serving

Croquettes are a great way to use up all the scraps of ham that cling to the bone and I prefer them this way rather than in ham salad. The Mornay sauce and sweet and sour sauce on the Brussels sprouts are two rich dishes so I like to add plain baking powder biscuits for contrast. Quickest and easiest way is to use refrigerated dough or a biscuit mix.

MARKET LIST

2½ cups ground or minced cooked ham
¼ pound thinly sliced bacon
2½ cups milk
 1 egg
¼ cup plain yogurt or sour cream
¼ cup grated Parmesan cheese
1 rib celery
1 pint Brussels sprouts or 1 package
 (10 ounces) frozen
½ head red cabbage
1 small apple

4 small, firm ripe bananas
Lemon
1 can (8 ounces) crushed pineapple in
 pineapple juice
Honey
Cornstarch
¼ cup raisins
Horseradish
Packaged bread crumbs
Oil for frying
Refrigerated biscuits

WORK PLAN

1. The night before or early on the day make the ham croquette mixture through step 2; chill.
2. About 1 hour before serving make the croquettes; coat and allow to dry.
3. Prepare the Mornay sauce and keep warm.
4. Prepare the salad; chill. Prepare the sauce for the sprouts. Start frying the croquettes and keep warm. In between put sprouts on to cook. Bake biscuits.
5. Prepare the bananas and bake.

HAM CROQUETTES WITH MORNAY SAUCE
Makes 12 croquettes (4 servings)
Crisp and golden on the outside, moist and savory inside, and a delightful way to use bits of ham. Serve with a rich cheese sauce.

3 tablespoons butter or margarine
2 tablespoons finely chopped celery
2 tablespoons finely chopped onion
⅓ cup flour
1 cup milk
2½ cups finely ground or minced
 cooked ham
 Salt

Dash liquid hot pepper seasoning
¼ cup flour
½ cup packaged bread crumbs
1 egg
1 tablespoon water
 Vegetable oil for frying
 Mornay sauce (recipe follows)

1. Melt butter in a medium-size skillet; sauté celery and onion until tender. Stir in flour, cook 1 minute.
2. Remove from heat; gradually stir in milk until mixture is blended. Cook over low heat stirring constantly until thick and bubbly; remove from heat. Stir in ham. Taste, add salt and hot pepper seasoning if needed. Spread evenly in same pan; cover. Chill until cold, preferably overnight.
3. Divide ham mixture into 12 equal portions; form each to make a cone or cylinder shape. Place flour and crumbs on separate pieces of wax paper. Beat egg and water in a bowl.
4. Roll each croquette in flour, coat evenly with egg and roll in crumbs. Place each finished croquette on wax paper. Let dry 15 to 30 minutes or refrigerate until ready to cook.
5. Meanwhile, prepare Mornay sauce.
6. To cook croquettes: Heat 1 inch oil in large saucepan to 375°. Fry croquettes, 2 or 3 at a time, turning frequently with slotted spoon until golden brown on all sides. Drain on paper toweling. Keep warm while cooking rest. Serve with Mornay sauce.

MORNAY SAUCE
Makes about 1½ cups

---

3 tablespoons butter or margarine	Dash cayenne
3 tablespoons flour	1½ cups milk
¼ teaspoon salt	¼ cup grated Parmesan cheese

Melt butter in a medium-size saucepan. Stir in flour, salt and cayenne. Cook 1 minute. Remove from heat; gradually stir in milk until mixture is smooth. Cook over low heat, stirring constantly, until thickened and bubbly. Stir in cheese.

SWEET AND SOUR BRUSSELS SPROUTS
Makes 4 servings
Sweet and sour and crunchy with bacon bits, this dressing makes Brussels sprouts a favorite with everyone.

---

1 pint Brussels sprouts or 1 package (10 ounces) frozen Brussels sprouts	1 teaspoon granulated or maple sugar
¼ pound thinly sliced bacon	¼ teaspoon salt
2 teaspoons cider vinegar	⅛ teaspoon pepper

1. Trim stem ends and outer leaves from Brussels sprouts; cut a cross in stem with the tip of a small knife. Soak in cold water 15 minutes; drain.
2. Cook in boiling salted water to cover for 10 minutes or until tender; drain.
3. Meanwhile, sauté bacon until crisp in large skillet; remove, drain on paper toweling, then crumble. Pour drippings from skillet; measure approximately 5 tablespoons back into skillet; add vinegar, sugar, salt and pepper. Add Brussels sprouts; toss to coat and heat through. Sprinkle with reserved crumbled bacon.

RED CABBAGE SLAW
Makes 4 servings

½ head red cabbage, finely shredded
¾ cup grated fresh apple
¼ cup raisins
2 teaspoons horseradish

¼ teaspoon salt
¼ cup mayonnaise
¼ cup plain yogurt or sour cream

In a small bowl mix cabbage, apple and raisins. Combine the horseradish, plain yogurt and mayonnaise and stir into cabbage mixture. Chill.

BANANAS BAKED WITH PINEAPPLE AND HONEY
Bake at 375° for 20 minutes
Makes 4 servings

4 small firm-ripe bananas
1 can (8 ounces) crushed pineapple in
   pineapple juice
3 tablespoons honey

1 tablespoon lemon juice
1½ teaspoons cornstarch
1½ tablespoons butter or margarine

1. Peel bananas and place in single layer in baking dish just large enough to hold them.
2. Combine pineapple with juice, honey, lemon juice and cornstarch in a bowl; pour over bananas. Dot with butter.
3. Bake in a moderate oven (375°) for 20 minutes or just until bananas are softened.

MENU
Serves 4

FOR A CELEBRATION

Chicken Breasts in Champagne Sauce (with rice)
Baked Asparagus • Kiwi and Papaya Salad
Rhubarb and Raspberry Soufflé

TOTAL TIME
About 25 minutes ahead, plus about 45 minutes before serving

A festive occasion calls for a special menu and the mention of champagne makes a party out of any meal. If you can swing it serve champagne as an aperitif or with the meal and you will have an instant celebration. Enjoy the bonuses of spring such as fresh asparagus and rhubarb or use the frozen kind if you have to. Egg yolks are used in the main dish and whites in the dessert.

MARKET LIST

2 whole chicken breasts (2 to 2½ pounds)
4 eggs
⅓ cup grated Parmesan cheese
½ cup heavy cream
1½ pounds fresh asparagus or 1 package (10 ounces) frozen asparagus
Lemon
2 ripe kiwi fruit
2 ripe papayas
4 cups shredded lettuce
½ pound fresh rhubarb or half of a 1-pound package frozen rhubarb

½ cup chicken broth
1 package (6 ounces) long-grain and wild rice mix
Bottled or homemade salad dressing for fruit salad
Cornstarch
3 tablespoons orange-flavored liqueur or juice
1 envelope unflavored gelatin
1 package (10 ounces) frozen raspberries
1½ cups dry champagne or dry white wine

WORK PLAN

1. Night before, or early on the day, make the rhubarb and raspberry dessert; chill.
2. 45 minutes before serving start browning the chicken. In between turning the chicken prepare the fruits for the salad; chill.
3. Cook the asparagus. Add the other ingredients to the chicken as in step 2; cover and simmer.
4. Preheat oven to 400°. Start the rice mix cooking according to package directions.

5. Arrange asparagus in baking dish, drizzle over butter, lemon juice and cheese and bake.
6. Continue with chicken recipe after chicken is done and removed from skillet.
7. Toss salad. Remove collar from soufflé just before serving.

CHICKEN BREASTS IN CHAMPAGNE SAUCE
Makes 4 servings

2 whole chicken breasts, split (2 to 2½ pounds)
3 tablespoons butter or margarine
1 teaspoon salt
¼ teaspoon pepper
½ teaspoon leaf thyme, crumbled
½ cup chicken broth
1½ cups dry champagne or dry white wine
2 tablespoons flour
2 egg yolks
1 package (6 ounces) long-grain and wild rice mix, cooked following label directions

1. Brown chicken breasts in butter in a large skillet until golden brown, turning often (about 20 minutes).
2. Add salt, pepper, thyme, broth and 1¼ cups of the champagne to pan drippings in skillet. Bring to boiling; lower heat; cover. Simmer 20 minutes or until chicken is tender; remove chicken and keep warm.
3. Stir flour into remaining ¼ cup of champagne; stir mixture into liquid in skillet. Cook, stirring constantly, until mixture is thickened and bubbly.
4. Beat egg yolks in a small bowl; add about ½ cup of the hot sauce; stir back into skillet. Heat thoroughly, but do not boil.
5. To serve: Arrange chicken breasts on platter with hot rice; spoon a little sauce over each piece of chicken. Garnish with watercress and green grapes, if you wish.

BAKED ASPARAGUS
Bake at 400° for 10 minutes
Makes 4 servings

1½ pounds fresh asparagus or 1 package (10 ounces) frozen asparagus
⅓ cup melted butter
1 tablespoon lemon juice
⅓ cup grated Parmesan cheese

1. Cook the asparagus until firm-tender; drain well and place in a shallow baking dish. Pour over the butter mixed with the juice.
2. Sprinkle with the Parmesan cheese and bake in a hot oven (400°) for 10 minutes or until browned.

KIWI AND PAPAYA SALAD
Makes 4 servings
Two exotic fruits that are now carried in almost every supermarket and are a taste sensation worth exploring.

2 ripe kiwi fruit, peeled and sliced
2 ripe papayas, peeled, halved, seeded and sliced

4 cups shredded lettuce
Bottled or homemade salad dressing

Toss the fruits and lettuce together and just before serving add dressing to barely coat. Toss again and serve at once.

RHUBARB AND RASPBERRY SOUFFLÉ
Makes 4 servings
A refreshing light dessert for a spring dinner. There's no last-minute fuss because it's made ahead.

2 cups frozen unsweetened cut rhubarb (about ½ of a 1-pound package) or fresh rhubarb, if available
⅓ cup sugar
1 tablespoon cornstarch
Dash salt
½ cup water
3 tablespoons orange liqueur or juice
1½ teaspoons lemon juice

1 envelope unflavored gelatin
¼ cup cold water
1 package (10 ounces) frozen raspberries
2 large egg whites, at room temperature
¼ cup sugar
½ cup heavy cream

1. Mix rhubarb, ⅓ cup sugar, cornstarch and salt in a large saucepan; stir in ½ cup water. Cook mixture until rhubarb is tender, stirring often. Stir in orange liqueur and lemon juice; cook 1 minute more.
2. Remove 1 cup rhubarb mixture for sauce; chill. Sprinkle gelatin over the ¼ cup water; let stand a minute to soften. Stir into rhubarb remaining in pan; stir in raspberries. Cook mixture over low heat just until gelatin is dissolved and raspberries are thawed. Pour mixture into container of electric blender. Cover; whirl until smooth. Strain to remove seeds. Cool slightly.
3. Beat egg whites until foamy in large bowl with electric mixer. Beat in the ¼ cup sugar, 1 tablespoon at a time, until soft peaks form. Fold rhubarb mixture gently into whites.
4. Wash and dry beaters. Whip cream in a small bowl until stiff. Fold into rhubarb mixture. Pour into a glass bowl or a 4-cup soufflé dish with a 2-inch foil collar. Chill until firm. Spoon rhubarb sauce on top or serve in bowl along with the soufflé.

MENU
Serves 4
* *Inexpensive*

PRETTY AS A PICTURE

Lamb Ragout with Apricots
Noodles • Steamed Spinach
Marinated Asparagus Salad
Strawberries Romanoff

TOTAL TIME
About 1 hour

Combining meat and fruit in a main dish has been a European tradition for centuries and here's a way to prove that the idea is adaptable to our palates too. When fresh asparagus is in season, I believe in enjoying it in every way possible and in this menu it shows up in the salad.

MARKET LIST

1 pound boneless lamb shoulder
1 egg
1 cup heavy cream
1½ pounds fresh spinach or 1½ bags (10 ounces each) spinach or 2 packages (10 ounces each) frozen chopped spinach
2 lemons
1½ pounds asparagus (about 16 spears)
Lettuce leaves

1 quart fresh strawberries
Chives
1 can (17 ounces) Italian plum tomatoes
½ cup dried apricot halves
2 tablespoons dry sherry
Cornstarch
¼ cup Cointreau
½ pound fine noodles

WORK PLAN

1. Start the preparation of the lamb ragout. Cook the asparagus until crisp-tender.
2. While lamb is cooking, slice and sugar the strawberries; chill.
3. Prepare the dressing for the asparagus and pour over cooled vegetables; chill.
4. 15 minutes before lamb is due to be done, cook the noodles according to package directions. Drain and toss with a little butter. While noodles are cooking, cook the spinach.
5. Thicken the ragout and finish the dessert.

LAMB RAGOUT WITH APRICOTS
Makes 4 servings
Rosemary unites the unusual ingredients in this tasty, quick-to-make dish.

1 pound boneless lamb shoulder, trimmed
2 tablespoons butter or margarine
1 can (17 ounces) Italian plum tomatoes with juice

½ cup dried apricot halves
½ teaspoon rosemary, crumbled
2 tablespoons dry sherry mixed with 1½ teaspoons cornstarch to thicken sauce (optional)

1. Cut meat into 1-inch cubes; pat dry on paper toweling.
2. Heat butter in large skillet. Brown lamb cubes.
3. Stir tomatoes, apricots and rosemary into skillet.
4. Bring to boiling; lower heat; simmer, covered, for 45 minutes. If too much liquid, uncover last 15 minutes, or thicken with sherry-cornstarch mixture. Taste; add salt and pepper if needed.

STEAMED SPINACH
Makes 4 servings

1½ pounds fresh spinach or 1½ 10-ounce bags spinach or 2 packages (10 ounces each) frozen chopped spinach
3 tablespoons butter
¼ cup finely chopped onion

1 small clove garlic, finely chopped
Salt and freshly ground black pepper to taste
⅛ teaspoon nutmeg
2 teaspoons lemon juice

1. Trim, wash, drain and chop fresh spinach.
2. Melt the butter in a large saucepan and sauté the onion and garlic until tender. Add fresh or frozen spinach, cover tightly and cook until wilted or thawed and heated.
3. Remove cover and evaporate extra moisture. Season with salt, pepper, nutmeg and lemon juice.

MARINATED ASPARAGUS SALAD
Makes 4 servings

6 tablespoons oil
2 tablespoons lemon juice
½ teaspoon salt
¼ teaspoon freshly ground black pepper

2 teaspoons chopped chives
1 hard-cooked egg
1½ pounds asparagus (about 16 stalks)
Lettuce leaves

Beat together the oil, lemon juice, salt, pepper and chives. Chill. Separate the yolk and sieve; chop the white finely and add to dressing. Cook the spears until crisp-tender, about 5 minutes; drain, cool, chill. Arrange chilled asparagus over lettuce leaves on two plates. Drizzle dressing over and sprinkle with sieved yolk.

STRAWBERRIES ROMANOFF
Makes 4 servings

1 quart fresh strawberries
½ cup sugar

¼ cup Cointreau
1 cup heavy cream, whipped

Reserve 4 perfect berries. Slice remaining berries into a bowl. Sprinkle with sugar, stir gently and chill well. Just before serving stir Cointreau into cream and stir into berries. Spoon into serving dishes and top with whole berries.

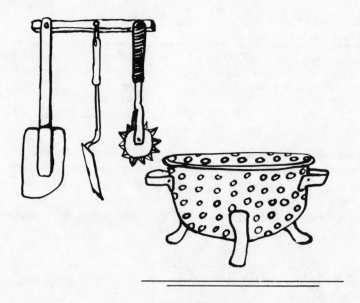

MENU
Serves 4

ENJOY AROMAS AND
TASTES FROM THE ORIENT

Curried Cream of Chicken Soup
Indonesian Satays • Rice (see page 137)
Eggplant Salad
Poached Apple Slices and Cookies

TOTAL TIME
About 30 minutes ahead, plus 25 minutes before serving

Satays are skewered morsels with a definite taste of peanut butter either in the marinade mixture or in the sauce served separately. To save time I suggest that you take a good, not too sweet, pepper relish from the store and pep it up with red pepper flakes to taste.

MARKET LIST

½ cup finely chopped cooked chicken (optional)

1½ pounds boneless chicken breasts or 1½ pounds lean boneless pork, cut into ½-inch cubes

1 cup half-and-half or light cream

6 small apples

3 tomatoes

1 medium-size eggplant

Chopped chives

Parsley

Lemon

Lettuce leaves

Peanut butter

2 cans (13¾ ounces each) chicken broth

1 can (6 ounces) tomato paste

Crushed red pepper

Not-too-sweet pepper relish

½ cup dry white wine

Garlic salad dressing

Rice

Cookies

WORK PLAN

1. The night before or early on the day make the satays through step 2; chill.
2. Prepare the apple slices and cook; chill. Fix the eggplant salad; chill.
3. About 25 minutes before serving, prepare the chicken soup. Thread the satays onto skewers.
4. Cook the rice. Finish off the soup.
5. Arrange salad on plates and drizzle over dressing. Cook satays.

CURRIED CREAM OF CHICKEN SOUP
Makes 4 servings

1 tablespoon butter or margarine
1 medium-size onion, sliced
2 small apples, peeled, quartered, cored and sliced (1½ cups)
1 tablespoon flour
2 teaspoons curry powder
¼ teaspoon salt

2 cups hot chicken stock or 1 can condensed chicken broth, plus water
½ cup dry white wine
1 cup half-and-half or light cream
½ cup finely chopped cooked chicken (optional)

1. Melt butter or margarine in large heavy saucepan; add onion and apple and sauté until soft but not brown.
2. Combine flour, curry and salt; blend into sautéed mixture. Gradually add hot broth, stirring constantly; stir in wine. Bring to boiling, stirring constantly, over medium heat. Simmer, stirring often, 10 minutes or until thickened. Cool.
3. Puree mixture through a food mill or in container of electric blender. Return to saucepan; stir in half-and-half. Add chicken, if you wish. Serve hot or chilled. This soup is great served with garlic bread.

INDONESIAN SATAYS
Makes 4 servings

¼ cup peanut oil
1 medium-size onion, chopped (½ cup)
2 cloves garlic, minced
1 tomato, peeled and chopped
2 tablespoons peanut butter
1 can (13¾ ounces) chicken broth
1 can (6 ounces) tomato paste

½ teaspoon crushed red pepper
1 teaspoon salt
1½ pounds boneless chicken breasts, skinned or 1½ pounds lean boneless pork, cut into ½-inch cubes
Pepper relish
Crushed red pepper

1. Heat oil in large skillet; sauté onion, garlic and tomato until very thick. Stir in peanut butter, chicken broth and tomato paste; stir in red pepper. Simmer, stirring constantly, 5 minutes. Add salt; cool.
2. Spear 2 cubes of chicken on each heat-proof skewer. Place skewers side by side in a shallow glass pan. Spoon sauce over chicken; cover and let stand in refrigerator until ready to serve.
3. Broil 5 to 6 minutes on each side or until chicken is lightly browned and hot, or until pork pieces are thoroughly cooked. Add red pepper flakes to pepper relish and spoon over each skewer and serve immediately.

EGGPLANT SALAD
Makes 4 servings

1 medium-size eggplant, peeled and cut into ½-inch cubes
3 tablespoons oil
2 tablespoons chopped chives
3 tablespoons chopped parsley
½ teaspoon salt
⅛ teaspoon freshly ground black pepper
1 tablespoon lemon juice
Garlic salad dressing
Lettuce leaves
2 tomatoes, cut into wedges

1. Cook the eggplant in the oil, stirring often until eggplant is crisp-tender, about 7 minutes. Stir in chives, parsley, salt, pepper and lemon juice. Chill.
2. Moisten eggplant with about ¼ cup dressing. Serve on lettuce leaves garnished with tomato wedges.

POACHED APPLE SLICES
Makes 4 cups
Apple slices hold their shape when poached this way.

1 cup water
1 cup sugar
2 tablespoons shredded lemon rind
4 tablespoons lemon juice
1 4-inch piece stick cinnamon, broken in half
4 small eating apples

1. Combine water and sugar in saucepan; bring to boiling, stirring until sugar dissolves. Add lemon rind, lemon juice and cinnamon; boil 1 minute.
2. Wash, quarter and core apples; slice into wedges about ¼-inch thick. Add to boiling syrup. Cover and continue cooking, shaking pan gently to distribute apple slices evenly in syrup, 3 to 5 minutes or until apples are barely tender. Remove from heat; cool, then chill.

MENU
Serves 4

BIRTHDAY CELEBRATION

Broiled Lemon Chicken
Stir-Fried Snow Peas and Cucumber
Butter Tossed Noodles
Strawberry Ice Cream Shortcake

TOTAL TIME

1 hour to assemble shortcake 1 to 5 days ahead; 5 minutes to marinate chicken, plus 35 minutes before serving

Colors and flavors are just two of the things that should be balanced in every menu and the delicate flavor and gradation of green colors in this stir-fried vegetable melange are just right with the tangy lemon chicken. Garnish it with a slice of lemon for more emphasis. Ice cream shortcake leftovers will keep for a week or two in the freezer.

MARKET LIST

1 broiler-fryer (3 to 3½ pounds)
2 cups heavy cream
2 lemons
½ pound fresh snow peas or 1 package (7 ounces) frozen snow peas
1 cucumber
1 pint strawberries
1 pound thin noodles

3 pints strawberry ice cream
12 dry Italian almond macaroons
3 tablespoons cream sherry
1 8-inch sponge cake (purchased)
1 jar (8 ounces) strawberry ice cream topping
¼ cup strawberry or red currant jelly

WORK PLAN

1. 1 to 5 days ahead prepare the shortcake through step 3.
2. Early in the day place chicken in marinade; refrigerate.
3. 30 minutes before serving time start broiling chicken.
4. Decorate shortcake; return to freezer only if kitchen is very warm.
5. Cook noodles according to package directions, drain and toss with butter.
6. Stir-fry snow peas and cucumber.

BROILED LEMON CHICKEN
Broil for 35 minutes
Makes 4 servings

1 broiler-fryer, split (3 to 3½ pounds)
½ cup lemon juice
1 clove garlic, crushed
1 teaspoon salt
½ teaspoon leaf rosemary, crumbled
Pinch ground pepper

1. Place chicken, skin side down, in a shallow dish. Combine remaining ingredients; pour over chicken. Cover; refrigerate 8 hours, turning chicken often.
2. Place chicken, skin side down, on rack in broiler pan about 8 to 10 inches from heat (see note). Broil 15 to 20 minutes, basting 2 or 3 times with marinade. Turn chicken skin side up. Baste. Continue to broil 15 minutes longer or until chicken is tender, basting from time to time.
3. When ready to serve, cut chicken to make 4 servings. Serve with hot cooked noodles and pan drippings.

Note: When lowest setting for broiler rack is 5 to 6 inches from heat, lower heat to medium to prevent over-browning.

STIR-FRIED SNOW PEAS AND CUCUMBER
Makes 4 servings
A tasty way to enhance, and stretch, delectable Chinese snow peas is to cook them with cucumber.

½ pound fresh snow peas or 1 package
   (7 ounces) frozen snow peas
1 cucumber
2 tablespoons peanut oil
1 small onion, finely chopped (¼ cup)
¼ teaspoon crushed red pepper
1 tablespoon cider vinegar
½ teaspoon sugar
1 teaspoon salt
⅛ teaspoon ground ginger

1. Snip off tips and remove strings from pea pods; if large, cut each in half diagonally.
2. Peel cucumber; cut in half lengthwise; scoop out and discard seeds. Cut crosswise into about ¼-inch-thick slices.
3. Heat oil in large skillet or wok. Stir in onion; stir-fry 2 minutes; stir in crushed pepper; cook 5 seconds. Add cucumber slices; stir-fry 1 minute. Stir in snow peas; cook, stirring and tossing, 2 minutes or just until crisply tender. Stir in vinegar, sugar, salt and ginger; serve at once.

STRAWBERRY ICE CREAM SHORTCAKE
Makes 12 to 16 servings

The first juicy red strawberries of spring are usually reserved for strawberry shortcake. We have made a frosty ice cream version of that all-American favorite.

3 pints strawberry ice cream
1 cup heavy cream
12 dry Italian almond macaroons
3 tablespoons cream sherry
1 8-inch bought sponge or chiffon cake layer

1 jar (8 ounces) strawberry ice cream topping
1 cup heavy cream
¼ cup strawberry or red currant jelly (optional)
1 pint strawberries

1. Soften ice cream in chilled large bowl; whip 1 cup heavy cream in a small bowl; fold into ice cream. Spread into 2 8-by-2-inch layer pans lined with plastic wrap; freeze 1 hour or until almost firm.
2. Crumble macaroons into a small bowl; sprinkle with sherry; let stand 15 minutes.
3. Split cake layer horizontally to make 2 layers. Place 1 layer, cut side up, on small cooky sheet; spread with about ⅓ of strawberry topping. Top with 1 ice cream layer. Sprinkle macaroon crumbs evenly over; spoon ⅓ of strawberry topping over. Top with remaining ice cream, strawberry topping and cake layer, cut side down, in that order; press lightly together. Freeze until firm, several hours or overnight.
4. To decorate: Whip the 1 cup cream in a medium-size bowl. Spread or pipe whipped cream onto sides of cake. Just before serving, melt jelly in small saucepan over low heat. Wash, dry, hull and halve strawberries; arrange over top of cake; brush with melted jelly, if you wish.

MENU
Serves 4
* Inexpensive

A NEW LOOK FOR SPRING'S FAVORITE VEGETABLE

Egg and Sausage Cake
Stir-Fried Asparagus Mimosa
Quick Herbed Bread
Green Salad with Dressing
Ricotta with Chocolate

TOTAL TIME
About 40 minutes

Dinner doesn't always have to be red meat and potatoes. Stretch the budget and try sausages with eggs in a tasty frittata to serve with local asparagus when it is at its best. The dessert is so easy and good you'll wonder why you never thought of it.

MARKET LIST

3 hot Italian sausages
15 ounces whole milk ricotta
6 eggs
1½ pounds fresh asparagus
1 lemon
Parsley

Lettuce (6 cups iceberg, Romaine, Boston, Chicory)
3 medium-size potatoes
⅓ cup confectioners' sugar
½ square semisweet chocolate
1 loaf French bread

WORK PLAN

1. Wash and dry salad greens; refrigerate. Prepare dressing; refrigerate.
2. Prepare dessert; refrigerate.
3. Slice, butter and season bread; wrap in foil. Preheat oven to 375°.
4. Prepare and cut asparagus. Assemble remainder of ingredients for dish.
5. Cook sausage; assemble remaining ingredients for main dish.
6. Prepare egg and sausage cake. Heat bread.
7. Stir-fry asparagus.
8. Tear salad greens; toss salad.

EGG AND SAUSAGE CAKE
Makes 4 servings
Spicy Italian sausages provide the seasoning in this unusual main dish.

3 hot Italian sausages	2 teaspoons salt
½ cup (1 stick) butter or margarine	½ cup chopped white onions
¼ cup olive oil	5 eggs
3 medium-size potatoes, pared and cut into ⅛-inch-thick slices (2 cups)	

1. Prick sausages with a fork; plunge into boiling water and parboil 5 minutes. Place sausages on rack under broiler for 10 minutes, turning once. Cut into ¼-inch-thick rounds.
2. Melt ¼ cup of the butter with 2 tablespoons of the olive oil in a large skillet. Add potatoes; sprinkle with 1 teaspoon salt and turn them several times until they are well coated with the butter-oil mixture. Cook over medium heat for 10 minutes until potatoes are lightly browned. Push potatoes to one side of the pan; add onions and cook 5 minutes. Add sausages; mix potatoes, onions and sausage together and cook 5 minutes longer. Remove to a sieve to drain off all fat.
3. Beat eggs with remaining 1 teaspoon salt in a large bowl; add vegetable and sausage mixture.
4. Heat the remaining butter and oil in a 9-inch skillet over medium heat. When very hot, pour in the egg mixture, spreading it so it will cook evenly. From time to time remove the skillet from the heat and give it a vigorous shake to prevent the eggs from sticking. When eggs become firm, in about 4 minutes, remove skillet from heat.
5. Place a plate over the skillet. Flip the egg cake onto the plate and slide back into the skillet, uncooked side down. Cook 3 minutes longer. Cut into wedges to serve.

STIR-FRIED ASPARAGUS MIMOSA
Makes 4 servings

1 bunch fresh asparagus (about 1½ pounds)	¼ teaspoon pepper
3 tablespoons peanut oil	1 yolk from hard-cooked egg
2 tablespoons lemon juice	Chopped parsley
½ teaspoon salt	Lemon wedges

1. Break woody ends from asparagus and discard; wash stalks well under running cold water. If sandy, cut off scales with the tip of a sharp knife, then wash stalks again. Cut off tips and set aside; cut stalks diagonally into bias slices about ¼ inch thick and 1 inch long.
2. Heat oil in large skillet or wok. Add sliced stalks; stir-fry 4 to 5 minutes or just until crisply tender. Add asparagus tips; stir-fry 2 to 3 minutes longer. Stir in lemon juice, salt and pepper. Cook 30 seconds.
3. Spoon asparagus into heated serving dish; sprinkle with chopped or sieved egg yolk and parsley. Serve with lemon wedges.

QUICK HERBED BREAD
Bake at 375° for 10 minutes
Makes 4 to 6 servings
You can make the herb butter ahead of time and refrigerate.

½ cup (1 stick) butter or margarine
1 clove garlic, finely chopped
2 tablespoons instant minced onion
¼ teaspoon leaf marjoram, crumbled

¼ teaspoon leaf thyme, crumbled
1 loaf French or Italian bread, 12 to 14 inches long

1. Preheat oven to moderate (375°).
2. Combine butter, garlic, onion, marjoram and thyme in bowl until well mixed.
3. Cut bread into 1-inch-thick slices, but do not cut all the way through bottom crust. Spread herb butter on cut surface of slices. Wrap loaf in heavy-duty or double-thick regular aluminum foil.
4. Bake bread until heated through, about 10 minutes. Unwrap, and break into slices to serve.

GREEN SALAD
Makes 4 servings

Separate salad greens into leaves. Rinse under cold water, and shake off as much of the water as possible. Now roll the greens in lots of paper toweling until thoroughly dry. If you want to prepare the greens before you start cooking dinner, put them in a plastic bag and place in refrigerator until ready to toss with the dressing (recipe follows). Otherwise, break into bite-size pieces (about 6 cups), toss the greens with the dressing and serve immediately.

BASIC SALAD DRESSING
Makes 4 servings

6 tablespoons olive oil or corn oil
2 tablespoons vinegar (see note)
½ teaspoon mustard (dry or prepared type)
½ teaspoon salt

¼ teaspoon pepper
1 teaspoon crumbled, dried herbs (basil, thyme, tarragon, parsley or dill)

Combine oil, vinegar, mustard, salt and pepper in the bottom of your salad bowl and blend with the flat of a fork or a small whisk. Stir in one or more herbs, if you wish. Place in refrigerator.

Note: You can use any kind of vinegar—distilled white, cider, red wine, white wine or tarragon-flavored.

RICOTTA WITH CHOCOLATE
Makes 4 servings

1 container (15 ounces) whole milk ricotta (2 cups)
⅓ cup confectioners' sugar

¼ teaspoon ground cinnamon
½ square (½ ounce) semisweet chocolate

In a medium-size bowl combine ricotta, sugar and cinnamon, blending well. Mound mixture into serving bowl. With vegetable peeler shave chocolate thickly over dessert. Cover with plastic wrap. Refrigerate until serving. Spoon into individual dessert dishes at table.

MENU
Serves 6
* Inexpensive

SPRING SPECTACULAR

Gougere with Mushrooms and Ham
Orange Avocado Salad with Lemon Dressing
Strawberry Bavarian or Fresh Strawberries

TOTAL TIME
About 25 minutes ahead if making bavarian, plus 1¼ hours before serving

This menu is great for lunch, brunch or a pleasantly light dinner. Make the dessert the day before and then you'll find that the gougere, which is only a fancy name for a savory cream puff dough, goes together easily and only takes 40 minutes to bake. The sauce is built into the middle and, best of all, it is not an expensive meal to fix but looks and tastes fantastic.

MARKET LIST

6 ounces cooked ham
4 eggs
½ cup plus 2 tablespoons grated
    sharp Cheddar cheese
2 cups heavy cream
½ pound mushrooms
2 large tomatoes
Parsley
1 head romaine

3 large navel oranges
1 large firm ripe avocado
    Lemon
1 quart strawberries
⅓ cup orange juice
1 envelope or teaspoon instant chicken
    broth
2 envelopes unflavored gelatin

WORK PLAN

1. Day before, or early on the day, make the bavarian and refrigerate.
2. About 1¼ hours before serving time preheat oven to 400°.
3. Follow the recipe for the gougere and set in oven to bake.
4. Prepare the lemon salad dressing; refrigerate. Follow through step 1 for the salad and refrigerate lettuce and orange sections.
5. Unmold bavarian onto serving plate and return to refrigerator.
6. When gougere is baked finish the salad and toss with the dressing.

GOUGERE WITH MUSHROOMS AND HAM
Bake at 400° for 40 minutes
Makes 6 servings

Pâte à choux

1 cup sifted all-purpose flour
  Pinch each salt and pepper
1 cup water
½ cup (1 stick) butter or margarine,
  cut up

4 eggs
⅛ pound sharp Cheddar cheese,
  diced (about ½ cup)

Filling

4 tablespoons butter or margarine
2 medium-size onions, chopped (1
  cup)
½ pound mushrooms, sliced
1½ tablespoons flour
1 teaspoon salt
¼ teaspoon pepper
1 envelope or teaspoon instant
  chicken broth

1 cup hot water
2 large tomatoes, peeled, quartered
  and seeded (2 cups)
6 ounces cooked ham, cut into thin
  strips (1½ cups)
2 tablespoons shredded Cheddar
  cheese
2 tablespoons chopped parsley

1. To make pâte à choux: Sift the flour, salt and pepper onto a sheet of wax paper. Heat the water and butter in a large saucepan until the butter melts.
2. Turn up the heat and bring water to boiling. Add flour mixture all at once and stir vigorously until mixture forms a ball in the center of the pan. (This will take about a minute.)
3. Allow mixture to cool for 5 minutes. Add the eggs one at a time, beating well with a wooden spoon after each addition. (This beating is important as the gougere will not puff otherwise.) Stir in the diced cheese.
4. To make filling: Melt the butter in a large skillet; sauté the onion until soft but not browned. Add the mushrooms and continue cooking 2 minutes.
5. Sprinkle with flour, salt and pepper; mix and cook an additional 2 minutes. Add the instant chicken broth and water, mix well; bring to boil, stirring constantly. Simmer 4 minutes. Remove sauce from heat. Cut each tomato quarter into 4 strips and add to the sauce with the ham strips. Taste; add additional seasoning, if you wish.

6. Butter a 10- to 11-inch ovenproof skillet, pie pan or shallow baking dish. Spoon the pâte à choux in a ring around the edge, leaving the center open. Pour the filling into the center and sprinkle all over with the cheese. Bake in a hot oven (400°) for 40 minutes or until gougere is puffed and brown and the filling is bubbling. Sprinkle with parsley and serve at once cutting into wedges as for a pie.

ORANGE AVOCADO SALAD
Makes 6 servings

1 medium-size head romaine	1 large firm ripe avocado
3 large navel oranges	Lemon Dressing (recipe follows)

1. Break the romaine into bite-size pieces in a large salad bowl (about 6 cups.) Pare and section oranges into a small bowl (2 cups.) Refrigerate both.
2. Just before serving, peel, pit and slice avocado. Arrange avocado and orange over romaine. Drizzle ⅓ to ½ cup Lemon Dressing over salad; toss gently to coat with dressing.

LEMON DRESSING
Makes ¾ cup

¼ cup fresh lemon juice	¼ teaspoon sugar
½ teaspoon salt	¼ teaspoon dry mustard
⅛ teaspoon pepper	½ cup vegetable oil

1. Beat lemon juice, salt, pepper, sugar and dry mustard together in a medium-size bowl.
2. Beat in vegetable oil in a slow steady stream until mixture is thick and slightly creamy; refrigerate. Shake well just before serving.

STRAWBERRY BAVARIAN
Makes 6 servings

2 envelopes unflavored gelatin	½ cup sugar
⅓ cup orange juice	2 cups heavy cream, whipped
1 quart strawberries, washed and hulled	Whole strawberries for garnish

1. Sprinkle gelatin over orange juice in a 1 cup measure. Let stand 5 minutes to soften. Place cup in saucepan of simmering water; stir until gelatin is dissolved; cool.

2. Reserve a few whole strawberries for garnish. Puree rest of strawberries in container of electric blender, or press through food mill or sieve. Stir in gelatin mixture and sugar. Chill, stirring occasionally, until mixture begins to thicken. Fold in whipped cream and spoon into an 8-cup mold or serving bowl. Refrigerate until mixture is set, several hours or overnight. Unmold, if molded. Garnish with reserved whole berries, if you wish.

MENU
Serves 6
* Inexpensive

FOR DISCERNING GUESTS

Spinach Roll with Creamed Mushrooms
French Bread • Marinated Vegetables or Tossed Green Salad
Walnut Supreme Pie

TOTAL TIME
About 45 minutes ahead, plus 40 minutes before serving

When the budget is low but the need is for an elegant, light meal that you are willing to work at here's the answer.

MARKET LIST

7 eggs
⅓ cup grated Parmesan cheese
1¼ sticks butter or margarine
¾ cup heavy cream
¾ pound mushrooms
    Parsley
2 green onions
1 pint cherry tomatoes
    Bibb or Boston lettuce
3 packages (10 ounces each) frozen
    spinach

Packaged bread crumbs
Olive oil
1 can (16 ounces) pitted ripe olives,
    drained
28 (2-inch) round buttery crackers
¾ cup finely chopped walnuts
1 quart vanilla ice cream
    Walnuts

WORK PLAN

1. Night before, or early on the day, make the meringue pie shell; bake and cool. Prepare the marinated vegetables; refrigerate.
2. 30 to 40 minutes before serving start to make the spinach roll. Preparation time depends on skill and confidence of the cook because the cooking time is only 12 minutes plus another 8 minutes to fill and roll. Heat bread while filling roll. Serve salad.
3. Scoop ice cream into pie shell just before serving dessert.

SPINACH ROLL WITH CREAMED MUSHROOMS
Bake at 350° for 12 minutes
Makes 6 servings

---

3 packages (10 ounces each) frozen spinach	6 tablespoons grated Parmesan cheese
¼ cup packaged bread crumbs	¾ pound mushrooms, sliced
1 teaspoon salt	4 tablespoons butter or margarine
¼ teaspoon pepper	3 tablespoons flour
Pinch ground nutmeg	1 teaspoon salt
6 tablespoons butter or margarine, melted	½ teaspoon pepper
4 eggs, separated	¾ cup heavy cream
	2 tablespoons chopped parsley

1. Thaw the spinach in a large skillet over low heat; drain and chop. Butter a 15-by-10-by-1-inch jelly-roll pan; line with wax paper. Butter again and sprinkle with the bread crumbs.
2. When the spinach is cool enough to handle, squeeze out all excess water. Place spinach in a bowl; add salt, pepper, nutmeg and 6 table- spoons melted butter.
3. Beat in the egg yolks one at a time. Beat the egg whites in a small bowl until they hold soft peaks; fold into the spinach mixture. Spoon mixture into prepared pan and smooth top evenly with a spatula. Sprinkle with 4 tablespoons of the Parmesan.
4. Bake in a moderate oven (350°) for 12 minutes or until the center feels barely firm when touched lightly.
5. While roll is baking, make filling: Sauté the mushrooms quickly in the 4 tablespoons butter in a large skillet. Shake the skillet occasionally. Sprinkle mushrooms with flour, salt and pepper; stir in the cream. Mix gently in the pan just until thickened.

6. When roll is baked, place a sheet of buttered wax paper, butter side down over the roll. Invert onto a warm cooky sheet, and carefully remove bottom paper.
7. Spread mushroom mixture over the hot spinach roll. Roll up, jelly-roll fashion, starting at a short end, and using the paper to aid in rolling. Ease the roll onto a warm platter, seam side down.
8. Sprinkle roll with remaining cheese and parsley.

MARINATED VEGETABLES
Makes 6 servings

¾ teaspoon dry mustard
¾ teaspoon sugar
¾ teaspoon salt
¼ teaspoon black pepper
¼ cup cider vinegar
¼ cup olive oil
¼ cup vegetable oil

¼ cup chopped green onion
¾ teaspoon minced parsley
1 pint cherry tomatoes
1 can (16 ounces) pitted ripe olives, drained
Bibb or Boston lettuce

1. Mix mustard, sugar, salt and pepper together in a medium-size bowl. Slowly stir in vinegar until dry ingredients are absorbed. Stir in olive and vegetable oils, onion and parsley; beat with spoon until well-blended.
2. Plunge tomatoes in boiling water for 10 seconds; peel and cut in half. Add tomatoes and olives to oil-vinegar mixture; marinate overnight in refrigerator.
3. To serve, remove vegetables from marinade with a slotted spoon and serve in lettuce cups.

WALNUT SUPREME PIE
Bake at 350° for 30 minutes
Makes one 9-inch pie
The trick to this meringue shell is the long, slow beating while you add sugar.

28 (2-inch) round buttery crackers
¾ cup finely chopped walnuts
¾ cup sugar
1 teaspoon baking powder

3 egg whites
1 teaspoon vanilla
1 quart vanilla ice cream
Coarsely chopped walnuts

1. Crumble crackers into container of electric blender. Cover and whirl until fine crumbs form. Measure 1 cup and mix with walnuts in a small bowl.
2. Combine the ¾ cup sugar with baking powder.
3. Beat egg whites until foamy-white and double in volume in a small bowl with an electric mixer at high speed. Beat in sugar-baking powder mixture, one tablespoon at a time, beating 1 minute before adding additional sugar, until meringue stands in firm peaks. (This beating is important to make a stiff meringue.)
4. Fold in vanilla, and cracker-walnut mixture.
5. Spread into a well-buttered 9-inch pie plate, leaving a slight depression in center and spreading meringue to edges of pie plate.
6. Bake in a moderate oven (350°) for 30 minutes or just until firm. Cool thoroughly on wire rack.
7. Scoop vanilla ice cream into center of pie and sprinkle with coarsely chopped walnuts.

MENU
Serves 6

DISTINCTIVELY CHINESE

Chicken with Walnuts
Rice (see page 137) • Broccoli with Sesame Seeds
Cucumber Salad
Oriental Sherbet Mold

TOTAL TIME
30 minutes ahead, plus 30 minutes before serving

You couldn't call this menu humdrum by any standards but it is surprisingly easy to get together and the only last-minute preparation is stir-frying the broccoli which takes less than 10 minutes if you have all the ingredients lined up. The dessert has to be made at least a day ahead.

MARKET LIST

1½ pounds boneless chicken breasts
   4 green onions
   1 bunch fresh broccoli (about 1½
      pounds)
   Fresh mint
   1 cup coarsely chopped walnuts
   Dry sherry
   Soy sauce
   2 tablespoons sesame seeds
   1 small can water chestnuts (optional)
   1 quart lemon sherbet

2 tablespoons minced preserved
   ginger
3 tablespoons finely chopped, pitted
   kumquats, fresh or preserved
   Orange-flavored liqueur
1 quart orange sherbet
1 can (5½ ounces) lichee nuts
1 can (11 ounces) mandarin orange
   sections
   Rice

WORK PLAN

1. Prepare dessert day before or several days ahead.
2. Set chicken in marinade about 30 minutes before serving.
3. Make the cucumber salad and refrigerate.
4. Cook rice. Unmold the Oriental Sherbet Mold and put back in freezer. Cook chicken.
5. Assemble ingredients for broccoli and cook just before serving meal.

CHICKEN WITH WALNUTS
Makes 6 servings

⅓ cup soy sauce
1½ tablespoons dry sherry
¾ teaspoon ground ginger
1½ pounds boneless chicken breast,
   cut into 1-inch pieces

7 tablespoons oil
½ cup sliced green onions
1 large clove garlic, crushed
1½ cups walnuts, coarsely chopped

1. Combine soy sauce, sherry, ginger and chicken in a small bowl. Mix and let stand 15 minutes.
2. Heat wok or large skillet. Add 4 tablespoons oil. Add green onion, garlic and walnuts and cook while stirring 3 minutes. Discard garlic. Transfer walnut-onion mixture to small bowl.
3. Add remaining oil to wok. Heat. Add chicken-soy mixture and stir-fry 6 minutes or until chicken is cooked and coated with soy mixture. Return walnut-onion mixture to wok and toss to mix.

BROCCOLI WITH SESAME SEEDS
Makes 6 servings
Sesame seeds provide the perfect Oriental accent for stir-fried broccoli.

1 bunch fresh broccoli (about 1½ pounds)	3 tablespoons white wine, chicken broth or water
2 tablespoons sesame seeds	3 tablespoons soy sauce
3 tablespoons peanut or vegetable oil	½ teaspoon salt
2 teaspoons finely chopped garlic	½ teaspoon sugar
½ cup sliced water chestnuts (optional)	

1. Trim outer leaves and tough ends from broccoli. Cut off flowerettes and set aside; slice stalks thinly.
2. Heat sesame seeds in large skillet or wok over medium heat, shaking pan constantly, just until lighty toasted; pour into small dish.
3. Heat oil in same skillet or wok over medium-high heat, stir in garlic and cook 15 seconds. Add sliced stalks and stir-fry 4 to 5 minutes. Stir in water chestnuts, wine, soy sauce, salt and sugar. Add flowerettes; cover. Lower heat; steam 3 to 4 minutes, stirring once or twice, or until broccoli is crisply tender. Turn into a heated serving dish; sprinkle with sesame seeds. Serve with additional soy sauce to sprinkle over each serving, if you wish.

CUCUMBER SALAD
Makes 6 servings

3 medium-size cucumbers	1½ teaspoons sugar
1½ tablespoons sliced green onion	½ teaspoon salt
3 talespoons white vinegar	¼ teaspoon pepper

1. Peel and thinly slice cucumbers; place in serving dish.
2. Add green onion, vinegar, sugar, salt and pepper; toss gently to coat. Cover with plastic wrap. Place in freezer section of refrigerator for a few minutes.

ORIENTAL SHERBET MOLD
Makes 10 servings

2 tablespoons minced preserved ginger	1 quart orange sherbet, softened
1 quart lemon sherbet, softened	1 can (5½ ounces) lichee nuts, drained
3 tablespoons finely chopped, pitted kumquats	1 can (11 ounces) mandarin orange sections, drained
2 tablespoons orange liqueur	Several sprigs fresh mint

1. Stir ginger into softened lemon sherbet. Spoon mixture onto bottom and side of a tall well-chilled 2-quart mold. Freeze until firm.
2. Stir kumquats and orange liqueur into softened orange sherbet in a well-chilled bowl. Spoon mixture into center of lemon sherbet-lined mold; freeze until firm, preferably overnight.
3. To unmold, cover mold with towel wrung out of hot water, repeating several times, if necessary. Turn out onto chilled serving plate. Return to freezer for at least an hour before serving. Garnish with lichee nuts, mandarin orange sections and mint. Leftover mold can be covered and stored in the freezer.

MENU
Serves 6
* Inexpensive

FAMILY FARE

So-Easy Rigatoni Bake
Crusty Italian Bread • Tossed Green Salad
Easy Apricot Pie or Fresh Fruit Compote

TOTAL TIME
About 45 minutes ahead if making pie or 20 minutes ahead for fruit plus 45 minutes before serving

Many families do not feel that they have had a decent meal unless there is a home-made baked dessert so this menu was put together to allow the busy cook to fulfill that obligation without spending half a day in the kitchen.

MARKET LIST

8 ounces sharp Cheddar or Swiss
  cheese in 1 piece
  Grated Parmesan
2 small heads Romaine, Boston or 1
  head iceberg lettuce
1 package radishes
1 cucumber
2 cups dried apricots

1 pound package #27 rigatoni macaroni
1 jar (15½ ounces) marinara sauce
1 loaf Italian bread
  Bottled dressing
  Pastry for 2-crust pie
  Cornstarch
  Light brown sugar
1 cup orange juice

WORK PLAN

1. The night before or early on the day put the apricots to soak for the pie and make the pastry; line pie plate; chill.
2. Early on the day or 45 minutes before serving preheat oven to 400°.
3. Complete the pie and bake.
4. 45 minutes before serving, preheat oven to 400° if baking pie and main dish, or 350° if baking main dish only.
5. Finish making pie if not done; put together rigatoni dish and place both in oven at the same time. Reduce heat to 325° after 12 minutes. Remove main dish when cheese has melted and mixture is bubbly hot.
6. Meanwhile, wash and drain salad ingredients; chill. Slice the bread and butter; sprinkle with garlic powder or garlic salt. Wrap in foil and put in oven for last 15 to 20 minutes cooking time.
7. Toss salad.

SO-EASY RIGATONI BAKE
Bake at 350° for 30 minutes
Makes 6 servings

---

3 cups #27 rigatoni macaroni (from a 16-ounce package)

8 ounces sharp Cheddar or Swiss cheese, in one piece

2 cups homemade marinara sauce or 1 jar (15½ ounces) marinara sauce

2 tablespoons grated Parmesan cheese, or half Parmesan and half mozzarella

1. Cook rigatoni in rapidly boiling salted water 12 to 15 minutes, or until barely tender. Drain.
2. Cut cheese into strips 1¼-inch long and ¼-inch thick. Insert a piece of cheese in each rigatoni. Place in shallow greased 6-cup baking dish. Pour sauce over; sprinkle with cheese.
3. Bake, uncovered, in a moderate oven (350°) for 30 minutes or until cheese is melted and sauce is bubbling hot.

EASY APRICOT PIE
Bake at 400° for 12 minutes, then at 325° for 20 minutes
Makes 1 8-inch pie

---

2 cups dried apricots
1 cup orange juice
    Pastry for a 2-crust pie
1 tablespoon cornstarch

½ cup firmly packed light brown sugar
¼ teaspoon salt
1 tablespoon butter

1. Soak dried apricots in orange juice for 2 hours.
2. Prepare pastry for 2-crust pie, using your favorite pastry recipe. Line an 8-inch pie plate with pastry and let it chill while the apricots soak.
3. In 2 hours drain the fruit, saving ⅔ cup of the liquid (see note).
4. Put cornstarch, light brown sugar and salt into a saucepan and gradually stir in the reserved orange juice. Cook mixture over moderate heat until slightly thickened, stirring constantly.
5. Spread the apricots around in the chilled pie-shell, pour the syrup over them and dot with butter. Cover with a lattice pastry top or a plain top slit plentifully for the juice to bubble through.
6. Bake in a hot oven (400°) for 12 minutes. Reduce oven temperature to 325° and bake another 20 minutes, or until the pastry is a delicate golden brown. Serve warm or cold.

Note: Use additional orange juice to make ⅔ cup liquid, if necessary.

MENU
Serves 6
* Inexpensive

GREEK ACCENTS TO AN IRISH DISH

Cabbage and Lamb in Lemon Sauce
Orange Cucumber Salad
Quick Chocolate Cream Pie

TOTAL TIME
1 hour, 20 minutes

One-pot meals that cook in an hour or less are a boon to every busy cook and there are many other rewards, such as economy and great compliments, for fixing this simple meal.

MARKET LIST

6 lamb shoulder chops (2 to 2½ pounds)	2 cucumbers
2 cups milk	6 navel oranges
5 eggs	1 small green pepper
1 cabbage (2½ to 3 pounds)	Lettuce
1 pound small new potatoes	1 can (13¾ ounces) chicken broth
3 lemons	14 chocolate sandwich cookies
Parsley	2 squares unsweetened chocolate

WORK PLAN

1. Prepare the cabbage dish through step 2 and set it to cook.
2. Make the chocolate cream pie; refrigerate.
3. Prepare salad on platter; cover with transparent plastic wrap and refrigerate. Make the oil and vinegar dressing and refrigerate separately.
4. Proceed with step 3 of the cabbage dish. Dinner's ready.

CABBAGE AND LAMB IN LEMON SAUCE
Makes 6 servings
Lemon and egg sauce is a delightful complement to lamb and cabbage.

---

2 tablespoons flour	1 cabbage (2½ to 3 pounds), cut in 6
1½ teaspoons salt	wedges
¼ teaspoon pepper	1 pound small new potatoes, pared or
2 tablespoons vegetable oil	scrubbed, with a 1-inch strip
6 lamb shoulder chops (2 to 2½	pared from around the middle
pounds)	2 eggs
1 large onion, sliced	¼ cup lemon juice
1 clove garlic, crushed	Lemon wedges
1 can (13¾ ounces) chicken broth	Parsley

1. Mix flour, salt and pepper on wax paper. Coat chops evenly with mixture, shaking off excess; reserve any remaining mixture.
2. Heat oil in large deep skillet; add chops and brown evenly on both sides; remove as they brown. Add onion and garlic to skillet; sauté until soft. Sprinkle any flour mixture left from chops over onion. Stir in broth; bring to boiling. Arrange chops, cabbage and potatoes in skillet; lower heat and cover. Cook, basting occasionally with sauce, 45 to 50 minutes or until chops and vegetables are tender.
3. Arrange chops and vegetables in a deep platter; keep warm. Beat eggs in a small deep bowl until light and foamy; beat in lemon juice. Gradually add hot sauce to eggs while beating; pour back into skillet. Cook over low to medium heat, stirring constantly, just until slightly thickened. Do not boil. Pour over chops and vegetables immediately. Garnish with lemon and parsley, if you wish.

ORANGE CUCUMBER SALAD
Makes 6 servings

2 cucumbers
6 navel oranges
1 small onion, chopped (¼ cup)
1 green pepper, chopped (¼ cup)

Lettuce
Oil and vinegar dressing
Salt and pepper to taste

Groove cucumbers with tines of a fork, and slice them thin. Peel and slice oranges. Chop onion and green pepper into small pieces. Arrange a lot of lettuce on a flat plate or platter, and alternate the orange and cucumber slices on top. Sprinkle with chopped onion and green pepper. Serve with an oil and vinegar dressing (⅔ cup oil, ⅓ cup vinegar, with some salt and pepper to taste).

QUICK CHOCOLATE CREAM PIE
Makes one 9-inch pie

14 chocolate sandwich cookies
 4 tablespoons butter or margarine
 2 tablespoons flour
 2 tablespoons cornstarch
½ teaspoon salt
¾ cup sugar

3 egg yolks
1 teaspoon vanilla
2 squares unsweetened cholate, diced
  or shredded
2 cups hot milk

1. Crush the cookies in a plastic bag with a rolling pin. If the filling from the cookies sticks to the sides of the bag, scrape it off with a spatula and mix into the crumbs.
2. Melt 3 tablespoons of the butter in a small skillet. Stir in the cookie crumbs; remove from heat and stir one minute. Press crumb mixture against sides and bottom of a 9-inch pie plate. Chill while preparing filling.
3. Place remaining tablespoon of butter, softened, in container of electric blender with the flour, cornstarch, salt, sugar, yolks, vanilla and chocolate. Cover and whirl for 5 seconds.
4. While the blender is still running gradually pour in the hot milk. Turn mixture into a saucepan and heat stirring until mixture is thick and bubbles. Cook, stirring 2 to 3 minutes over low heat. Cool quickly by setting pan in ice water; stir often. Pour into pie shell. Chill.

MENU
Serves 6

FOR SPECIAL GUESTS

Beets, Herring and Potato Salad in Mustard Mayonnaise
Chicken Breasts in Vermouth
Noodles • Quick Green Beans
Dutch Rhubarb Cream or Fresh Pears

TOTAL TIME
1 hour ahead plus 30 minutes before serving

In a rut with menu planning? Then this simple meal will get you out in a hurry with no tremendous outlay of money, time or effort. Surprise your family and your guests with a completely different kind of first course. You can add a green salad, if you wish, but I find it a relief to skip the expected once in a while.

MARKET LIST

3 whole chicken breasts
2 eggs
1½ cups milk
¾ cup shredded Cheddar cheese
½ cup heavy cream
1 bunch beets (about 1 pound)
6 small new potatoes
2 green onions
Dill
1½ pounds green beans

1 pound rhubarb or 1 package (about 1 pound) frozen rhubarb
Lemon
1 jar (8 ounces) herring in wine sauce, drained
1 cup mayonnaise
¼ cup dry vermouth
¼ cup undiluted frozen orange juice concentrate
2 envelopes unflavored gelatin
1 pound noodles

WORK PLAN

1. The night before or early in the day make the rhubarb dessert; chill. While dessert is chilling make the herring salad, chill and fix the marinade for the chicken but do not put the chicken in until early on the day it is to be served.
2. 30 minutes before serving, remove herring salad and dessert from refrigerator. Have coals in hibachi or grill ready to cook, or cook the breasts under the broiler.
3. Cook the green beans and finish as recipe directs. Cook noodles according to package directions; drain and toss with pat of butter.

BEETS, HERRING AND POTATO SALAD IN MUSTARD MAYONNAISE
Makes 6 servings
Here's a handsome, deep-pink salad of Scandinavian origin.

4 medium-size beets (1 pound)
6 small new potatoes
1 jar (8 ounces) herring in wine sauce, drained
3 tablespoons minced green onions
1 cup mayonnaise

1 teaspoon dry mustard
1 teaspoon vinegar
½ teaspoon salt
⅛ teaspoon freshly ground pepper
2 hard-cooked eggs, sliced
Dill

1. Scrub beets and trim, leaving 1 inch of the tops and the root end attached. Cook, covered, in boiling salted water to cover, 45 minutes or until tender when pierced with the tip of a sharp knife. Drain; rinse in cold running water and slip off skins, root and top. Cube and put into a large bowl.
2. While beets are cooking, cook potatoes in boiling salted water 30 minutes, or until tender. Drain, peel and cube. Add to beets together with herring and green onions.
3. Combine mayonnaise, mustard, vinegar, salt and pepper in a small bowl, stirring until smooth. Pour over beet mixture and toss gently to mix. Chill at least 2 hours or overnight.
4. Remove from refrigerator 30 minutes before serving; garnish with sliced egg and dill.

CHICKEN BREASTS IN VERMOUTH
Makes 6 servings

¼ cup dry vermouth
1 tablespoon leaf rosemary, crumbled
1 teaspoon salt
½ teaspoon pepper

3 whole chicken breasts, halved
¼ cup butter or margarine, melted
¼ cup undiluted frozen orange juice, concentrate, thawed

1. Combine vermouth, rosemary, salt and pepper; pour over chicken breasts. Marinate for 2 hours or more in refrigerator, turning occasionally. Remove chicken from marinade; combine marinade with butter and orange juice concentrate.
2. Broil chicken 6 inches from heat or grill chicken 5 inches from hot coals about 30 minutes, turning and basting frequently with orange mixture. Serve with any remaining marinade, heated in pan on the grill.

QUICK GREEN BEANS
Makes 6 servings

3½ tablespoons flour
  ½ teaspoon salt
  Dash pepper
3½ tablespoons melted butter

1½ cups milk
1½ pounds hot, cooked green beans
  ¾ cup shredded Cheddar cheese

Stir flour, salt and pepper into melted butter in saucepan. Stir in milk; cook until thickened. Pour over cooked green beans. Sprinkle with Cheddar cheese; brown under broiler.

DUTCH RHUBARB CREAM
Makes 6 servings
Serve this soft and creamy dessert in your best sherbet dishes.

1 pound rhubarb, cut into 1-inch
  pieces or 1 package (about 1 pound)
  frozen rhubarb
1½ cups water

1 cup sugar
1 teaspoon grated lemon rind
2 envelopes unflavored gelatin
  ½ cup heavy cream

1. Combine rhubarb, 1 cup of the water, sugar and lemon rind in a medium-size saucepan. Cover and bring to boiling; lower heat and simmer until tender (about 5 minutes for frozen).
2. Sprinkle gelatin over the ½ cup water in a 1-cup measure; let stand 5 minutes to soften. Stir into hot mixture. Cook 5 more minutes, mashing rhubarb.
3. Pour into bowl; chill until mixture will hold its shape softly when spooned.
4. Beat cream in a small bowl with electric mixer until stiff; fold into rhubarb until no white streaks remain. Spoon into 5-cup dish or individual sherbets. Chill 4 hours or until soft-set. Or chill longer and remove from refrigerator 30 to 60 minutes before serving.

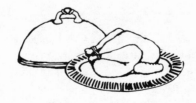

MENU
Serves 8

PREPARE AHEAD FIESTA

Broiled Mushrooms Stuffed with Beer Cheese
Fiesta Chicken Kiev
Ratatouille • Tossed Green Salad
Spiced Peaches

TOTAL TIME
40 minutes ahead of time, plus 45 minutes before serving

If you've ever dreamed of serving a dinner without the last minute frantic panic pattern here's a menu you'll love. The main dish, Chicken Kiev, actually improves as a result of being frozen so it can be made up to 4 months ahead. A great dish to have stashed away for unexpected dinner guests too. The dessert is put together up to a week before. So all that's left to do during the 45 minutes it takes to thaw and cook the frozen chicken is fix the appetizer, vegetable and salad.

MARKET LIST

½ cup finely chopped cooked ham
4 whole chicken breasts, halved, skinned and boned (about 3½ pounds)
5 ounces sharp Cheddar cheese
3 tablespoons pasteurized process cheese spread
24 medium-size mushrooms (about 1¾ pounds)
Lettuce
Tomato
1 green pepper
1 cucumber
1 medium-size eggplant (about 1 pound)

Parsley
½ pint cherry tomatoes
½ cup light beer
2 tablespoons chopped, seeded canned green chili pepper
1 cup Cheddar cheese crackers
Taco seasoning mix
Ripe olives
5 tablespoons oil
2 cans (1 pound, 14 ounces each) cling peach halves
1⅓ cups sugar
1 cup cider vinegar
4 cinnamon sticks
2 teaspoons whole cloves

WORK PLAN

1. Up to 4 months ahead fix the Fiesta Chicken Kiev; freeze.
2. Up to a week ahead place peaches in spicy syrup; refrigerate.
3. 45 minutes before serving, bake chicken. While chicken is baking, prepare broiled mushrooms.
4. Wash, drain and refrigerate salad greens; chill. Cook the Ratatouille.
5. Broil the mushrooms and serve with aperitifs or spritzers.

BROILED MUSHROOMS STUFFED WITH BEER CHEESE
Makes ¾ cup stuffing, or enough for 24 medium-size mushrooms caps
This beer cheese is also good spread on toast triangles and broiled.

24 medium-size mushrooms (about 1½ pounds)
2 tablespoons butter or margarine
½ bar (5 ounces) sharp Cheddar cheese, shredded
1 clove garlic, mashed
1½ teaspoons Worchestershire sauce
½ teaspoon dry mustard
Light beer (about ¼ cup)
¼ cup finely chopped cooked ham

1. Wipe mushrooms with damp towel if necessary. Remove stems and chop, reserving caps. Saute stems in 2 tablespoons of the butter in large skillet until tender. Sauté caps in remaining butter, adding more butter if necessary, until tender.
2. Mix sautéed stems with cheese, garlic, Worcestershire, mustard and beer; stuff mushrooms caps with mixture. Arrange on cooky sheets.
3. Broil 4 inches from heat for 2 minutes, or until cheese is melted and bubbly. Sprinkle with ham.

FIESTA CHICKEN KIEV
Makes 8 servings
A Southwestern version of classic butter-stuffed chicken fillets.

4 whole chicken breasts, halved, skinned and boned (about 3½ pounds)

3 tablespoons butter or margarine, softened

3 tablespoons pasteurized process cheese spread

2 teaspoons instant minced onion

1 teaspoon salt

2 tablespoons chopped seeded canned green chili peppers

¼ cup (½ stick) butter or margarine

1 cup Cheddar cheese crackers, crushed to fine crumbs

1½ tablespoons taco seasoning mix

Shredded lettuce

Diced tomatoes

Chopped black olives

1. Place each chicken breast half between wax paper on a board; pound with mallet or rolling pin to flatten to about ¼-inch thickness.
2. Beat the 3 tablespoons butter, cheese spread, onion, salt and chilies in a small bowl until well blended; divide mixture into 8 equal portions. Place one portion on each of the chicken pieces close to one of the sides. Roll up chicken, tucking in ends to completely enclose the filling. Fasten with wooden picks or tie with kitchen string.
3. Melt remaining butter in a small skillet. Combine cheese cracker crumbs with taco seasoning on a piece of wax paper. Dip rolled chicken into butter, then into crumbs to coat well.

To freeze: Freeze chicken rolls on a jelly-roll pan until frozen solid. Remove from pan and pack into containers. Seal, label and return to freezer. Maximum recommended freezer storage: 4 months. To serve, place frozen rolls on jelly roll pan and bake in a hot oven (425°) for 45 minutes.

RATATOUILLE
Makes 8 servings
Here's a crisp spring version of the popular French eggplant-based vegetable combination.

1 green pepper

1 cucumber

¼ pound mushrooms

1 medium eggplant (1 pound)

5 tablespoons olive or vegetable oil

1 large onion, sliced

1 clove garlic, crushed

1½ teaspoons salt

¼ teaspoon pepper

1 teaspoon dried basil

1 tablespoon fresh chopped parsley

½ pint cherry tomatoes, halved

1. Wash pepper and halve. Remove ribs and seeds; cut into 1-inch dice. Peel cucumber and halve lengthwise; scoop out and discard seeds. Slice cucumber ¼- to ½-inch thick. Wipe mushrooms with damp cloth; cut into quarters through stems. Wash eggplant; cut into about ½-inch dice (do not peel).
2. Heat 2 tablespoons of the oil in large skillet or wok. Add onion, garlic, pepper, cucumber and mushrooms. Stir-fry over high heat 4 to 5 minutes. Remove with slotted utensil to bowl.
3. Heat remaining oil in skillet or wok. Add eggplant; stir and toss 3 to 4 minutes or just until tender.
4. Return vegetables to pan; sprinkle with salt, pepper, basil and parsley. Add tomatoes; stir gently. Cover; simmer 3 to 5 minutes.

SPICED PEACHES
Makes 8 servings

2 cans (1 pound, 14 ounces each) cling peach halves	1 cup cider vinegar
1⅓ cups sugar	4 3-inch pieces stick cinnamon
	2 teaspoons whole cloves

1. Drain syrup from peaches into a large saucepan. Put peach halves into a large bowl.
2. Add sugar, vinegar, cinnamon and cloves to peach syrup. Bring to boiling; lower heat; simmer gently 10 minutes.
3. Pour hot syrup over peach halves; cover and cool thoroughly. Refrigerate several hours or overnight. (This is not a preserve; it will keep in refrigerator about 1 week.)

Note: Leftover peach syrup can be used as part of the liquid in preparing a gelatin salad.

Summer

QUICKEST OF THE QUICK

Egg Drop Soup
Stir-Fried Chicken and Vegetables
Rice (see page 137) • Sweet and Sour Radishes
Fresh Pears with Yogurt

TOTAL TIME
About 30 minutes

I bet the second time you make this meal you could pare the fixing time down to 20 minutes. It goes together fast.

MARKET LIST

2 halves boneless chicken breast
  (about 8 ounces)
1 egg
1 container plain or flavored yogurt
  Lemon
½ cup chopped spinach or 2
  tablespoons cooked peas
2 bunches red radishes or 3 white
  radishes

Watercress
2 ripe pears
2 cups chicken broth
1 package (10 ounces) frozen Chinese-
  style stir-fry vegetables with
  seasonings
Rice
Soy sauce

WORK PLAN

1. Put the rice on to cook.
2. Prepare the radishes, dressing and wash watercress. Chill separately.
3. Assemble all the ingredients for the soup and the chicken dish. 10 minutes before rice is due to be cooked, heat the broth for the soup.
4. Stir-fry the chicken and vegetable dish; keep warm.
5. Finish the soup. Toss the radishes and dressing and arrange on watercress.
6. Peel, core and slice pears just before serving; brush with lemon juice to prevent browning, if you wish, and spoon the yogurt over.

EGG DROP SOUP
Makes 2 servings

2 cups chicken broth
1 egg, beaten
½ teaspoon lemon juice
½ teaspoon soy sauce

½ cup chopped fresh spinach or 2
tablespoons fresh or frozen cooked
peas

Heat the broth to boiling. Beat the egg with the lemon juice and soy sauce. Add spinach or peas to broth, return to the boil and with a fork gradually stir in the egg mixture until it is set. Do not overcook.

STIR-FRIED CHICKEN AND VEGETABLES
Makes 2 servings

3 teaspoons vegetable oil
1 package (10 ounces) frozen Chinese-
style stir-fry vegetables with
seasonings

2 chicken breast fillets (about 8
ounces), cut into ¼-inch slices
¼ cup water
Soy sauce

1. Heat 2 teaspoons of the oil in a heavy skillet. Remove and reserve seasoning envelope from vegetables. Add frozen vegetables to hot oil and stir to break up pieces. Cover and let cook 2 minutes. Remove to small bowl; keep warm.
2. Heat remaining teaspoon oil in skillet. Add chicken; cook 5 minutes, stirring constantly with wooden spoon. There should be no pink left in the chicken.
3. Return vegetables to skillet; sprinkle seasonings over and stir in water until sauce thickens (about 1 minute). Season to taste with soy sauce and serve with hot cooked rice.

SWEET AND SOUR RADISHES
Makes 2 servings

2 bunches red radishes or 3 white
radishes
¼ teaspoon salt
1 tablespoon light brown sugar

2 teaspoons soy sauce
1 tablespoon sesame oil or salad oil
2 tablespoons wine vinegar
Watercress

1. Trim off ends of radishes; scrub well and slice thinly into a bowl.
2. Combine remaining ingredients and toss with radish slices just before serving. Serve over watercress or other salad greens.

MENU
Serves 2

HOT AND COLD CHINESE

Chicken and Chinese Cabbage Salad
Stir-Fried Shrimp • Rice (see page 137)
Coffee Ice or Fresh Berries and Cream

TOTAL TIME
About 1 hour

This is a versatile menu. You can serve the shrimp and rice before the chicken salad, if you prefer, and with this sequence it would be freshly cooked. With both shrimp and chicken the menu is high in protein and low in saturated fat for a satisfying repast without lots of calories. Adding fresh fruit to the dessert would increase the amount of food for anyone who was not satisfied.

MARKET LIST

1 chicken breast (about 12 ounces)
½ pound raw shrimp, shelled and
  deveined or frozen, shelled and
  deveined
  Fresh ginger root (optional)
3 green onions
1 cup bean sprouts
1 medium-size head Chinese cabbage
  Dry sherry

1 package (7 ounces) frozen snow peas
1 tablespoon toasted sesame seeds
½ cup coarsely chopped walnuts
¼ cup thinly sliced water chestnuts
  Rice
  Instant espresso coffee
1 envelope unflavored gelatin
½ pint vanilla ice cream

WORK PLAN

1. Prepare the ice and freeze. Cook chicken, defrost snow peas, make dressing; chill.
2. 20 minutes before serving time cook the rice. Mix chicken, snow peas, onion and sprouts with dressing; chill. Slice cabbage. Don't forget to stir the ice every 10 to 15 minutes.
3. Assemble ingredients for stir-fried shrimp and cook 5 minutes before serving.

CHICKEN AND CHINESE CABBAGE SALAD
Makes 2 servings

1 chicken breast (about 12 ounces)
1 package (7 ounces) frozen snow peas
¼ cup peanut or vegetable oil
2 tablespoons cider vinegar
4½ teaspoons soy sauce
¾ teaspoon ground ginger
Pinch sugar and salt
¼ cup sliced green onion
1 cup bean sprouts
1 medium head Chinese cabbage
1 tablespoon toasted sesame seeds
½ cup coarsely chopped walnuts

1. Simmer chicken breast in salted water until tender, about 10 minutes. Skin, bone and cube (1½ cups).
2. Defrost snow peas; dry on paper toweling.
3. Make dressing: Shake oil, vinegar, soy sauce, ginger, sugar and salt in a screw-top jar.
4. Toss chicken, snow peas, green onion and bean sprouts with the soy dressing. Cover and refrigerate.
5. Slice enough cabbage to make 4 cups. Place in bowl; arrange chicken mixture on top. Sprinkle sesame seeds and walnuts over top. Toss lightly.

STIR-FRIED SHRIMP
Makes 2 servings

2 teaspoons oil
½ pound shelled and deveined raw shrimp or frozen shelled and deveined shrimp
½ green onion, finely chopped
2 tablespoons water
¼ cup thinly sliced water chestnuts
1 thin slice fresh ginger root or pinch ground ginger
¼ teaspoon salt
2 teaspoons soy sauce
2 teaspoons dry sherry
½ teaspoon cornstarch
2 teaspoons water

1. Heat the oil in a wok or skillet. Add the shrimp and onion and stir-fry until shrimp turns pink, about 1 minute.
2. Add the water, water chestnuts, ginger, and salt. Cover and cook 1 minute. Stir in soy sauce, sherry and cornstarch mixed with the water. Cook, stirring until sauce is clear and slightly thickened.

COFFEE ICE
Makes 2 servings

1 cup hot, double strength espresso made from instant espresso coffee
1 tablespoon sugar

½ teaspoon unflavored gelatin
1 tablespoon cold water
½ pint vanilla ice cream

1. Soften the gelatin in the cold water. Add softened gelatin and sugar to hot coffee; stir to dissolve sugar and gelatin.
2. Pour into an ice cube tray and freeze, or in a small metal bowl. As it starts to freeze break up the crystals with a fork or wooden spoon and repeat about every 15 minutes until mixture is frozen into small crystals.
3. Place a scoop of ice cream in individual dishes or parfait glasses and spoon the coffee ice over.

MENU
Serves 2

PORCH SUPPER

Bacon-Spinach Junior Club Sandwiches
Vegetables Vinaigrette
Oranges in Wine

TOTAL TIME
30 minutes ahead, plus 20 minutes before serving

Hearty sandwiches are a nice change of pace when the weather is hot, and here's a menu that lets you do half the preparation early in the morning. The sandwiches are a bacon and spinach salad between slices of toast.

MARKET LIST

6 slices bacon
2 eggs
Spinach leaves
6 cherry tomatoes
2 green onions
1 small zucchini
1 small cucumber

1 carrot
Lettuce leaves
2 navel oranges
Lemon
4 slices firm white bread
¼ cup dry red wine
Mayonnaise

WORK PLAN

1. Night before or early on the day prepare Vegetables Vinaigrette and chill. Prepare Oranges in Wine and chill.
2. 20 minutes before serving make the club sandwiches.

BACON-SPINACH JUNIOR CLUB SANDWICHES
Makes 2 servings
The flavor of this sandwich is reminiscent of the popular sweet-sour spinach salad with chopped egg and bacon bits. Called a "junior club," it consists of 2 slices of bread rather than the usual 3.

---

6 slices bacon	1½ teaspoons sugar
2 eggs	¼ teaspoon salt
½ medium-size onion, finely chopped	Dash pepper
(¼ cup)	4 slices firm white bread, toasted
¼ cup mayonnaise	Spinach leaves
1 tablespoon red wine vinegar	6 cherry tomatoes

1. Fry bacon until crisp in large skillet; drain on paper toweling. Remove all but about 2 tablespoons fat from pan. Break eggs, one at a time, into hot fat; fry until firm, breaking yolks with a pancake turner, and turning them over. Transfer to warm platter. Remove and discard all but 1 tablespoon of the fat from pan.
2. Cook onion in remaining fat until tender. Remove from heat. Stir in mayonnaise, vinegar, sugar, salt and pepper.
3. Spread mayonnaise mixture on each slice of toast. Cover 2 slices with a layer of spinach leaves, 3 slices bacon, a fried egg and top with more spinach leaves. Cover with remaining slices of toast, mayonnaise-coated side down. With serrated knife, cut sandwiches into 4 triangles.
4. Alternately spear triangles with cherry tomatoes on 8-inch skewers.

VEGETABLES VINAIGRETTE
Makes 2 servings

---

2 green onions, chopped	¼ cup oil
1 small zucchini, cut into julienne strips	1 tablespoon red wine vinegar
	¼ teaspoon salt
1 small cucumber, pared, halved, seeded and cut into thin slices	⅛ teaspoon pepper
	¼ teaspoon Italian herbs
1 carrot, cut into julienne strips	Lettuce leaves

In a small bowl combine the green onion, zucchini, cucumber and carrot. In a second small bowl beat together the oil, vinegar, salt, pepper and herbs. Pour over vegetables and chill at least 2 hours.

ORANGES IN WINE
Makes 2 servings

2 navel oranges, peeled and thinly sliced
¼ cup water
¼ cup dry red wine
2 tablespoons light brown sugar

½ teaspoon grated lemon rind
1 whole clove
1 small piece stick cinnamon or ¼ teaspoon ground cinnamon

Place the orange slices in a bowl. Combine remaining ingredients in a small saucepan; bring to boiling, stirring to dissolve sugar. Pour over oranges. Chill several hours or overnight.

MENU
Serves 2

BACON 'N EGGS IN DISGUISE

Corn Omelet
Popovers • Marinated Artichoke Salad
Quick Cherry Cobbler

TOTAL TIME
About 55 minutes

I'm suggesting this menu for a cool day in the summer or when you come home chilled from a breezy sail or swim in the ocean. If you feel it is not hearty enough for your dinner companion cook a package of frozen chopped spinach to go with the omelet.

MARKET LIST

6 slices bacon
7 eggs
½ cup milk
2 large ears of corn or 1 cup drained canned kernels
1 large green pepper
Lettuce leaves
2 green onions

2 stalks celery
Lemon
1 jar (6 ounces) marinated artichoke hearts
2 tablespoons sliced ripe olives
½ can (21 ounces) cherry pie filling
½ cup buttermilk baking mix
2 tablespoons orange juice

WORK PLAN

1. Preheat the oven to 400°. Make the popovers, heat pans and start popovers baking.
2. Prepare Quick Cherry Cobbler and put in oven with popovers opening and closing the oven door carefully and slowly. Remove cobbler when done and let popovers stay in turned-off oven an extra 5 minutes.
3. Meanwhile fix the salad; chill.
4. Prepare the omelet. The oven will still be warm enough without being turned-on again to finish cooking the omelet as indicated in step 4.

CORN OMELET
Makes 2 servings
Pick the corn right from the garden or use canned corn to make this unusual omelet.

---

2 large ears of corn or 1 cup drained canned kernels	6 eggs
6 slices bacon	1 teaspoon salt
4 tablespoons butter	¼ teaspoon black pepper
1 large onion, thinly sliced	Few drops liquid hot pepper
1 cup diced green pepper	seasoning

1. Scrape corn from cobs (you should have 1 cup). Cook corn in boiling unsalted water to cover in a small saucepan 3 to 5 minutes or until tender; drain and spoon into a large bowl. Preheat oven to 325°.
2. Cook bacon in a large skillet until crisp and brown. Remove, crumble and add to corn. Pour off fat into a 1-cup measure. Measure and return 1 tablespoon to skillet. Add 2 tablespoons of the butter and heat until melted. Sauté onion and pepper until tender; add to corn.
3. Beat the eggs with salt, pepper and liquid hot pepper seasoning in a large bowl until just blended. Add the corn mixture.
4. Wipe the skillet out with paper toweling. Heat the remaining 2 tablespoons butter with 1 tablespoon of the bacon fat until very hot. Add the egg mixture and cook until bottom is set but top is still liquid. Transfer skillet to oven and bake 2 minutes or until top is set.

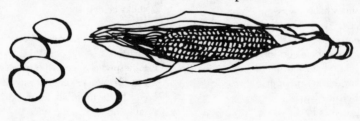

POPOVERS
Bake at 400° for 40 minutes
Makes 4 popovers

Shortening	½ cup milk
½ cup flour	2 teaspoons oil
¼ teaspoon salt	1 egg

1. Preheat the oven to hot (400°). Grease 4 medium-size metal muffin tins very well with shortening.
2. Place flour and salt in a small bowl. In a measuring cup beat together the milk, oil and egg. Gradually beat egg mixture into flour to make a smooth batter.
3. Heat muffin tins in oven 5 minutes. Half fill with batter and bake 40 minutes or until well puffed and brown. Pierce each one with a skewer or tip of sharp knife and close oven door. Turn off heat and leave in oven 5 minutes longer for extra crispness.

MARINATED ARTICHOKE SALAD
Makes 2 servings

1 jar (6 ounces) marinated artichoke hearts, drained	½ cup chopped celery
	Lemon
2 tablespoons chopped green onion	Freshly ground black pepper to taste
2 tablespoons sliced ripe olives	Lettuce leaves

In a small bowl combine the artichoke hearts, green onion, olives and celery. Squeeze lemon juice and add pepper to taste. Chill. Arrange salad in lettuce cups to serve.

QUICK CHERRY COBBLER
Bake at 400° for 20 minutes
Makes 2 servings

½ can (21 ounces) cherry pie filling	1 tablespoon sugar
½ teaspoon grated lemon rind	2 tablespoons orange juice
½ cup buttermilk baking mix	2 teaspoons soft butter or margarine

1. Heat the cherry pie filling and lemon rind in a small saucepan. Spoon into a small (2½-cup) baking dish.
2. In a small bowl mix together the baking mix, sugar, juice and butter. Drop by spoonfuls onto hot cherry mixture. Bake 20 minutes or until lightly brown.

MENU
Serves 2
* *Inexpensive*

OLÉ

Quick Chili for Two
Corn Chips • Cucumber Radish Salad
Guavas with Cream Cheese

TOTAL TIME
About 35 minutes

This chili may not be fantastic enough to win a chili cooking contest, but it goes together fast and sure tastes good when the two of you are starving after a hard day's work. Don't like guavas? Then substitute some delicious fresh fruit topped with ice cream, if you wish.

MARKET LIST

½ pound ground chuck
1 package (3 ounces) cream cheese
1 small cucumber
½ bag radishes
 Watercress
1 can (16 ounces) tomatoes

1 can (8 ounces) tomato sauce
1 can (8 ounces) kidney beans
 Bottled oil and vinegar dressing
1 small can guavas or guava paste
 Corn chips

WORK PLAN

1. Make the chili and set to simmer. Meanwhile fix the salad ingredients; chill.
2. Make up the dessert plates; chill. And that's all there is to it.

QUICK CHILI FOR TWO
Makes 2 servings

½ pound ground chuck
1 medium-size onion, chopped (about ½ cup)
1 clove garlic, finely chopped
1 can (16 ounces) tomatoes

1 can (8 ounces) tomato sauce
¾ teaspoon salt
2 teaspoons chili powder
½ teaspoon cumin
1 can (8 ounces) kidney beans

In a medium-size skillet cook the meat, onion and garlic until the meat has lost all its pink color and is lightly brown. Remove extra fat. Stir in the tomatoes, tomato sauce, salt, chili powder and cumin. Bring to boiling and cook, uncovered, over low heat about 25 minutes. Stir in the kidney beans and liquid. Reheat.

CUCUMBER RADISH SALAD
Makes 2 servings

1 small cucumber	Watercress
½ bag radishes	Bottled oil and vinegar dressing

Peel the cucumber, halve, remove seeds and cut remaining halves into thin slices. Thinly slice radishes and toss with cucumbers. Chill. Arrange watercress on two salad plates, top with cucumber mixture and pour over dressing.

GUAVAS WITH CREAM CHEESE

1 small can guavas or guava paste	1 package (3 ounces) cream cheese

Place chilled guavas or slices of paste on dessert plates. Divide the cream cheese between plates and serve with knife and fork.

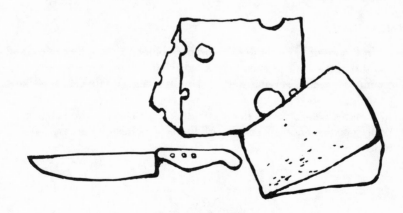

MENU
Serves 4

SOME UNUSUAL AND DELICIOUS FLAVOR COMBINATIONS

Spanish Veal with Almonds and Green Noodles
Fresh Corn Sautéed • Nectarine and Cucumber Salad
Blueberry Fool

TOTAL TIME
About 25 minutes ahead, plus 30 minutes before serving

Fresh fruits and vegetables are one of the joys of summertime dining and here they are combined in an unusual salad which I'm betting you will like well enough to serve as a luncheon main dish. The veal dish calls for boneless shoulder which is considerably cheaper than cutlets or scallopini but equally delicious.

MARKET LIST

1 pound boneless veal shoulder, cubed	8 ears corn
1 cup plain yogurt	Parsley
1 cup heavy cream	¼ cup blanched almonds
1 package (3 ounces) cream cheese	2 tablespoons dry sherry
Fresh mint	⅔ cup canned condensed beef broth
1 cucumber	1 pound fine green spinach noodles
1½ pounds nectarines	Confectioners' sugar

WORK PLAN

1. Night before or early on the day prepare blueberry fool through step 2 and the nectarine and cucumber salad mixture; chill.
2. 30 minutes before serving start cooking the veal. While veal is cooking toast the almonds and grind.
3. 15 minutes before veal is due to be done start cooking the noodles.
4. While noodles are cooking prepare the corn. Finish blueberry fool.
5. Finish veal dish.

SPANISH VEAL WITH ALMONDS AND GREEN NOODLES
Makes 4 servings

¼ cup blanched almonds
2 cloves garlic, mashed
1 teaspoon plus 1 tablespoon vegetable oil
1 pound boneless veal shoulder, cubed

2 tablespoons dry sherry
⅔ cup canned condensed beef broth
1 pound fine green spinach noodles, cooked al dente, drained

1. Toast almonds in a moderate oven (350°) for about 15 minutes or until golden brown.
2. Sauté garlic in 1 teaspoon oil in a large skillet; remove to small cup.
3. Add remaining tablespoon oil to skillet. Brown meat, part at a time, removing cubes to a bowl. Stir in veal, sherry and all but 1 tablespoon of broth. (Add remaining broth to cup with garlic.) Simmer meat, covered, until tender (about 20 minutes).
4. Meanwhile, grind toasted almonds in blender; stir into garlic and broth in cup. When veal is tender, stir in almond mixture; cook uncovered 10 more minutes. Taste; add salt and pepper, if needed. Serve over hot noodles.

FRESH CORN SAUTÉED
Makes 4 servings

8 ears fresh corn, shucked and kernels cut off
¼ cup (½ stick) butter or margarine
½ teaspoon salt

¼ teaspoon pepper
1 tablespoon water
1 tablespoon chopped parsley

Sauté the corn kernels in the butter over low heat 5 minutes. Add the water, cover tightly, and cook 3 minutes. Add remaining ingredients.

NECTARINE AND CUCUMBER SALAD
Makes 4 servings

1 cup plain yogurt
1 tablespoon chopped fresh mint
½ teaspoon salt
¼ teaspoon sugar
1 small clove garlic, minced

1½ pounds nectarine, sliced or ½ can (1 pound, 14 ounces) canned peaches, drained and sliced
1 cucumber, pared and thinly sliced

Combine yogurt, mint, salt, sugar and garlic; mix well. Place a layer of nectarines, then a layer of cucumbers in a shallow serving dish. Spoon on some of yogurt mixture; repeat layering until all are used. Cover and refrigerate for at least 2 hours or overnight. Serve with slotted spoon.

BLUEBERRY FOOL
Makes 4 to 6 servings
Juicy blueberries plus a light touch of lemon are blended with a fluffy cream and cream cheese mixture. Serve this lovely dessert in your prettiest glass bowl.

1 pint blueberries	1 package (3 ounces) cream cheese
¼ cup sugar	¼ cup confectioners' sugar
1½ teaspoons cornstarch	1 teaspoon vanilla
1 teaspoon grated lemon rind	1 cup heavy cream

1. Place blueberries in medium-size saucepan; mix sugar and cornstarch; sprinkle over berries. Cook over medium heat, stirring often and crushing a few berries, until mixture thickens slightly and bubbles 1 minute.
2. Remove from heat, stir in lemon rind, and cool completely. Pour into a 4- to 5-cup glass bowl, cover, and refrigerate several hours.
3. To serve, beat cream cheese until soft in medium-size bowl with electric hand mixer or rotary beater. Blend in confectioners' sugar and vanilla; add cream, and beat until fluffy and soft peaks form.
4. Spoon cream mixture on top of blueberries; then gently fold in, leaving streaks of blue and white. Sprinkle with additional lemon rind, if you wish. Refrigerate until serving time.

MENU
Serves 4

A REAL QUICKIE WITH AN ORIENTAL FLAVOR

Mushrooms and Chicken Lo Mein
Stir-Fried Asparagus
Lichees and Pineapple

TOTAL TIME
About 30 minutes

One of the more interesting new products to appear in supermarkets recently are instant Oriental soup mixes which come in several flavors and are also known as Ramen noodles. In this menu they are used in a traditional Chinese noodle dish. Add a stir-fried, bright green vegetable and fruit dessert for a colorful, not-too-heavy meal for summer.

MARKET LIST

2 whole chicken breasts or 1 pound
boneless chicken

½ small head bok choy or ½ pound
Swiss chard

¼ pound fresh snow peas or 1 package
(7 ounces) frozen snow peas,
thawed

1½ pounds asparagus or 1 package (10
ounces) frozen asparagus tips

½ fresh pineapple or 1 can (1 pound,
4 ounces) pineapple chunks in
pineapple juice

Soy sauce

4 packages (3 ounces each) chicken-
flavored Oriental instant noodle
soup (also known as Ramen)

Cornstarch

2 cups chicken broth

1 can (4 ounces) water chestnuts

1 can (15 ounces) straw mushrooms
(available in Oriental grocery
stores) or 2 cans (4½ ounces each)
whole mushrooms

1 can (20 ounces) lichees

WORK PLAN

1. Assemble all of the ingredients for the lo mein dish in the order they
will be used.
2. Prepare the asparagus ready for stir-frying.
3. Skewer the fruits for the dessert kabobs; chill.
4. Prepare the Mushrooms and Chicken Lo Mein dish. Keep warm while
stir-frying the asparagus.

MUSHROOMS AND CHICKEN LO MEIN
Makes 4 servings

2 whole chicken breasts, skinned and
boned or 1 pound boneless chicken
breasts

½ small head bok choy or ½ pound
Swiss chard

¼ pound snow peas or 1 package (7
ounces) frozen snow peas, thawed

½ cup vegetable oil

4 packages (3 ounces each) chicken-
flavored Oriental instant noodle soup
(also known as Ramen noodles)

Boiling water

2 tablespoons cornstarch

2 cups water or chicken broth

½ cup sliced water chestnuts

1 tablespoon soy sauce

1 can (15 ounces) straw mushrooms,
drained (available in Oriental
grocery stores) or 2 cans (4½ ounces
each) whole mushrooms, drained

1. Cut chicken into thin slices. Cut white part of bok choy or chard stalks into diagonal slices; cut green tops into 1-inch lengths; keep them in separate bowls. Remove any strings from fresh snow pea pods.
2. Heat large deep skillet, Dutch oven or wok over high heat. Add oil; heat 30 seconds. Add uncooked blocks of instant noodles; fry until browned on broad sides, and remove to large bowl with slotted spoon, leaving oil in pan. Sprinkle 2 seasoning packets from noodles over browned noodles; add boiling water to barely cover. Let stand while preparing sauce, tossing occasionally.
3. Combine cornstarch, water and remaining 2 seasoning packets in a 4-cup measure. If using chicken broth, omit packets. Reheat pan; add white part of bok choy or chard and pea pods; stir-fry until browned. Add water chestnuts and green leaves; stir-fry 15 seconds.
4. Restir cornstarch mixture; pour into pan, and bring to boiling. Return vegetables to pan; add soy sauce and mushrooms. Drain noodles; add to sauce. Toss and serve in warm dish.

STIR-FRIED ASPARAGUS
Makes 4 servings

1½ pounds asparagus, trimmed and cut into 1-inch lengths or 1 package (10 ounces) frozen asparagus tips, partially thawed

3 tablespoons oil
1 tablespoon soy sauce
2 tablespoons water

1. Prepare the asparagus. Heat the oil in a wok or medium-size skillet. Add asparagus and fry stirring rapidly for 2 minutes or until asparagus turns bright green.
2. Add the soy sauce and water. Cover and cook 3 to 5 minutes or until asparagus is crisp-tender.

LICHEES AND PINEAPPLE
Makes 4 servings

½ fresh pineapple or 1 can (1 pound, 4 ounces) pineapple chunks in pineapple juice

1 can (20 ounces) lichees, drained

If using canned pineapple, alternate lichees and chunks on four skewers. If using fresh pineapple cut into 2 wedges and loosen the pineapple from the skin, cut into chunks but leave on the skin. Arrange on plate and surround with lichees.

MENU
Serves 4

EAT IN OR OUT

Lemony Chicken Wings and Shrimp Kabobs
Broiled Potato Slices
Lima Beans à la Française
Sliced Tomatoes with Basil
Summer Pudding Surprise

Total Time
About 40 minutes ahead, plus about 40 minutes before serving

You won't have to worry about leftovers of this dessert, it is so good everyone will want seconds or will demand a piece for lunch the next day. The oven doesn't have to be turned on at all for this menu, which can be a blessing when the weather is warm, and it saves energy. A small hibachi fire will be big enough to cook the kabobs and the potatoes.

MARKET LIST

6 chicken wings
1 pound frozen shelled and deveined
  shrimp, thawed
1 cup heavy cream
4 large tomatoes
  Fresh basil
3 lemons
6 medium-size potatoes
  Parsley
1 pint fresh blueberries or frozen
  unsweetened blueberries

3 cups sliced fresh strawberries
  Large head Boston lettuce
1 package (10 ounces) frozen
  raspberries
10 slices firm bread
2 packages (10 ounces) frozen lima
  beans
⅓ cup olive oil
  Leaf tarragon
  Seasoned salt

WORK PLAN

1. The night before put the fruits and sugar to macerate for the dessert while lining the bowl with the bread for the summer pudding. Prepare the kabob marinade and add the trimmed wings and shrimp; cover and chill. Finish dessert.
2. About 40 minutes before serving light the charcoal fire. Cook the potatoes and then slice and grill. Keep warm.
3. While the potatoes are cooking prepare the lima beans.

4. Skin and slice the 4 tomatoes, season with salt, pepper, chopped fresh basil and a drizzle of olive oil and wine vinegar. Cover and chill.
5. Skewer the wings and shrimp and cook as soon as potatoes are done. If you are using a larger grill the potatoes and skewers can be cooked simultaneously and it will save 10 to 15 minutes total time.
6. Unmold the dessert and garnish with whipped cream.

LEMONY CHICKEN WINGS AND SHRIMP KABOBS
Makes 4 servings
Here's an unusual kabob combination with a wonderful lemon-herb flavor.

6 chicken wings (about 1½ pounds)
1 pound frozen shelled and deveined shrimp, thawed
Lemon-Herb Marinade (recipe follows)

¼ cup (½ stick) butter or margarine, melted

1. Divide chicken wings by cutting through joints. Remove wing tips and save for soup. Combine wings and shrimp with Lemon-Herb Marinade in a bowl. Marinate for 2 hours at room temperature, or in refrigerator overnight.
2. Drain wings and shrimp, reserving marinade. Place wings on foil-lined grill. Grill 15 minutes over gray coals, turning once or twice or until golden brown and almost tender. Spear chicken and shrimp alternately on 6 skewers.
3. Grill directly over coals, brushing with butter and marinade and turning often until shrimp and chicken are tender, about 5 minutes.

LEMON-HERB MARINADE
Makes 1 cup

⅔ cup lemon juice
⅓ cup olive oil
1 teaspoon salt

1 teaspoon sugar
1½ teaspoons crumbled leaf tarragon

Combine all ingredients in a small bowl. Stir well.

BROILED POTATO SLICES
Makes 4 servings

6 medium-size potatoes, pared
⅓ cup butter or margarine, melted

1 teaspoon seasoned salt

1. Cook the potatoes in boiling salted water to cover until barely tender, about 20 minutes. Drain and cool slightly.
2. Slice the potatoes into ⅓-inch thick slices and place on grill while kabobs are cooking. Mix butter and seasoned salt and brush both sides of potato slices on each side as they are cooking. Grill until golden and crisp.

LIMA BEANS A LA FRANÇAISE
Makes 4 servings

3 tablespoons butter or margarine
1 medium-size onion, finely chopped
1 clove garlic, finely chopped
2 packages (10 ounces each) frozen
lima beans, partially thawed
1 large head Boston lettuce, shredded

1 cup water
¾ teaspoon salt
¼ teaspoon freshly ground black
pepper
1 teaspoon crushed rosemary
2 tablespoons chopped parsley

1. Melt the butter in a saucepan and sauté the onion and garlic until tender but not browned.
2. Add the lima beans, lettuce, water, salt, pepper and rosemary; cover. Bring to boiling and cook 15 minutes or until beans are tender.
3. Remove cover and boil until liquid is reduced to an amount that is just enough to moisten the mixture, about 20 minutes. Sprinkle with parsley. Leftover beans can be added to a salad.

SUMMER PUDDING SURPRISE
Makes 6 servings
This traditional English dessert does not require any cooking. The juices of the fresh sugared berries spooned inside the bread-lined mold soak into the bread when refrigerated overnight.

3 cups fresh sliced strawberries
1 pint fresh or frozen unsweetened
blueberries
⅓ to ½ cup sugar

1 package (10 ounces) frozen
raspberries, partially thawed
10 slices firm white bread
1 cup heavy cream

1. Place strawberries and blueberries in large bowl; stir in sugar. Let stand, stirring often, until juicy and sugar is dissolved, about 30 minutes. Stir in raspberries.
2. Meanwhile, remove crusts from bread slices. Line a 1½-quart deep mixing bowl with 6 or 7 overlapping bread slices. Cut 1 slice to fit bottom. Fill bowl with berry mixture; cover top completely with remaining bread. Cover with wax paper; set a small flat plate or pie plate on top and place a 3- or 4-pound weight on the plate. (Several large cans of fruit or vegetables will do.) The weighted plate presses on the bread to compact the mixture. Refrigerate overnight.
3. To serve, invert pudding onto a chilled serving plate. Garnish with a few extra berries, if you wish. Cut pudding in wedges to serve. Beat the cream just until softly whipped. Serve with the pudding.

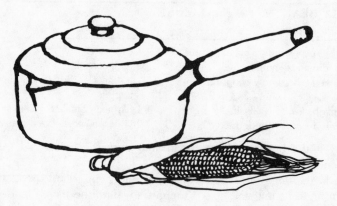

MENU
Serves 4
* *Inexpensive*

SOUP AND SANDWICH DINNER

Curried Cream of Corn Soup
Provençal Pan Bagna (with cold cuts, optional)
Melon and Berries with Yogurt Mint Dip

TOTAL TIME
About 40 minutes

Hot soup made with fresh corn and a sandwich scented with garlic and dripping with olive oil would be a pleasant repast on a summer evening. If the people gathered at your table must have meat at every meal make some cornets out of Genoa salami or spicy ham and garnish the sandwich platters with them.

MARKET LIST

6 ounces hard salami or spicy ham
4 eggs
¼ cup heavy cream
2 cups plain yogurt
6 large ears corn
2 medium-size tomatoes
1 small green pepper
1 small red onion
1 small honeydew
1 pint strawberries
1 orange
Fresh pineapple spears (optional)

Fresh mint
2 cans (13¾ ounces each) chicken
broth
4 hard-crusted French rolls or hero
rolls
Olive oil
1 can (2 ounces) flat anchovy fillets
10 pitted ripe olives
¼ cup thawed frozen orange juice
concentrate
Honey

WORK PLAN

1. Prepare the soup according to recipe.
2. Fix the sandwiches and set aside at room temperature to mellow.
3. Prepare the dip for the fruits and arrange fruits on platter around dip; chill.

CURRIED CREAM OF CORN SOUP
Makes 4 servings

---

6 large ears of corn
1 medium-size onion, chopped (½ cup)
2 tablespoons butter
½ teaspoon curry powder
1½ tablespoons flour

¾ teaspoon salt
¼ teaspoon freshly ground pepper
2 cans (13¾ ounces each) chicken broth
¼ cup heavy cream

1. Scrape corn from cobs (you should have 3 cups); reserve.
2. Sauté onion in butter in a large saucepan until tender, about 3 minutes. Stir in curry powder, flour, salt and pepper and cook 1 minute, stirring constantly. Add the chicken broth; bring to boiling, stirring until smooth and slightly thickened.
3. Add the corn. Lower heat and cook, partly covered, until corn is tender, about 3 to 5 minutes; cool.
4. Puree, part at a time, in container of electric blender. Return puree to saucepan; bring to boiling; stir in cream.

PROVENÇAL PAN BAGNA
Makes 4 servings
This appealing French sandwich is ideal for a picnic in a park or at the beach. Also called "pan bagnat" or "pain baigne," the name means "bathed bread" as the bread is bathed in olive oil for flavor.

4 hard-crusted French rolls or hero rolls
½ cup olive oil
2 tablespoons red wine vinegar
2 cloves garlic, minced
¼ teaspoon leaf basil, crumbled
2 medium-size tomatoes, halved and thinly sliced
1 small green pepper, halved, seeded and cut into thin strips
1 small red onion, sliced and separated into rings
Salt
Pepper
4 hard-cooked eggs, sliced
1 can (2 ounces) flat anchovy fillets, drained (12)
10 pitted ripe olives, halved

1. Cut rolls in half horizontally. Combine oil, vinegar, garlic and basil in a 1-cup measure; stir until blended. Drizzle 1 tablespoon mixture on each cut side of rolls.
2. Arrange tomato slices on bottom halves of rolls, overlapping to fit; top with green pepper strips and onion rings. Sprinkle with salt and pepper. Arrange egg slices over onion rings; top with anchovy fillets and olives. Sprinkle with more salt and pepper; drizzle with any leftover dressing.
3. Carefully place tops of rolls over filled bottoms; press down gently. The flavor of these sandwiches improves on standing a short while. For picnics, wrap in foil or plastic.

MELON AND BERRIES WITH YOGURT MINT DIP
Makes 2 cups dip

1 small honeydew, peeled, halved and seeded
1 pint strawberries, hulled
Orange slices, halved
Fresh pineapple fingers (optional)
2 cups (1 pint) plain yogurt
2 tablespoons finely chopped fresh mint or 2 teaspoons dried mint leaves
¼ cup thawed frozen orange juice concentrate, undiluted
2 tablespoons honey

Cut melon into 1-inch cubes; leave strawberries whole; wrap and chill fruit. Combine yogurt, mint, orange juice and honey in a medium-size bowl; stir until well-blended; cover and chill. When ready to serve, spoon dip into a glass bowl or a hollowed-out melon shell and place in the center of a large bowl filled with crushed ice. Place fruits on crushed ice to serve. Spear fruits on skewers for dipping.

MENU
Serves 4
* Inexpensive

SEASONED FOR SUMMER

Cold Zucchini Soup
Orange Ginger Soy Chicken
Rice (see page 137) • Minted Tomato Salad
Frozen Fruit Sherbet

TOTAL TIME
About 30 minutes early on the day, plus 55 minutes before serving

The chicken can be cooked over charcoal or under the broiler and during most of that time you can relax and only get up to turn it once in awhile. The soup is a wonderful way to use up some of the zucchini you've been collecting from the garden.

MARKET LIST

1 broiler-fryer (about 3 pounds), quartered
1 cup dairy sour cream
6 medium-size zucchini
2 tablespoons chopped chives or 1 green onion
2 large ripe tomatoes
1 large green or red sweet pepper
2 ribs celery
1 medium-size sweet onion

Fresh mint
Lettuce leaves
3 cans (13¾ ounces each) chicken broth (about 5 cups)
1 can (6 ounces) frozen orange juice concentrate
Sherry
Rice
Cookies

WORK PLAN

1. Night before, or early in the day make the soup. Prepare the marinade for the chicken; pour over and refrigerate.
2. About 55 minutes before serving start to cook the chicken.
3. Prepare the salad; chill.
4. Cook the rice.
5. Make the sherbet just before serving.

COLD ZUCCHINI SOUP
Makes 4 servings
This soup can be kept frozen for several weeks. If you use homemade chicken broth, omit flour.

1 medium-size onion, chopped
  (½ cup)
1 large clove garlic, minced
2 tablespoons butter
1 tablespoon vegetable oil
6 medium-size zucchini, chopped
  (2 pounds)
1 teaspoon salt

¼ teaspoon freshly ground pepper
1 tablespoon flour
3 cans (13¾ ounces each) chicken
  broth (about 5¼ cups)
1 cup dairy sour cream
2 tablespoons minced chives or green
  onions

1. Sauté onions and garlic in the butter and oil in a large saucepan until tender but not brown. Add zucchini, salt and pepper; cover. Cook over low heat for 10 minutes or until very tender.
2. Stir in the flour; cook 1 minute. Stir in the broth; bring to boiling. Cook 5 minutes; cool.
3. Puree mixture, part at a time, in container of electric blender. Taste and add additional salt and pepper, if necessary. Chill several hours.
4. To serve: Top each serving with a dollop of sour cream mixed with either chive or green onion.

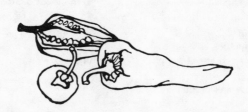

ORANGE GINGER SOY CHICKEN
Makes 4 servings
A zingy combination of sweet and tangy makes the marinade for this chicken.

1 broiler-fryer (about 3 pounds,
  quartered)
3 ounces frozen orange juice
  concentrate, undiluted and thawed
3 tablespoons dry sherry

3 tablespoons soy sauce
½ teaspoon ground ginger
1 clove garlic, mashed
½ teaspoon salt
⅛ teaspoon pepper

1. Arrange chicken in shallow glass or enamel dish. Combine orange juice, sherry, soy sauce, ginger, garlic, salt and pepper in a 4-cup measure. Pour orange mixture evenly over chicken. Marinate at least 2 hours at room temperature or in refrigerator overnight, turning chicken occasionally.
2. Drain chicken, reserving marinade. Place chicken on grill, bone side down. Grill 40 minutes, turning often and brushing generously with reserved marinade until chicken is fork-tender. Heat any remaining marinade to serve with chicken. Serve with hot cooked rice.

MINTED TOMATO SALAD
Makes 4 servings

2 large ripe tomatoes, peeled, seeded and roughly chopped
1 large green or red sweet pepper, cored, seeded and diced
2 ribs celery, diced
1 medium-size sweet onion, chopped
¼ cup olive or salad oil
1½ tablespoons wine vinegar
½ teaspoon salt
¼ teaspoon freshly ground black pepper
2 tablespoons chopped fresh mint leaves or 1 tablespoon crumbled dried mint
Lettuce leaves

Combine all the ingredients except for the lettuce; mix well. Serve in lettuce cups or over shredded lettuce.

FROZEN FRUIT SHERBET
Makes 4 servings

1 small can (6 ounces) frozen orange juice concentrate
4 tablespoons sugar
3 heaping cups crushed ice

1. Place all the ingredients in the container of an electric blender; cover and whirl, stopping to push the mixture away from the sides with a rubber spatula. Do not push down into the ice.
2. Continue blending until mixture looks like snow. Serve at once. Blending will take about 1 minute.

MENU
Serves 4

MIX AND MATCH MENU

Honeydew Melon with Lime Wedges
Teriyaki • Rice (see page 137)
Stir-Fried Peas Plus
Fruit-Glazed Tarts

TOTAL TIME
About 15 minutes ahead, plus 30 minutes before serving

Here is a way to enjoy beef round or chuck simply grilled because it has been marinated to make it tender and flavorful. Cook it out over the barbecue grill or hibachi or under the broiler.

MARKET LIST

1½ pounds beef round or chuck, well-
   trimmed and cut into 1-inch cubes
  2 slices bacon
  1 package (3 ounces) cream cheese
  ¼ cup dairy sour cream
  1 honeydew melon
    Lime
    Fresh ginger root, if available
  2 cloves garlic
18 tiny white onions (½ pound)
  2 pounds fresh peas, shelled (2 cups)

1 small green pepper, cut into strips
  Parsley
  Lemon
  Fresh fruits: strawberries, grapes,
  blueberries, peaches or nectarines
  Soy sauce
1 envelope instant chicken broth
  Rice
1 can water chestnuts (optional)
4 3-inch baked tart shells
  White grape or apple jelly

WORK PLAN

1. 24 to 48 hours before serving prepare marinade for teriyaki; add meat; toss and refrigerate.
2. About 30 minutes before serving time prepare the tarts; chill.
3. Cook the rice. Skewer the meat and start cooking.
4. While the meat is cooking cook the stir-fried peas.
5. Cut melon into 4 wedges, remove seeds and fibers. Serve with lime wedges.

TERIYAKI
Makes 4 servings
By marinating a less tender cut of meat for 24 hours, you can have teriyaki at less than sirloin steak prices.

1½ pounds beef round or chuck, well-trimmed and cut in 1-inch cubes	2 tablespoons brown sugar
1 tablespoon grated fresh ginger root or 1 teaspoon ground ginger	½ cup soy sauce
	2 tablespoons vegetable oil
2 cloves garlic, mashed	Freshly ground black pepper to taste

1. Place meat in deep nonmetal bowl. Combine remaining ingredients in a 1-cup measure; pour over meat and stir to coat well. Allow meat to marinate in refrigerator for 24 to 48 hours, turning occasionally.
2. Place meat on skewers; grill about 4 inches from hot coals or under a preheated broiler, turning and basting frequently with reserved marinade, for 12 to 15 minutes.

STIR-FRIED PEAS PLUS
Makes 4 servings
Tiny white onions, bacon and green pepper make this a tasty accompaniment for springtime dinners.

2 slices bacon	1 envelope instant chicken broth
18 tiny white onions (½ pound), peeled (see note)	1 teaspoon flour
	½ cup water
2 pounds fresh peas, shelled (2 cups)	2 tablespoons chopped parsley
1 small green pepper, cut into strips	1 tablespoon butter or margarine

1. Cook bacon until crisp in large skillet; remove and reserve. Add onions to drippings in skillet; sauté over medium heat 10 minutes, stirring often.
2. Add peas to skillet; stir-fry 5 minutes or until peas become bright green. Add green pepper.
3. Blend instant chicken broth, flour and water in small bowl until smooth. Stir into skillet; add 1 tablespoon parsley. Cover and cook 3 minutes longer. Stir in remaining parsley and butter until melted. Spoon into heated serving dish; crumble bacon over top.

Note: If tiny white onions are not available, use larger ones, halved or quartered.

FRUIT-GLAZED TARTS
Makes 4 tarts

1 package (3 ounces) cream cheese, softened	Fresh fruits (grapes, strawberries, peaches, nectarines)
¼ cup dairy sour cream	¼ cup white grape or apple jelly
1 tablespoon sugar	1 tablespoon sugar
½ teaspoon grated lemon rind	4 purchased 3-inch baked tart shells
¼ teaspoon vanilla	

1. Beat cream cheese, sour cream, sugar, lemon rind and vanilla until light and fluffy; spoon into tart shells, dividing evenly. Chill until firm.
2. Decorate with fruits of your choice. Heat white grape jelly with remaining sugar in a small saucepan until melted and bubbly; cool slightly; spoon over fruits to glaze. Chill tarts.

MENU
Serves 6
* *Inexpensive*

FIX AHEAD FOR OUTDOOR ENJOYMENT

Jellied Tomato and Zucchini Soup
Moussaka Burgers • Creamy Coleslaw
Frozen Papaya Cream

TOTAL TIME
1 hour ahead, plus 30 minutes before serving

Plan to cook the Greek-inspired burgers over an outdoor grill or hibachi. Everything else is ready to go. A terrific menu for the dog days of summer.

MARKET LIST

1½ pounds ground round or chuck	3 papayas
¼ cup light cream or half-and-half	1 quart tomato juice
¾ cup heavy cream	1 cup (13¾ ounces) chicken broth
2 small zucchini	2 envelopes unflavored gelatin
2 to 3 limes	2 cans (4¾ ounces each) eggplant appetizer
Parsley	
1 large head cabbage	3 tablespoons seasoned bread crumbs
Lemon	6 sesame seed buns
1 cup grated carrots (about 2)	¼ cup mayonnaise
½ green pepper	

WORK PLAN

1. Early on day or night before make papaya cream; freeze 1 hour. Beat and return to freezer.
2. While papaya cream is freezing make jellied soup; chill.
3. 30 minutes before serving make cole slaw; chill. Take out papaya cream to soften; stir and refreeze if necessary.
4. Prepare the moussaka burgers; cook.
5. Serve soup.

JELLIED TOMATO AND ZUCCHINI SOUP
Makes 6 servings
A sunny Mediterranean-style soup.

1 medium-size onion, chopped	1 teaspoon sugar
2 tablespoons olive or vegetable oil	⅛ to ¼ teaspoon liquid red pepper
2 small zucchini, finely diced	seasoning
4 cups tomato juice	2 envelopes unflavored gelatin
1 can (13¾ ounces) chicken broth	½ cup cold water
3 tablespoons lime juice	2 tablespoons chopped parsley
2 teaspoons Worcestershire sauce	Lime slices
1 teaspoon salt	

1. Sauté onion in oil in large saucepan until soft, about 5 minutes. Stir in zucchini; saute 2 to 3 minutes. Add tomato juice, chicken broth, lime juice, Worcestershire, salt, sugar and pepper seasoning.
2. Heat to boiling; lower heat and cover. Simmer 5 minutes. Soften gelatin in ½ cup cold water 5 minutes; stir into hot soup. Cool completely and chill several hours or overnight until jellied. To serve, break up with a fork and spoon into chilled glasses or soup bowls. Garnish with chopped parsley and lime slices.

MOUSSAKA BURGERS
Makes 6 servings
*The combination of seasoned eggplant mixture and beef resembles the
classic Greek dish, moussaka.*

1½ pounds ground round or chuck
  2 cans (4¾ ounces each) eggplant
    appetizer
  3 tablespoons chopped parsley
  3 tablespoons seasoned bread crumbs

1½ teaspoons salt
  ½ teaspoon pepper
1½ tablespoons vegetable oil
  6 sesame seed rolls, split, toasted and
    buttered

1. Lightly mix ground round with eggplant appetizer (reserving ½ can for
   garnish), parsley, bread crumbs, salt and pepper, and then shape this
   mixture into 6 equal-size patties.
2. Heat oil in large skillet. Pan-fry burgers over medium heat 4 minutes
   on each side or until done as you like them. Or broil or grill 5 to 6
   inches from heat, turning once.
3. Place each hamburger on bottom half of each roll; top with dollop of
   reserved eggplant appetizer and remaining half of roll. Garnish with
   olives, if you wish.

CREAMY COLESLAW
Makes about 8 cups
What would a barbecue be without a big bowl of creamy coleslaw?

1 large head cabbage, about 4 pounds,
  shredded (about 4 quarts)
¼ cup sugar
¼ cup lemon juice
¼ cup mayonnaise or salad dressing

¼ cup light cream or half-and-half
½ teaspoon salt
¼ teaspoon pepper
1 cup grated carrots
½ cup diced green pepper

1. Place shredded cabbage in a very large bowl, sprinkle with sugar and
   toss just until mixed. Cover and chill 30 minutes.
2. Mix lemon juice, mayonnaise and cream in a 1-cup measure; pour over
   cabbage. Sprinkle with salt and pepper. Add carrots and green pepper;
   toss to mix well.

FROZEN PAPAYA CREAM
Makes 6 servings
This unusual and delicious dessert is made from the tropical papaya fruit, a newcomer to the supermarket. Freezing the mixture till soft brings out its flavor.

3 papayas
6 tablespoons lime juice
½ cup sugar

¾ cup heavy cream
Lime wedges

1. Cut papayas in half lengthwise; scoop out and discard seeds. Scoop out 6 small balls with a melon baller, reserving for garnish. Carefully scoop out remaining pulp, reserving papaya shells. Puree papaya with lime juice and sugar in container of electric blender until smooth or beat with a fork or rotary beater until fairly smooth.
2. Beat the cream until stiff; quickly but gently fold papaya into cream (do not overmix). Pour mixture into a shallow 9-inch cake pan. Place in freezer 1 hour or until frozen 1 inch around edge. Stir with a spoon. Return to freezer another 30 minutes to 1 hour or until soft-frozen.
3. To serve: Spoon mixture into reserved papaya shells, dividing evenly (or spoon into sherbet glasses for serving). Garnish with a wedge of lime and reserved papaya balls. Serve at once or return to freezer a few minutes until ready to serve.

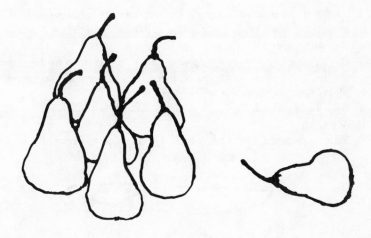

MENU
Serves 6

MEMORIES OF PROVENCE

Mediterranean Tuna Salad
Quick Refrigerated Dough Biscuits or Brown and Serve Rolls
Nectarines with Sour Cream Sauce

TOTAL TIME
About 25 minutes ahead, plus 20 minutes before serving

When the weather is unbearably hot the less cooking the better, but hot biscuits from the toaster oven take no time or effort at all and complement the main dish salad perfectly.

MARKET LIST

2 eggs
1 cup dairy sour cream
Parsley
1½ pounds new red potatoes
3 ribs celery
Lettuce
Lemon
6 to 8 nectarines or peaches, peeled
Tarragon vinegar

2 cans (7 ounces each) tuna
1 jar (7 ounces) roasted red peppers
1 can (2 ounces) flat anchovy fillets
3 tablespoons white creme de cacao
1 package refrigerated biscuit dough
  or brown and serve rolls, croissants
  or bread
3 tablespoons Seville orange marmalade or 1 tablespoon orange rind

WORK PLAN

1. Early on the day, or the night before, mix the salad dressing. Cook potatoes and hard-cook eggs. Slice potatoes, pour marinade over them and refrigerate.
2. 20 minutes before serving preheat oven according to package directions for heating/cooking refrigerator biscuits or brown and serve rolls.
3. Make sour cream sauce for nectarines.
4. Bake biscuits or rolls.
5. Assemble salad.
6. Slice nectarines; toss with a little lemon juice to prevent discoloration.

MEDITERRANEAN TUNA SALAD
Makes 6 servings
Tuna prepared with Mediterranean accents makes a zesty and colorful salad.

¼ cup tarragon vinegar
2 tablespoons lemon juice
1 clove garlic, minced
2 tablespoons chopped parsley
½ teaspoon leaf basil, crumbled
½ teaspoon salt
⅛ teaspoon pepper
½ cup olive oil
1½ pounds new red potatoes

1 cup sliced celery
2 cans (7 ounces each) tuna, drained
   and broken into chunks
1 jar (7 ounces) roasted red peppers
2 hard-cooked eggs, cut into wedges
1 can (2 ounces) flat anchovy fillets
Lettuce
Lemon

1. Combine vinegar, lemon juice, garlic, parsley, basil, salt, pepper and oil in jar with tight-fitting lid; shake until well combined.
2. Wash potatoes well in cold water; cook in boiling salted water 20 minutes or until tender. Drain, cool and slice. (Peel potatoes before slicing, if you wish.) Place potatoes and celery in a shallow bowl; pour dressing over. Toss gently to coat potatoes well. Refrigerate and allow to marinate at least 2 hours. Refrigerate tuna, peppers, eggs and anchovies separately.
3. To serve: Line a deep platter or shallow bowl with lettuce. Lift potatoes from dressing and arrange on top of lettuce; reserve dressing. Top with tuna, peppers and eggs. Arrange anchovies on top; drizzle with reserved dressing. Garnish with lemon slices, if you wish.

NECTARINES WITH SOUR CREAM SAUCE
Makes 6 servings
The sauce is excellent on peaches, too.

1 cup dairy sour cream
3 tablespoons Seville orange
   marmalade or 1 tablespoon grated
   orange rind

3 tablespoons white creme de cacao
Dash salt
6 to 8 nectarines or peaches, peeled

Combine sour cream, marmalade, creme de cacao and salt in a small bowl; chill. To serve, slice nectarines into serving bowl. Pass sauce in separate bowl.

MENU
Serves 6

PATIO DINING

Chilled Gazpacho
Prize-Winning Barbecued Chicken
Corn Roasted in Foil
Potato Packages
Blueberry/Strawberry-Topped Sponge Flan or Watermelon

TOTAL TIME

About 25 minutes ahead, plus 1 hour before serving

Traditional enough for a July 4th cookout but this menu is quick and easy enough to serve often all summer long.

MARKET LIST

2 broiler-fryers (3 pounds each), cut up
Milk
3 eggs
2 ribs celery
4 green onions
1 small cucumber
Chopped chives
6 ears corn
6 medium potatoes (2 pounds)
½ cup chopped green pepper
2 cups (1 pint) fresh blueberries

7 to 8 large strawberries
2 cans (14½ ounces each) sliced baby tomatoes
1 can (5¾ ounces drained weight) pitted black olives
1 can condensed beef broth
¾ cup dry white wine
Croutons
1 ten-inch sponge flan ring
½ cup strawberry jelly
1 package vanilla pudding mix

WORK PLAN

1. The night before, prepare the gazpacho and refrigerate. Make vanilla pudding according to package directions and chill, covered.
2. Prepare the chicken marinade. Pour over chicken, cover and refrigerate.
3. About 1½ hours before serving time start charcoal fire. Start chicken cooking.
4. Prepare corn and potato packages for grill.
5. Heat strawberry jelly and glaze flan ring. Assemble flan ring.
6. About 20 minutes before chicken is done, add corn and potatoes to grill.

CHILLED GAZPACHO
Makes about 6 servings

2 cans (14½ ounces each) sliced baby tomatoes
1 can (5¾ ounces drained weight) pitted black olives
¾ cup chopped celery
¾ cup chopped green onions
¾ cup chopped cucumber
2 cloves garlic, minced
3 tablespoons red-wine vinegar
1½ tablespoons liquid seasoning for meats
1 teaspoon Worcestershire sauce
6 drops liquid red pepper seasoning (or to taste)
1 can condensed beef broth
¾ cup dry white wine
Croutons
Chopped chives

1. Drain tomatoes over a large bowl. Cut tomato slices into large pieces; add to juice in bowl.
2. Drain olives; cut each into 3 slices. Add with celery, green onion, cucumber and garlic to bowl. Stir in vinegar, liquid seasoning, Worcestershire sauce, red pepper seasoning, beef broth and wine; cover. Chill.
3. To serve: Ladle into chilled soup bowls; garnish with chives and croutons.

PRIZE-WINNING BARBECUED CHICKEN
Makes 6 servings

1 cup vegetable oil
⅔ cup wine vinegar
3 tablespoons sugar
3 tablespoons catsup
1 tablespoon grated onion
1½ teaspoons salt
1 teaspoon dry mustard
1 tablespoon Worcestershire sauce
1 clove garlic, minced
Dash liquid hot pepper seasoning
2 broiler-fryers (3 pounds each), cut up

1. Combine all ingredients except chicken in a 2-cup measure. Place chicken in a shallow glass baking dish. Pour marinade over and marinate in refrigerator 6 to 8 hours or overnight, turning occasionally, if possible.
2. Grill chicken 5 to 6 inches from coals 20 to 30 minutes on each side, turning and brushing often with marinade. If you have any remaining marinade, skim fat, then heat and serve hot with chicken.

CORN ROASTED IN FOIL
Makes 6 servings

1 quart water	¼ pound (1 stick) melted butter or
2 tablespoons sugar	margarine
6 ears corn, in husks	Seasoned salt or table salt

Combine water and sugar; soak corn in mixture for 15 minutes. Remove from water and wrap each ear, still in its husk, in a piece of aluminum foil; twist ends to close. Grill 5 inches from heat for 15 to 20 minutes, turning often. Remove foil; wearing protective gloves, strip husks from corn and roll ears in shallow platter of melted butter seasoned with salt.

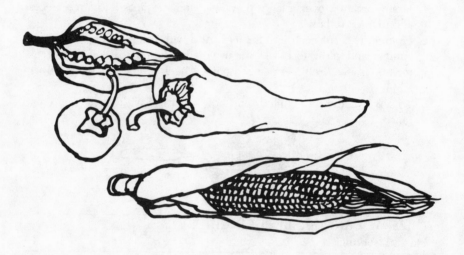

POTATO PACKAGES
Makes 6 servings

6 medium potatoes, pared and cut into ½-inch cubes (2 pounds)	2 teaspoons salt
1 large onion, chopped (1 cup)	½ teaspoon pepper
½ cup chopped green pepper	¼ teaspoon caraway seeds
	⅓ cup butter or margarine

Place potatoes in center of 18-by-22-inch rectangle of heavy duty aluminum foil. Sprinkle with onion, green pepper, salt, pepper and caraway seeds; dot with butter. Fold foil to seal package securely; grill seam side down, 5 inches from coals, for 20 minutes. Turn package and grill 20 minutes longer or until potatoes are tender. Toss lightly with fork and serve.

BLUEBERRY/STRAWBERRY-TOPPED SPONGE FLAN
Makes 6 to 8 servings

½ cup strawberry jelly
1 tablespoon water
1 ten-inch sponge flan ring from
   supermarket

1 package vanilla pudding mix, made
   according to package directions and
   chilled
2 cups (1 pint) fresh blueberries
7 to 8 large strawberries

1. Heat strawberry jelly and water in a small saucepan until melted and bubbly. Brush over interior of shell and sides of cake and allow to set for 5 minutes.
2. To assemble: Fill center of sponge flan with chilled vanilla pudding. Arrange 7 or 8 strawberries in center, stem ends down; arrange blueberries around top. Glaze berries with additional melted strawberry jelly, if you wish.

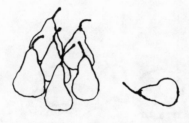

MENU
Serves 6

OUTDOOR GRILL SPECIAL

Beef and Sausage Kabobs
Carrots and Kasha • Corn-on-the-Cob
Onion Cheese Rolls
Baked Apples or Pears

TOTAL TIME
About 15 minutes ahead, plus 45 minutes before serving

The only dish you have to fix in the kitchen is the carrots and kasha and this can be done ahead, if you wish. The rest of the menu including the dessert is cooked over a barbecue grill for extra flavor and fun.

MARKET LIST

1½ pounds boneless chuck, sirloin or
  round steak, cut into 1-inch cubes
1 pound sweet Italian sausage,
  cooked, cooled and cut into 1-inch
  chunks
3 slices bacon
1 cup (2 sticks) butter or margarine
½ cup freshly grated Parmesan cheese
1 egg
2 green onions
5 carrots
4 medium-size mushrooms
6 ears corn
3 cloves garlic

1 cup thinly sliced white onions
  (about 4)
6 large cooking apples or pears
  Parsley
1 cup dry red wine
½ cup kasha (buckwheat groats)
1 can (13¾ ounces) chicken broth
6 crusty oblong rolls about 5 inches
  in diameter
½ cup chopped walnuts
⅓ cup raisins
⅓ cup orange marmalade
1 cup maple syrup

WORK PLAN

1. Start carrots and kasha cooking.
2. Prepare kabobs and basting sauce; start cooking. Fix corn in foil; start cooking.
3. Make the rolls; begin cooking. Prepare the apple or pear packages; start cooking.

BEEF AND SAUSAGE KABOBS
Makes 6 servings
Sweet sausage is a great flavor addition for these juicy beef kabobs.

1½ pounds boneless chuck, sirloin or
  round steak, cut into 1-inch cubes
1 pound sweet Italian sausage,
  cooked, cooled and cut into 1-inch
  chunks
1 cup dry red wine
2 tablespoons vegetable oil

1 clove garlic, crushed
1 teaspoon salt
½ teaspoon leaf rosemary, crumbled
3 slices bacon, finely diced
2 tablespoons flour
2 tablespoons water

1. Combine beef, sausage, wine, oil, garlic, salt and rosemary in glass or stainless steel bowl. Toss until well mixed. Marinate for 2 hours at room temperature or in refrigerator overnight.
2. Drain beef and sausages, reserving marinade. Cook bacon in small saucepan until crisp. Stir in flour; cook 1 minute. Stir in reserved marinade. Cook over low heat until bubbly. If mixture is very thick, add water a tablespoon at a time until it is of a thin sauce consistency. Remove from heat.
3. Spear cubes of beef and sausages alternately on 6 long skewers. Place kabobs on grill. Brush with marinade. Grill 15 minutes for rare, 20 minutes for medium or longer for well done beef.

CARROTS AND KASHA
Makes 6 servings
This unusual combination can be served as a vegetable or used as a stuffing for chicken or Cornish hens.

¼ cup chopped green onions	½ cup kasha
5 carrots, scraped and cut into 1½-inch cubes (about 2 cups)	1 can (13¾ ounces) chicken broth
4 medium-size mushrooms, chopped	½ teaspoon salt
2 tablespoons vegetable oil	⅛ teaspoon freshly ground pepper
1 egg	1 tablespoon chopped parsley

1. Sauté onions, carrots and mushrooms in vegetable oil in a large skillet until tender, about 10 minutes.
2. Beat egg slightly in a small bowl; add the kasha and mix well. Add mixture to skillet; cook, stirring, until kasha separates. Stir in broth, salt and pepper; cover. Simmer 20 minutes or until broth is absorbed and kasha is tender. Sprinkle with parsley.

SWEET CORN-ON-THE-COB
Makes 6 servings
Grilling corn in its own husk is a great flavor saver.

---

6 ears fresh corn	Salt
Softened butter or margarine	Pepper

1. To roast corn in husks, remove only outer husks, fold back inner ones, being careful not to split them, and remove silks. Spread corn with butter; sprinkle with salt and pepper. Pull husks back up over ears; tie tips with string to keep corn covered and moist.

2. To roast corn in aluminum foil, husk and remove silks; spread with butter and season with salt and pepper. Wrap well in heavy-duty or double-thick regular aluminum foil.
3. Place corn on grill over gray coals. Roast 15 to 25 minutes, turning several times to grill evenly.

ONION CHEESE ROLLS
Makes 6 servings

---

6 crusty oblong rolls, about 5 inches in length
½ cup (1 stick) butter or margarine, softened

2 cloves garlic, minced
½ cup freshly grated Parmesan cheese
⅓ cup finely chopped parsley
1 cup thinly sliced white onions

1. Split each roll in half lengthwise but not all the way through.
2. Combine butter, garlic, Parmesan cheese and parsley in a bowl.
3. Spread cut side of rolls with butter-cheese mixture; cover with onion slices. Close rolls, wrap individually in aluminum foil, and grill over hot coals for about 15 minutes, turning once or twice.

BAKED APPLES OR PEARS WITH SYRUP
Makes 6 servings
Warm fruit with a simple syrup is a refreshing finish for a barbecue.

---

6 large cooking apples or pears
½ cup chopped walnuts
⅓ cup raisins
⅓ cup orange marmalade
1 cup water

¼ cup (½ stick) butter or margarine
1 cup maple or maple-blended syrup
½ teaspoon ground cinnamon
½ teaspoon ground nutmeg

1. Pare apples or pears ⅓ of the way down and remove core. Combine walnuts, raisins and marmalade in small bowl. Fill cored centers of apples or pears with mixture.
2. Place each apple or pear on a square of heavy-duty foil and add 2 tablespoons of the water. Wrap and seal. Repeat with remaining apples or pears.
3. Place packages directly on coals along the sides of the grill pan; bake 40 minutes or until tender, turning packages every 10 minutes. Time will depend on size of fruit and heat of coals. To test for doneness, unwrap one package. Fruit is done when easily pierced with a fork.
4. Combine butter, syrup, cinnamon and nutmeg in small saucepan. Heat on grill until butter is melted and syrup bubbly. Place fruit on serving plate; top each with syrup. Serve with ice cream, if you wish.

MENU
Serves 6

LET'S HAVE A BARBECUE

Mushroom-Stuffed Tomatoes
Mediterranean Lamb Kabobs
Rice (see page 137)
Lebanese Tossed Salad
Pineapple, Luau Style

TOTAL TIME
About 15 minutes ahead, plus about 40 minutes before serving

A leisurely barbecue with a minimum of kitchen preparation is the secret of entertaining outdoors. And it doesn't have to be hotdogs and hamburgers. Here's a fairly sophisticated meal that goes together fast.

MARKET LIST

2 pounds boneless leg of lamb	1 medium-size cucumber
1 4-ounce package cream cheese	1 large ripe pineapple
¾ cup dairy sour cream	Lime
5 small zucchini	Lemon
9 medium-size ripe tomatoes	1 bottle (8 ounces) Italian salad
¾ pound mushrooms	dressing
1 bunch green onions	Italian seasoning mix
Fresh dill weed	Dried mint leaves
1 medium-size head iceberg lettuce	Honey

WORK PLAN

1. Night before or early on the day prepare the kabobs through step 1; refrigerate.
2. 40 minutes before serving start the charcoal fire.
3. Prepare the mushroom-stuffed tomatoes; chill.
4. Fix the salad and dressing; chill. Cut the pineapple and prepare it for grilling once the meat is finished.
5. Cook the rice and start cooking the kabobs.

MUSHROOM-STUFFED TOMATOES
Makes 6 servings
These make an excellent appetizer, but are also good with sautéed fish and barbecued chicken.

6 medium-size ripe tomatoes (about 2 pounds)
¾ pound mushrooms, finely chopped
4 tablespoons butter or margarine
¾ teaspoon salt
¼ teaspoon freshly ground pepper
4 tablespoons minced green onion

½ package (8 ounces) cream cheese, softened
¾ cup dairy sour cream
3 tablespoons finely chopped fresh dill or 1½ teaspoons dried dillweed
Dill sprigs

1. Cut ¼ inch slice off top of tomato each, discarding any seeds and chop coarsely reserving 2 tablespoons. With a paring knife remove about 2 tablespoons of the pulp from each tomato to make a pocket.
2. Sauté mushrooms in butter in a large skillet, stirring constantly until lightly browned. Add salt, pepper and green onion; cook for 1 minute.
3. Whip cream cheese and sour cream in a medium-size bowl until smooth. Stir in remaining tomato-mushroom mixture and dill.
4. Spoon mushroom mixture into tomato shells. Arrange on a serving platter and garnish with reserved chopped tomato and a sprig of fresh dill. Serve chilled.

Note: You can stuff the tomatoes several hours before serving.

MEDITERRANEAN LAMB KABOBS
Makes 6 servings

2 pounds boneless leg of lamb, cut into 1-inch cubes
5 small zucchini (about 1 pound), cut into 1-inch chunks
2 tablespoons instant minced onion
1 bottle (8 ounces) Italian salad dressing
1 teaspoon Italian seasoning mix
½ teaspoon salt

1. Combine all ingredients in large glass or stainless steel bowl. Let mixture marinate for 2 hours at room temperature or in refrigerator overnight.
2. Drain lamb and zucchini, reserving marinade. Spear cubes of lamb and zucchini alternately on 6 long skewers. Place kabobs on grill. Grill 20 minutes for medium, turning often and brushing kabobs with reserved marinade.

LEBANESE TOSSED SALAD
Makes 6 servings
The Lebanese people are fond of salads, and this minty version is a popular one.

1 medium-sized head of lettuce
3 medium-size ripe tomatoes, cut in wedges
1 medium-size cucumber, pared and sliced
1 small onion, thinly sliced
1 teaspoon dried mint leaves, crumbled
Lemon Dressing (recipe follows)

1. Wash lettuce and dry thoroughly. Tear bite-size pieces into salad bowl. Add tomato, cucumber and onion; toss lightly. Sprinkle crumbled mint leaves over salad.
2. Cover salad bowl tightly with plastic wrap. Chill in refrigerator.
3. Just before serving toss with only enough dressing to lightly coat lettuce leaves.

LEMON DRESSING
Makes ⅓ cup

1 clove garlic, crushed
1 teaspoon salt
1 tablespoon olive oil
¼ cup lemon juice

Combine ingredients in a screw-top jar; shake until well mixed.

PINEAPPLE, LUAU STYLE
Makes 6 servings

1 large ripe pineapple	2 tablespoons lime juice
⅓ cup butter or margarine	¼ teaspoon ground ginger
⅓ cup honey	

1. Remove leafy top of pineapple; reserve. Cut pineapple lengthwise into 6 wedges. Cut off core of each wedge, then slash vertically 1 inch apart down to but not through skin.
2. Heat butter in small saucepan on grill until melted. Add honey, lime juice and ginger. Brush cut surfaces of pineapple with lime mixture. Place spears on grill. Grill 15 minutes, turning every 5 minutes and brushing with lime mixture.
3. Line serving platter with lemon leaves; place reserved pineapple top in center. Arrange spears on leaves. Serve hot with remaining lime mixture. Garnish with lime slices, if you wish.

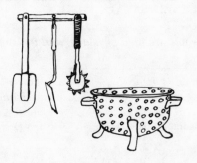

MENU
Serves 8

FOR THE HOTTEST DAY

Cold Glazed Ham Loaf
Old-Fashioned Potato Salad • Caesar Salad
Iced Strawberry Soup

TOTAL TIME
1 hour ahead, plus 30 minutes before serving

Fruit soup for dessert is a Scandinavian custom and a pleasant change from pies and cakes. A super ham loaf made ahead and chilled is almost like a gourmet deli's country-style pâté and fine enough to please the most finicky guest.

MARKET LIST

6 cups ground ham
¼ cup Parmesan cheese
4 eggs
½ cup light cream or milk
3 cups plain yogurt
  Parsley
3 heads small Romaine lettuce
8 medium-size potatoes
1 medium-size red onion
3 pints strawberries

1 cup soft bread crumbs
1 cup mashed potato
  Frozen orange juice concentrate
1 cup olive oil
  White wine vinegar
2 cans (2 ounces each) anchovy fillets
  Garlic croutons
1 cup orange juice
  Ground cardamom
  Honey

WORK PLAN

1. Night before make the ham loaf; cool and refrigerate. Cook potatoes; make dressing; toss; chill. Make strawberry soup; chill.
2. 30 minutes before serving, assemble all ingredients for salad; refrigerate greens and dressing.
3. Toss salad at table or buffet.

COLD GLAZED HAM LOAF
Makes 8 servings

6 cups ground ham
1 cup soft bread crumbs
1 cup mashed potato
2 eggs, lightly beaten
2 tablespoons chopped parsley
1 small onion, finely chopped
1 tablespoon butter or margarine

2 teaspoons Dijon-style mustard
½ teaspoon salt
⅛ teaspoon pepper
2 tablespoons frozen orange juice
  concentrate
2 tablespoons honey

1. Combine ham, bread crumbs, potato, eggs and parsley in a large bowl.
2. Sauté onion in butter; stir in mustard, salt and pepper. Add to ham mixture and mix. Pack into a 9-by-5-by-3-inch loaf pan rinsed with cold water.
3. Turn out ham loaf onto greased shallow baking pan. Mix orange juice concentrate and honey and brush over loaf.
4. Bake in a hot oven (400°) for 20 minutes. Brush with remaining orange mixture and bake 20 minutes longer. Cool, cover and refrigerate.

OLD-FASHIONED POTATO SALAD
Makes 8 servings
A mild potato salad with a creamy cooked dressing.

Boiled Dressing (recipe follows)
8 medium-size potatoes (about 2 pounds)
1 medium-size red onion, chopped (½ cup)

¼ cup chopped parsley
1 teaspoon salt
⅛ teaspoon pepper

1. Prepare Boiled Dressing; cool.
2. Cook potatoes in boiling salted water to cover in a large saucepan until tender, about 20 minutes. Drain, peel and slice into a large bowl.
3. Add onion, parsley, salt, pepper and Boiled Dressing. Toss, just until potatoes are coated with dressing. Chill until serving time.

BOILED DRESSING
Makes 1¼ cups

2 tablespoons flour
¾ teaspoon dry mustard
½ teaspoon salt
2 tablespoons sugar
½ cup cold water

¼ cup vinegar
2 egg yolks, lightly beaten
1 tablespoon butter or margarine
½ cup light cream or milk

1. Combine flour, dry mustard, salt and sugar in top of a double boiler. Stir in water, vinegar and egg yolks.
2. Cook over hot, not boiling, water, stirring constantly until thickened. Remove from heat; stir in butter and cream.
3. Chill in screw-top jar or plastic container. This dressing is very good on potato salad, cole slaw or egg salad. If necessary, thin with added cream or milk.

CAESAR SALAD
Makes 8 servings

3 small heads Romaine lettuce
1 cup olive oil
7 tablespoons white wine vinegar
3 teaspoons dry mustard
1½ teaspoons salt
¼ teaspoon pepper
2 cans (2 ounces each) anchovy fillets, well mashed

3 teaspoons Worcestershire sauce
3 cloves garlic, mashed
2 eggs
4 tablespoons freshly grated Parmesan cheese
Garlic croutons
Freshly ground black pepper

1. Wash lettuce, dry on paper toweling, then break into pieces. Roll up in fresh paper toweling; put in a plastic bag and refrigerate for several hours until crisp.
2. Combine the oil, vinegar, mustard, salt, pepper, anchovies and their oil, Worcestershire and garlic in a cup; beat well to blend.
3. Place lettuce in a salad bowl. Break the egg over the greens and toss to coat all leaves. Add dressing; toss again. Sprinkle over the Parmesan and garlic croutons. Top with a few turns of the pepper mill, toss and serve at once.

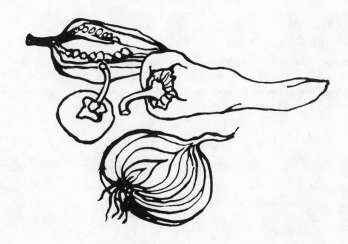

ICED STRAWBERRY SOUP
Makes 8 servings
Here's a cool and fruity treat for warm days.

3 pints strawberries	½ cup sugar, or to taste
½ cup cold water	⅛ teaspoon ground cardamom
1 cup orange juice	3 cups plain yogurt

1. Wash and hull strawberries. Puree strawberries with the water in container of electric blender. Pour mixture into large bowl; stir in orange juice, sugar and cardamom until sugar is dissolved. Blend in yogurt; chill.
2. Serve in chilled bowls garnished with additional sliced strawberries and sprigs of mint, if you wish.

MENU
Serves 12
* Inexpensive

FAMILY GET-TOGETHER

Raw Vegetables with Mayonnaise Dip
Hamburgers in Beer • Sesame Seed Buns
Fiesta Corn Casserole • Relishes and Pickles
Sliced Tomato and Fresh Basil Salad
Grilled Bananas

TOTAL TIME
1¼ hours

Adding a make-ahead casserole that will bake while everyone is outdoors tending the barbecue is an idea I find works well. It's a surprise for one thing and allows a less-than-expert barbecue cook to concentrate on one main dish. Great for family reunion backyard picnics.

MARKET LIST

3 pounds ground beef
4 eggs
½ cup milk
1 pound Cheddar cheese
12 bananas
6 to 8 ripe tomatoes
   Fresh basil
   Green pepper strips/ celery pieces/
   cucumber strips
1 can (12 ounces) beer

12 sesame seed hamburger buns
2 cups yellow cornmeal
2 cans (1 pound, 1 ounce each) cream-
   style corn
2 cans (4 ounces each) green chilies or
   1 green pepper
Bottled Italian Dressing
Relishes
Pickles
Mayonnaise

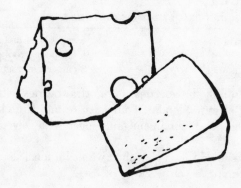

WORK PLAN

1. Up to 2 hours ahead prepare the two corn casseroles and refrigerate.
2. Mix and shape the hamburgers.
3. About 1 hour before serving (about the time you light the charcoal) preheat the oven and place the casseroles in. They will take 10 minutes longer at least to bake when they are cold from the refrigerator.
4. Slice tomatoes, arrange on platter, drizzle with dressing, sprinkle with chopped fresh basil; cover with transparent wrap and refrigerate.
5. Prepare raw vegetable dippers and arrange around dish of mayonnaise.
6. Grill hamburgers and then toast buns starting about 10 minutes before casserole is due to be cooked.
7. Grill bananas to order after hamburgers have been consumed. Have a happy burn-free barbecue.

HAMBURGERS IN BEER
Makes 12 hamburgers
This is an excellent way to keep hamburgers warm when cooking for a crowd.

---

3 pounds ground beef	1 can (12 ounces) beer
1 teaspoon salt	¼ teaspoon salt
½ teaspoon pepper	Dash liquid hot pepper seasoning
½ cup (1 stick) butter or margarine	

1. Mix meat lightly with the 1 teaspoon salt and pepper and shape into patties.
2. Melt butter in shallow baking pan on grill; add beer, ¼ teaspoon salt and hot pepper sauce
3. Grill hamburgers about 5 inches from coals to desired degree of doneness, about 5 minutes on one side and 3 minutes on the other for medium rare. As hamburgers cook, place them in beer mixture to keep them warm until all are cooked.

Note: Any extra beer mixture will add a special flavor to pot roast or stews. Boil mixture 5 minutes, cool and refrigerate.

FIESTA CORN CASSEROLE
Bake at 350° for 45 minutes
Makes 12 servings

4 eggs
2 cups yellow cornmeal
2 cans (1 pound, 1 ounce each) cream-style corn
½ cup milk
⅔ cup margarine, melted

1 teaspoon baking soda
2 teaspoons salt
1 pound shredded Cheddar cheese
2 cans (4 ounces each) green chilies or 1 green pepper, slivered and par-cooked 3 minutes

1. Beat the eggs lightly in a medium-size bowl; stir in the cornmeal. Add the corn, milk, margarine, baking soda and salt. Grease 2 6-cup casseroles with oil or margarine.
2. Place half the corn mixture in each of the two casseroles. Into each casserole divide half the cheese and the chilies, cut into chunks, or the green pepper. Add remaining corn mixture and top with remaining cheese. Bake in moderate oven (350°) 45 minutes or until set. (The time depends on the shape of the casserole.) Cut into wedges or spoon out.

GRILLED BANANAS
Makes 12 servings

12 green bananas   Confectioners' sugar

Grill unpeeled bananas 4 inches from medium coals, turning once, for 20 minutes or until peel is black and banana is soft. Split and sprinkle with sugar. Serve banana in peel, slit and topped with sour cream and toasted coconut.

Fall

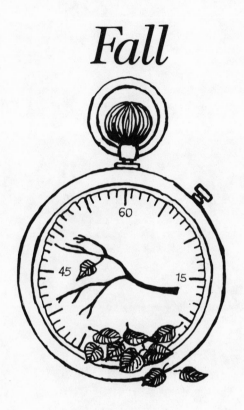

ONE SMALL BIRD SERVES TWO

Rock Cornish Game Hen
Baked Orange Sweet Potatoes • Fried Tomato Slices
Tossed Green Salad
Coffee Mousse

TOTAL TIME
About 1½ hours

One large Cornish game hen split in half will serve 2 with no leftovers and as long as there is stuffing, cooked separately to speed the cooking, and 2 vegetables, no one will feel hungry.

MARKET LIST

1 large rock Cornish game hen
4 strips bacon
2 eggs
1 cup heavy cream
1 rib celery
  Parsley
4 cups mixed salad greens
1 large green or red firm tomato

Orange
¼ package (7 ounces) stuffing mix
  Yellow cornmeal
1 small can (8 ounces) sweet potatoes
  Instant espresso
1 envelope unflavored gelatin
  Bottled dressing

WORK PLAN

1. Preheat the oven to 350°. Make the dessert; chill.
2. Prepare the game hen and start roasting. Make stuffing; reserve. Make sweet potatoes; reserve.
3. Wash the salad greens, dry and refrigerate.
4. 25 minutes before bird is cooked add 2 casseroles to oven.
5. Toss salad.

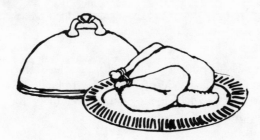

ROCK CORNISH GAME HEN
Roast at 350° for about 1¼ hours
Makes 2 servings

1 large rock cornish game hen (about
    1½ pounds)
Salt
Freshly ground pepper
4 strips bacon
2 tablespoons butter

1 tablespoon finely chopped onion
¼ cup finely chopped celery
¼ package (7 ounces) stuffing mix
1 tablespoon chopped parsley
    Pinch thyme

1. Sprinkle the inside of the bird with salt and pepper and place on a rack
   in a small roasting pan. Arrange the strips of bacon over the bird to
   cover all exposed surfaces.
2. Roast in a moderate oven (350°) (preferably a toaster oven to conserve
   energy) for 1¼ hours or until no pink juices run when thigh is pierced.
   Or cook on spit over grill.
3. Melt the butter in a small skillet and sauté the onion and celery until
   tender. Add ¼ the amount of the water needed for whole package of
   stuffing, bring to boiling. Stir in stuffing mix, parsley and thyme.
   Transfer to a large custard cup or small au gratin dish. Cover and bake
   alongside game hen for last 25 minutes of cooking time.

BAKED ORANGE SWEET POTATOES
Bake at 350° for 20 minutes
Makes 2 servings

1 small can (8 ounces) sweet potatoes
    or yams, drained
¼ cup orange juice
1 teaspoon orange rind
1 teaspoon cornstarch

1 tablespoon melted butter or
    margarine
2 tablespoons light brown sugar
⅛ teaspoon salt

Place the drained sweet potatoes in a small casserole. Combine the remaining ingredients in a small saucepan and bring to boiling, stirring constantly. Pour over potatoes. Bake in a moderate oven (350°) for the last 25
minutes of cooking time for the game hen.

FRIED TOMATO SLICES
Makes 2 servings

1 large firm green or red tomato
2 tablespoons yellow cornmeal
⅛ teaspoon salt

Pinch pepper
1½ tablespoons bacon drippings or
 shortening

Slice the tomato into 4 thick slices. Dip slices in cornmeal mixed with salt and pepper. Melt the bacon drippings in a medium-size skillet; when hot fry the tomato slices until browned on both sides.

COFFEE MOUSSE
Makes 2 servings

2 egg yolks
3 tablespoons sugar
½ cup espresso (made with instant
 powder)

2 teaspoons unflavored gelatin
3 tablespoons cold water
1 cup heavy cream, whipped

Beat the egg yolks and sugar until thick; then beat in the coffee. Soak the gelatin in the water 5 minutes. Heat the coffee mixture in the top of a double boiler over simmering water until it thickens slightly. Stir in the softened gelatin and stir to dissolve. Cool mixture until it starts to thicken. Fold in the whipped cream and spoon into 2 dessert dishes.

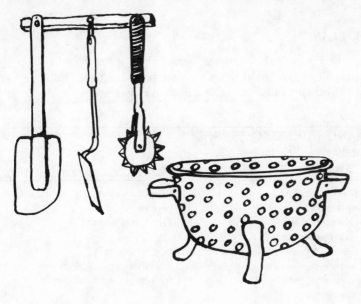

MENU
Serves 2

SIMPLE BUT SATISFYING

Ham and Cheese Casserole
Wax Bean Salad
Cantaloupe with Ricotta

TOTAL TIME
45 minutes

Dinner on the table in less than an hour after you come home with at least 30 minutes free to take a shower or watch the news on TV is the promise of this simple but tasty meal.

MARKET LIST

2 ounces prosciutto or ham
4 ounces Swiss or Gruyere cheese
1 egg
　Milk
　Grated Parmesan cheese
½ cup ricotta cheese
2 ounces mushrooms
　Parsley

½ pound wax beans
3 green onions
1 small red or green sweet pepper
1 cantaloupe, chopped
2 tablespoons crystallized ginger
1 cup noodles
　Dry bread crumbs

WORK PLAN

1. Cook the noodles. Cook the wax beans. Preheat the oven to 400°.
2. Finish off casserole and bake. Complete bean salad and chill.
3. Make ricotta mixture; chill. Cut and seed cantaloupe.

HAM AND CHEESE CASSEROLE
Bake at 400° for 30 minutes
Makes 2 servings

1 cup noodles, cooked and drained
1 tablespoon oil
½ cup chopped onion
1 cup sliced mushrooms
½ cup shredded prosciutto or ham
⅔ cup Swiss or Gruyere cheese, diced
½ teaspoon salt
½ teaspoon thyme

¼ teaspoon freshly ground black
　pepper
　Dry bread crumbs
1 egg
2 tablespoons milk
3 tablespoons grated Parmesan cheese
1 tablespoon chopped parsley

1. Toss drained noodles with 1 teaspoon of the oil. Heat remaining oil in a small skillet and sauté the onion until soft. Add the mushrooms and cook 1 minute longer.
2. Combine noodles, onion-mushroom mixture, prosciutto, cheese, salt, thyme and pepper. Transfer to a 1½-quart casserole that has been buttered and sprinkled with bread crumbs.
3. Combine the egg and milk and pour over noodle mixture. Sprinkle with the cheese and bake in a hot oven (400°) for 30 minutes or until browned and bubbly. Sprinkle with parsley.

WAX BEAN SALAD
Makes 2 servings

½ pound wax beans, cooked until crisp-tender
3 green onions, chopped
1 small red or green sweet pepper, diced
3 tablespoons oil

1 tablespoon wine vingear
¼ teaspoon salt
⅛ teaspoon pepper
1 tablespoon chopped parsley
¼ teaspoon oregano

Combine all the ingredients. Toss, cover and refrigerate at least 1 hour.

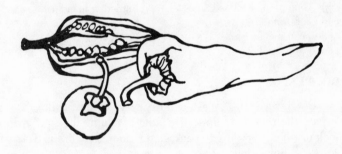

CANTALOUPE WITH RICOTTA
Makes 2 servings

½ cup ricotta cheese
1 tablespoon sugar
¼ teaspoon cinnamon
¼ teaspoon ground ginger

1 to 2 tablespoons chopped crystallized ginger
1 cantaloupe, halved and seeds removed

In a small bowl combine the ricotta, sugar, cinnamon, and ground and crystallized gingers. Spoon into the melon halves.

MENU
Serves 2

PLAIN AND GOOD

Beef Stroganoff
Poppyseed Noodles • Italian Beans with Almonds
Bread Sticks • Tossed Green Salad
Grapes and Sour Cream

TOTAL TIME
About 45 minutes

Quick but elegant, this menu would be complimented by the addition of a California Petit Sirah or Cabernet Sauvignon wine. Presto, you'll have a celebration dinner in less than an hour.

MARKET LIST

1 slice (½-inch thick) boneless sirloin (about ¾ pound)
1½ cups sour cream
¼ pound mushrooms
3 cups mixed salad greens
2 cups Thompson seedless grapes
¾ cup beef broth
1 tablespoon tomato paste
⅓ pound fine noodles

Poppy seeds
1 package (10 ounces) frozen Italian green beans
2 tablespoons sliced almonds
2 to 4 rolls
Bottled or homemade salad dressing
Bread sticks

WORK PLAN

1. Prepare dessert; chill. Wash and dry salad greens; chill.
2. Prepare the stroganoff up to the point of adding the sour cream.
3. Cook noodles according to package directions and drain. Toss with 2 tablespoons butter and 1 teaspoon poppy seeds.
4. While noodles are cooking, cook beans according to package directions. Brown almonds. Drain beans and toss with almonds.
5. Stir sour cream into stroganoff and reheat but do not boil.
6. Toss salad.

BEEF STROGANOFF
Makes 2 servings

1 slice (about ½-inch thick) boneless sirloin (about ¾ pound)
2 tablespoons flour
½ teaspoon salt
⅛ teaspoon pepper
3 tablespoons butter or margarine

1 small onion, chopped (¼ cup)
1 small clove garlic, finely chopped
¼ pound mushrooms, sliced
¾ cup beef broth
1 tablespoon tomato paste
½ cup sour cream

1. Cut the sirloin into 1½-inch long strips. Toss the strips in the flour mixed with the salt and pepper.
2. Heat the butter in a medium-size skillet. Brown the meat on all sides; remove to a bowl with a slotted spoon.
3. Add the oil to the skillet and sauté the onion and garlic until tender. Add the mushrooms and cook stirring 3 minutes.
4. Stir in the broth and tomato paste. Bring to boiling. Return meat to skillet and reheat. Stir in the sour cream and reheat but do not allow to boil.

ITALIAN GREEN BEANS WITH ALMONDS
Makes 2 servings

1 package (10 ounces) frozen Italian green beans
2 tablespoons butter or margarine

2 tablespoons sliced almonds
¼ teaspoon oregano

Cook beans according to package directions and drain. Meanwhile, heat butter in a small skillet and sauté almonds 3 minutes. Add oregano and toss with drained beans.

GRAPES AND SOUR CREAM
Makes 4 servings

2 cups Thompson seedless grapes, removed from stems

¾ cup dairy sour cream or yogurt
⅓ cup light brown sugar

Mix ingredients together and chill well.

MENU
Serves 2

HOMEMADE DELI SPECIAL

Italian Sausage and Peppers in Heros
Chick Pea Salad
Quickie Ice Cream Dessert

TOTAL TIME
30 minutes

When time is of the essence this menu can be put together in about 30 minutes and if you have 2 pairs of hands working in the kitchen you can cut it to 20 minutes.

MARKET LIST

½ pound sweet Italian sausage
½ pint vanilla ice cream
2 large sweet red or green peppers
2 ribs celery
½ cucumber
2 tablespoons chopped red onion
    Parsley

Lettuce leaves
1 loaf Italian bread
1 small can chick peas
    Coffee-flavored liqueur
    Powdered espresso (optional)
¼ cup chopped toasted almonds

WORK PLAN

1. Cook the sausages; fix peppers.
2. Make salad; chill.
3. Fix dessert; freeze.
4. Finish off sausage and pepper dish.

ITALIAN SAUSAGES AND PEPPERS IN HEROS
Makes 2 servings

½ pound sweet Italian sausages
2 large sweet red or green peppers,
    cored and seeded and cut into 1-
    inch-wide strips
2 tablespoons olive oil

1 clove garlic, crushed
⅛ teaspoon salt
    Pinch pepper
    Italian bread

1. In a small skillet cook the sausages until well done, about 20 minutes. Remove from skillet.
2. Add the oil to the skillet, along with pepper strips, garlic, salt and pepper. Cook, stirring until pepper strips are tender but not mushy. Slice sausages into 1-inch lengths and add to skillet. Remove garlic.
3. Reheat. Pile sausages and peppers into a 4- to 6-inch length of Italian bread that has been split in half lengthwise.

CHICK PEA SALAD
Makes 2 servings

1 can (1 pound, 1 ounce) chick peas, drained and rinsed
⅓ cup diced celery
⅓ cup diced pared cucumber
2 tablespoons chopped red onion
2 tablespoons chopped parsley

3 tablespoons olive oil
1 tablespoon wine vinegar
¼ teaspoon salt
⅛ teaspoon pepper
Lettuce leaves

In a small bowl combine the chick peas, celery, cucumber, onion and parsley. Beat together the oil, vinegar, salt and pepper and pour over chick pea mixture. Toss, chill and serve in lettuce cups.

QUICKIE ICE CREAM DESSERT
Makes 2 servings

½ pint vanilla ice cream
2 tablespoons coffee-flavored liqueur

¼ cup chopped toasted almonds
Powdered espresso coffee

Soften the ice cream. Stir in the liqueur and nuts. Spoon into two dessert dishes, sprinkle with a little espresso and freeze.

MENU
Serves 2

INTIMATE DINING FOR TWO

Steak Diane Flambé
Baked Potatoes with Sour Cream and Chives
Herbed Tomato Halves • Bibb or Boston Lettuce Salad
Fresh Pineapple Compote

TOTAL TIME

1 hour (but you're not working every minute)

When there's just the 2 of you and it's a special occasion forget the budget; splurge on filet mignon. Fix it and flame it tableside for dramatic effect.

MARKET LIST

2 mignonettes (fillets) of beef, about 4
   to 6 ounces each
½ cup sour cream
¼ pound mushrooms
3 shallots or green onions
   Chives
   Parsley
2 baking potatoes
1 large tomato
½ ripe pineapple
1 head Bibb or ½ head Boston lettuce

Cognac
Bottled meat sauce such as Escoffier-brand Sauce Robert
Beef broth
Madeira or Sherry
1 slice bread
¼ cup Kirsch (cherry brandy)
1 jar (1 pound, 1 ounce) pitted dark
   sweet cherries
Homemade salad dressing

WORK PLAN

1. Scrub potatoes, prick and place in a 400° oven or toaster oven to bake. Or 6 minutes in a microwave oven will do.
2. Prepare the fresh pineapple compote and refrigerate. Prepare tomato halves.
3. Wash, dry and refrigerate lettuce.
4. Assemble all the ingredients, utensils and serving plates for the Steak Diane.
5. When potatoes are almost done bake tomato halves.
6. Toss salad.
7. Prepare Steak Diane tableside.

STEAK DIANE FLAMBÉ
Makes 2 servings

2 tablespoons clarified butter (see note)
¼ pound mushrooms, sliced
2 tablespoons chopped shallots or green onions
½ teaspoon chopped chives
1 teaspoon chopped parsley
2 mignonettes (fillets) of beef, about 4 ounces each
¼ cup Cognac
¼ teaspoon Worcestershire sauce
1 tablespoon bottled meat sauce (such as Escoffier-brand Sauce Robert)
¼ cup beef broth
2 tablespoons Madeira or sherry
½ teaspoon salt
¼ teaspoon freshly ground pepper

1. Pour butter into blazer pan of chafing dish (or use a 10-inch skillet). Heat, and when very hot (but not brown), add mushrooms, shallots, chives and parsley. Cook, stirring constantly, 2 minutes.
2. Add beef. Cook 2 minutes on each side.
3. Pour in Cognac, warm gently, then ignite carefully. When flames die down, add Worcestershire sauce and meat sauce.
4. Stir in broth, Madeira, salt and pepper. Cook 2 minutes longer.

Note: To clarify butter, melt 2½ tablespoons butter in a small metal cup or saucepan. Pour off clear yellow liquid (the clarified butter) and discard the milky solids remaining.

HERBED TOMATO HALVES
Bake at 400° for 10 minutes or broil 5 to 10 minutes
Makes 2 servings

1 large tomato
1½ teaspoons chopped green onion
1 tablespoon butter or margarine
¼ teaspoon salt
⅛ teaspoon pepper
Pinch leaf marjoram, crumbled
Pinch leaf basil, crumbled
⅓ cup fresh bread crumbs

1. Core tomato; cut in half crosswise. Place cut side up in shallow baking pan.
2. Sauté onion in butter in a small skillet until soft. Add salt, pepper, marjoram, basil and bread crumbs. Stir with fork until crumbs are thoroughly moistened. Divide mixture evenly over tomato halves.
3. Bake in a hot oven (400°) for 10 minutes or until tomatoes are heated thoroughly. Or broil until bubbly hot and lightly browned.

FRESH PINEAPPLE COMPOTE
Makes 2 servings

½ ripe pineapple
2 tablespoons confectioners' sugar
¼ cup Kirsch (cherry brandy)

1 jar (1 pound, 1 ounce) pitted dark
  sweet cherries

1. Cut pineapple into 3 or 4 wedges. Loosen fruit in one piece from each wedge; trim core. Cut into ½-inch chunks.
2. Place pineapple in a large bowl, sprinkle with confectioners' sugar, add Kirsch. Toss gently. Cover with plastic wrap and refrigerate several hours for pineapple to absorb flavor of brandy, tossing once or twice. Chill the cherries.
3. Just before serving, drain juice from cherries. Add cherries to pineapple; toss thoroughly.

Make-ahead note: Sweet ripe pineapple takes on an extra taste dimension when marinated in Kirsch. You can make this compote a day or two in advance.

MENU
Serves 4

ISLAND MAGIC

Cucumber and Potato Soup
Sweet and Pungent Pork with Vegetables
Rice (see page 137) • Stir-Fried Snow Peas (optional)
Bananas Tropical

TOTAL TIME
About 50 minutes

An attractive and appetizing three-course meal in less than an hour is easy with this Asian-inspired menu that draws on several different cultures for inspiration.

MARKET LIST

1 pound lean boneless pork
2 cups milk
1 cup light cream or plain yogurt
1 medium-size green pepper
3 carrots
1 large cucumber
¼ cup green onion
3 bananas
1 can condensed cream of potato soup
1 can (1 pound, 4 ounces) pineapple
   chunks in pineapple juice

White vinegar
Vegetable oil for frying
Rice
1 package frozen snow peas
⅓ cup flaked coconut
¼ cup light brown sugar
½ cup dark rum
1 quart vanilla ice cream
Soy sauce

WORK PLAN

1. Prepare soup up to adding seasonings and yogurt.
2. Start rice cooking.
3. Prepare the Sweet and Pungent Pork. Stir-fry pea pods, if using. Finish soup.
4. Prepare bananas just before serving. Can be done over a tableside burner or in an electric skillet, if you wish.

CUCUMBER AND POTATO SOUP
Makes 4 servings
A creamy vichyssoise-type soup with an unusual ingredient—cucumber.

1 large cucumber, pared, seeded and
   diced (1½ cups)
¼ cup sliced green onion
2 tablespoons butter or margarine
2 cups milk

1 can condensed cream of potato soup
½ teaspoon salt
⅛ teaspoon cayenne pepper
⅛ teaspoon ground nutmeg
1 cup light cream or plain yogurt

1. Sauté cucumber and onion in butter in large saucepan until soft, about 5 minutes. Stir in milk and potato soup. Bring to boiling, stirring constantly. Lower heat and cover.
2. Simmer 5 minutes, stirring often. Stir in salt, cayenne, nutmeg and cream or yogurt; heat through. (Do not boil if using yogurt.) Serve hot in soup bowls; garnish with sliced green onion.

SWEET AND PUNGENT PORK WITH VEGETABLES
Makes 4 servings

A popular and uniquely Chinese concoction of pork (the most popular meat in China), pineapple and vegetables. The amber-colored sauce is achieved by caramelizing the sugar rather than adding catsup, which many restaurants use.

1 pound lean boneless pork	1 tablespoon cornstarch
½ cup flour	2 tablespoons distilled white vinegar
1¼ teaspoons salt	1 medium-size green pepper, seeded
½ teaspoon baking powder	3 carrots
½ cup cold water	Vegetable oil for frying
1 can (1 pound, 4 ounces) pineapple chunks in pineapple juice	¼ cup sugar

1. Cut pork into 1-inch cubes. Combine flour, 1 teaspoon of the salt and the baking powder in a medium-size bowl. Add water, stirring until smooth. Add pork cubes; stir until coated.
2. Drain juice from pineapple into a 1-cup measure. Stir in cornstarch, vinegar and remaining salt. Cut green pepper into 1-inch squares. Cut carrots into paper-thin diagonal slices.
3. Heat 1 inch of oil in 4-quart saucepan or Dutch oven to 370°. Fry pork cubes until golden brown, removing browned pieces with slotted spoon to paper toweling to drain. Cut one cube to make sure pork is thoroughly cooked.
4. Carefully pour off all oil from pan. (You can refrigerate the oil and reuse it in other recipes.) Return 1 tablespoon oil to pan. Add carrots and stir-fry 1 minute. Add green peppers; stir-fry 2 minutes. Remove to small bowl. Add sugar to pan. Heat until melted and amber in color, watching carefully so that it does not burn. Remove pan from heat.
5. Restir cornstarch mixture; pour over melted sugar. It will sizzle, but stir until smooth. Cook over medium heat until thickened and bubbly. Return vegetables; cook until carrots are tender. Add pineapple and pork cubes. Spoon onto platter and serve with rice.

STIR-FRIED SNOW PEAS
Makes 4 servings

2 tablespoons vegetable oil
1 package (10 ounces) frozen snow peas
2 tablespoons soy sauce

1 tablespoon water
1 teaspoon cornstarch

1. Heat the oil in a wok or skillet. Add frozen snow peas and cook stirring vigorously until peas turn bright green, about 3 minutes.
2. Mix soy sauce, water and cornstarch and add to wok or skillet while stirring. Serve as soon as snow peas are coated with glaze.

BANANAS TROPICAL
Makes 4 servings

⅓ cup flaked coconut
1½ tablespoons butter or margarine
¼ cup firmly packed brown sugar
½ cup dark rum

⅛ teaspoon ground cinnamon
3 bananas, peeled and sliced
1 quart vanilla ice cream

1. Heat coconut in large skillet until toasted; stir to brown evenly. Remove to a sheet of foil and cool.
2. Add butter, sugar, rum and cinnamon to skillet. Heat until bubbly. Add bananas and cook until slices are heated through.
3. Spoon ice cream into serving dishes and spoon hot bananas and juices over. Sprinkle with coconut. Serve at once.

MENU
Serves 4

STIR-FRY SPECIAL

Chili Shrimp on Chinese Cabbage
Rice • Chinese Mixed Vegetables
Melon in Sabayon Sauce

TOTAL TIME
About 40 minutes

The one international cuisine which lends itself to quick, last-minute cooking is Chinese stir-frying and in this simple menu two of the dishes are prepared just that way and, best of all, all the ingredients are available in the supermarket.

MARKET LIST

1 pound fresh shelled, deveined shrimp or 1 pound thawed frozen shrimp
2 eggs
1 small head Chinese celery cabbage
4 to 6 stalks celery
3 green onions
1 honeydew melon
Cornstarch
Dry sherry

4 to 6 dried red chili peppers
½ cup shelled roasted peanuts
Rice
2 packages (6 ounces each) snow peas or Italian green beans
1 can (4 ounces) water chestnuts
1 can (4 ounces) whole mushrooms or 1 cup fresh mushrooms
½ teaspoon unflavored gelatin
½ cup orange juice

WORK PLAN

1. Prepare the Sabayon Sauce; chill. Cut melon balls from the honeydew; chill.
2. Assemble the ingredients for both the stir-fried dishes.
3. Put the rice on to cook.
4. Cook the Chinese Mixed Vegetables; keep warm.
5. Cook the Chili Shrimp on Chinese Cabbage.

CHILI SHRIMP ON CHINESE CABBAGE
Makes 4 servings
This relatively hot Szechuan dish has been "cooled off" so that you can enjoy the shrimp and peanut flavors. Remove the hot peppers before serving, or warn eaters not to eat them.

1 pound fresh shelled and deveined shrimp or 1 pound thawed frozen shrimp
1 small head Chinese celery cabbage
3 green onions
¼ cup water
1 tablespoon cornstarch
3 tablespoons vegetable oil

½ teaspoon salt
½ teaspoon sugar
1 tablespoon soy sauce
1 clove garlic, minced
2 tablespoons dry sherry
4 to 6 dried red chili peppers
½ cup unsalted shelled roasted peanuts

1. Rinse shrimp; pat dry with paper toweling. Cut cabbage into 1-by-2-inch pieces (you should have about 8 cups). Cut onions into 1-inch lengths. Mix water and cornstarch in 1-cup measure.
2. Heat large deep skillet, Dutch oven or wok over high heat. Add 1 tablespoon of the oil; swirl to coat bottom and side. Add cabbage and stir-fry until coated with oil. Add salt, sugar and soy sauce. Stir-fry until just tender-crisp. Restir cornstarch mixture. Remove 1 tablespoon and add to cabbage. Stir until juices are thickened. Remove cabbage to platter; keep warm.
3. Reheat pan with remaining oil. Add shrimp and garlic. Stir-fry just until shrimp turns firm and pink. Add sherry and chili peppers. Stir-fry to loosen browned bits in pan. Restir cornstarch mixture. Pour over shrimp. Stir in green onions and peanuts. Taste for salt and add if needed. Spoon shrimp over cabbage.

RICE
Makes 4 servings

2½ cups water
1¼ cups long-grain rice

1 teaspoon salt

Combine water, rice and salt in a large saucepan. Bring to boiling over high heat. Cover and simmer 12 minutes or until liquid is absorbed. Fluff with fork.

CHINESE MIXED VEGETABLES
Makes 4 servings
A side dish to serve with a favorite Chinese main dish—quick to prepare with ingredients handy in the freezer or on the pantry shelf.

2 tablespoons vegetable oil
2 cups diagonally thinly sliced celery
2 packages (6 ounces each) frozen snow peas or Italian green beans
1 can (4 ounces) water chestnuts, drained and sliced
2 tablespoons soy sauce
2 tablespoons dry sherry
¾ teaspoons seasoned salt
¼ teaspoon pepper
¼ teaspoon sugar
1 can (4 ounces) whole mushrooms (or 1 cup fresh or frozen)
1 tablespoon cornstarch

1. Heat oil in large skillet. Add celery and stir-fry 2 minutes. Add snow peas and water chestnuts. Stir-fry until vegetables are crisp-tender.
2. Add soy sauce, sherry, salt, pepper and sugar. Heat 1 minute.
3. Drain mushrooms and add to skillet. Dissolve cornstarch in liquid. Add to skillet. Cook until thickened and vegetables are coated.

MELON IN SABAYON SAUCE
Makes 4 servings
Cool and refreshing honeydew melon balls served with a satin-smooth wine Sabayon Sauce—a perfect way to finish a summer meal.

½ teaspoon unflavored gelatin
¼ cup sugar
½ cup orange juice
¼ cup white port wine or dry sherry
2 eggs, slightly beaten
1 honeydew melon, chilled

1. Sprinkle gelatin and sugar over orange juice and port wine in large bowl or double boiler. Beat in eggs. Set over barely simmering water.
2. Cook about 8 to 12 minutes, beating constantly with a whisk or rotary hand beater until mixture thickens slightly and is double in volume. Remove from hot water and set in ice water. Beat mixture until cool, then remove from ice water.
3. Scoop enough melon balls from melon with melon baller to fill 4 dessert glasses; keep refrigerated. Just before serving, pour sauce over each serving.

MENU
Serves 4
* *Inexpensive*

PASS THE GRATED PARMESAN

Lemon-Parsley Clam Sauce with Linguini
Garlic Bread • Spinach and Mushroom Salad
Pots de Creme au Chocolat or Apples and Grapes

TOTAL TIME
About 40 minutes ahead, plus less than 30 minutes before serving

It's possible that you have all the ingredients for this quick menu in your pantry or refrigerator except for the salad makings, the cream for the dessert and a loaf of fresh bread.

MARKET LIST

4 slices bacon
Parmesan cheese
5 eggs
1¼ cups light or heavy cream
Parsley
Lemon
1 pound loose fresh spinach or 1 10-ounce bag
¼ pound mushrooms
2 medium-size carrots

2 cans (7 to 8 ounces each) minced clams
1 package (8 ounces) linguini or thin spaghetti
4 squares semi-sweet chocolate
Light brown sugar
1 package (1 pound) linguini or flat noodles
1 loaf Italian bread

WORK PLAN

1. Night before or early in the day make and bake the pots de creme. Cool and chill.
2. 30 minutes before serving, wash the spinach, prepare other salad ingredients and chill. Sauté bacon and make salad dressing. Keep warm. Slice and butter bread, sprinkle with garlic salt, wrap in foil and heat 10 minutes in 375° oven.
3. Cook the linguini and make lemon clam sauce.
4. Finish the salad. Pour sauce over drained linguini.

LEMON-PARSLEY CLAM SAUCE WITH LINGUINI
Makes 4 servings (1½ cups sauce)
The tangy flavor of lemon gives character to this quick clam sauce.

2 cans (7 to 8 ounces each) minced clams
1 small onion, chopped (¼ cup)
3 cloves garlic, minced
⅓ cup olive or vegetable oil
2 tablespoons butter or margarine
1 teaspoon leaf oregano, crumbled
½ teaspoon salt
⅛ teaspoon pepper
1 package (1 pound) linguini or thin spaghetti
2 tablespoons chopped parsley
1 teaspoon grated lemon rind
1 to 2 tablespoons lemon juice
Grated Parmesan cheese

1. Drain clam juice from clams; reserve.
2. Sauté onion and garlic in oil and butter in a saucepan until tender, but not brown, about 5 minutes.
3. Add reserved clam juice, oregano, salt and pepper; bring to boiling over high heat. Cook until reduced to one cup, about 5 minutes.
4. Meanwhile, cook linguini or thin spaghetti, following label directions, drain and keep hot in kettle.
5. Lower heat under clam juice mixture and add reserved clams, parsley, lemon rind and lemon juice. Heat thoroughly. Toss with hot linguini. Serve with grated Parmesan cheese.

SPINACH AND MUSHROOM SALAD
Makes 4 servings
Fresh spinach with a tangy dressing.

4 slices bacon
2 teaspoons sugar
2 tablespoons cider vinegar
2 tablespoons water
½ teaspoon salt
1 pound fresh loose spinach
¼ pound fresh mushrooms, sliced
2 medium-size carrots, shredded
2 hard-cooked eggs, cut into wedges

1. Cook bacon in skillet, remove to paper toweling, crumble and reserve. Measure bacon fat and return 2 tablespoons to skillet. Stir in sugar, vinegar, water and salt. Keep warm over low heat.
2. Wash and remove stems from spinach. Dry thoroughly and break into pieces in salad bowl. Pour warm dressing over and toss until coated and wilted.
3. Top with mushrooms, carrots and bacon. Toss. Garnish with eggs.

POTS DE CREME AU CHOCOLAT
Bake at 325° for 20 minutes
Makes 4 to 6 servings
This rich, satiny dessert is traditionally baked and served in pots de creme cups—but custard cups or individual soufflé dishes will serve as nicely.

4 squares semisweet chocolate	3 egg yolks
1¼ cups light or heavy cream	2 tablespoons light brown sugar

1. Place 4 4-ounce or 6 3-ounce pots de creme cups, custard cups or individual soufflé dishes in shallow baking pan.
2. Chop the chocolate coarsely. Place in small heavy saucepan and add cream. Cook, stirring constantly with wooden spoon, over medium-high heat until chocolate melts and mixture comes just to boiling (about 15 minutes). Remove from heat.
3. Beat egg yolks and sugar with wire whisk in medium-size bowl until blended. Gradually beat in hot cream mixture. Strain into 4-cup measure and pour into cups.
4. Set shallow baking pan on oven rack. Pour boiling water into pan, about half way up the sides of cups.
5. Bake in slow oven (325°) for 20 minutes or just until mixture begins to set around edges. Remove cups from water to a wire rack; let cool 30 minutes. Cover with lids or plastic wrap and refrigerate at least 4 hours or overnight. Decorate with rosettes of whipped cream, if you wish.

MENU
Serves 4

FOR VEGETABLE AND FRUIT LOVERS

Artichokes Hot with Lemon Butter or Cold with Vinaigrette Dressing
Helen's Yorkie Beef Pudding
Broccoli with Sour Cream • Parslied Carrots
Stuffed Baked Apples

TOTAL TIME
About 55 minutes

Artichokes, served hot or cold according to your mood, the weather or the amount of last-minute cooking you are willing to do, are an appetizer and they eliminate the need for a separate salad course. The Yorkie Beef Pudding is a variation on the British specialty, Toad-in-a-Hole.

MARKET LIST

¾ pound ground chuck
2 eggs
1 cup sour cream
2½ sticks butter
1 cup milk
4 small artichokes
2 lemons
1 bunch green onions
Parsley
1 small orange
5 to 6 navel oranges
1 bunch broccoli
4 large carrots

4 large baking apples
½ cup leftover cooked vegetables or frozen mixed vegetables
1 package (10 ounces) frozen raspberries
Honey
½ cup chopped slivered almonds or walnuts
2 tablespoons brandy
¾ cup raisins
¼ cup red currant jelly
Leaf tarragon
1 can (10½ ounces) beef gravy

WORK PLAN

1. If you wish to serve the artichokes cold they should be trimmed, cooked, cooled and chilled early in the day. Also make the vinaigrette dressing; chill.
2. Preheat oven to 425°. Prepare beef pudding and apples and bake together.
3. If you are serving the artichokes hot, trim them and cook in boiling water as directed.
4. Prepare and cook the carrots and the broccoli.
5. Make the sour cream sauce for the broccoli.

ARTICHOKES HOT WITH LEMON BUTTER
OR COLD WITH VINAIGRETTE DRESSING
Makes 4 servings

4 small artichokes   Lemon juice

Lemon Butter

½ cup (1 stick) melted butter   1 tablespoon lemon juice

Vinaigrette Dressing

¼ cup olive or salad oil   2 green onions, chopped
1 tablespoon lemon juice or wine   ¼ teaspoon salt
  vinegar   ⅛ teaspoon freshly ground black
2 drops liquid red pepper seasoning   pepper
1 clove garlic, crushed   ¼ cup chopped parsley

1. Trim the stem ends of the artichokes; rub with lemon juice or cut lemon. With scissors cut off the spines from the outside leaves; brush with lemon.
2. Add to a kettle of boiling salted water that will just accommodate the artichokes in an upright position resting against each other. Add half a lemon. Cover and simmer 30 minutes or until outer leaves come off easily and stem ends are tender.
3. Drain upside down a few minutes if serving hot with the lemon butter. Cool if serving cold. Open up center of artichoke and remove the choke. Brush with lemon and chill. Meanwhile combine all the ingredients for the vinaigrette and beat or shake to mix.
4. Serve the dressing in the center of the artichoke or separately.

HELEN'S YORKIE BEEF PUDDING
Bake at 425° for 30 minutes
Makes 4 servings

1 small onion, thinly sliced   ¼ teaspoon salt
3 tablespoons butter or margarine   ⅛ teaspoon pepper
¾ pound ground chuck   2 eggs
½ cup leftover cooked vegetables or   1 cup milk
  frozen mixed vegetables   1 cup sifted, all-purpose flour
1 can (10½ ounces) beef gravy   ½ teaspoon salt
½ cup water

1. Sauté onion in 1 tablespoon of the butter in a small skillet until tender. Add meat; cook until brown, breaking up with wooden spoon as it cooks; add vegetables.
2. Combine gravy and water in a 2-cup measure. Stir ¼ cup gravy mixture into meat-vegetable mixture; blend well and add salt and pepper.
3. Set oven to hot (425°). Melt remaining 2 tablespoons butter in a 10-inch quiche dish or pie plate in oven while it heats.
4. Beat eggs in medium-size bowl, add milk and beat until well-blended. Add flour and salt and beat until batter is smooth. Pour into quiche dish.
5. Spread meat-vegetable filling evenly over batter to within 1-inch of edge.
6. Bake for 30 minutes, or until brown and puffy. Heat remaining gravy to serve with pudding.

BROCCOLI WITH SOUR CREAM
Makes 4 servings

1 bunch broccoli, flowerettes removed and stalks reserved for soup	2 tablespoons flour
	1 cup sour cream, at room temperature
1 tablespoon butter or margarine	1 teaspoon lemon juice
1 tablespoon chopped onion	1 tablespoon Dijon-style mustard

1. Steam or cook the broccoli flowerettes until crisp-tender, about 8 minutes. Drain and arrange in serving dish.
2. While broccoli is cooking melt the butter in the top of a double boiler and sauté the onion until tender. Stir in the flour and gradually blend in the sour cream until smooth.
3. Heat the mixture over boiling water until it thickens, stirring constantly. Stir in the lemon juice and mustard and spoon over the broccoli.

PARSLIED CARROTS
Makes 4 servings

4 large carrots, cut into tiny matchstick pieces or julienne-style	⅛ teaspoon freshly ground black pepper
½ cup water	3 tablespoons butter or margarine
½ teaspoon salt	2 tablespoons chopped parsley

1. Cook the carrot pieces with the water, salt and pepper in a tightly covered saucepan until barely tender, about 8 minutes.
2. Remove cover and boil to evaporate all but 2 tablespoons liquid. Add butter and parsley.

STUFFED BAKED APPLES
Bake at 425° for 25 minutes
Makes 4 servings
These will bake along with the Yorkie Beef Pudding.

¾ cup raisins
2 tablespoons brandy
½ cup chopped or slivered almonds or walnuts
¼ cup honey

Lemon
4 large baking apples
1 package (10 ounces) frozen raspberries, partially thawed

1. Soak the raisins in the brandy until they have absorbed most of the liquid. Stir in the almonds, honey, grated rind of the lemon and 1 tablespoon lemon juice.
2. Cut a small slice from the base of the apples so that they stand upright. Core and cut a ½-inch strip of the peel away around the thickest part.
3. Place in a small shallow baking dish. Stuff with the raisin mixture. Pour ½ cup water around apples, cover tightly with aluminum foil and bake 30 minutes or until the apples are tender.
4. Whirl the raspberries and juice in an electric blender. Heat in a small saucepan to serve with warm apples or serve as is with chilled apples.

MENU
Serves 4
Inexpensive

MANGIA MANGIA

Stracciatella
Italian Pork • Sautéed Zucchini
Beet and Sour Cream Salad
Pears in Wine

TOTAL TIME
About 20 minutes ahead, plus 30 minutes before serving

Watching your weight? Serving a fairly low-calorie but satisfying soup before a simple main course with one vegetable can help. Use a low-calorie bottled dressing in place of the sour cream for the beets in the salad . . . it won't taste as good but it will be less caloric.

MARKET LIST

4 loin pork chops, cut ½-inch thick
3 eggs
Parmesan cheese
1 cup dairy sour cream
4 Bosc or other firm pears (about 1½ pounds)
Lettuce leaves
2 medium-size zucchini (about 20 ounces)
½ pound spinach or ½ package (10 ounces) frozen spinach

Lemon
3 cans (13¾ ounces each) chicken broth
1 can (5½ ounces) tomato juice
Seasoned bread crumbs
1 can (1 pound) tiny whole beets, drained
1½ cups dry red wine

WORK PLAN

1. Night before or early on the day prepare the pears; chill.
2. 30 minutes before serving cook and chop the spinach for the soup; set aside.
3. Prepare the beet salad. Chill.
4. Slice and coat zucchini ready for frying.
5. Make the pork dish.
6. Fry the zucchini. Keep warm.
7. Finish soup.

STRACCIATELLA
Makes 4 servings

½ pound spinach, washed and trimmed or ½ package (5 ounces) frozen spinach
2 eggs
Pinch salt

2 tablespoons grated Parmesan cheese
Pinch ground nutmeg
3 cans (13¾ ounces each) chicken broth (about 5 cups)
2 teaspoons lemon juice

1. Cook fresh spinach in a large saucepan, covered, until leaves just wilt; or cook frozen spinach following label directions. Drain; squeeze out as much water as possible; then chop coarsely.
2. Beat eggs in a medium-size bowl with salt, Parmesan and nutmeg. Stir in 1 cup of the chicken broth.
3. Heat remaining broth to boiling in a large saucepan. Pour egg mixture slowly into boiling broth, stirring gently with a wire whisk. Stir in spinach; lower heat. Add lemon juice and simmer about 3 minutes longer, beating constantly.

ITALIAN PORK
Makes 4 servings

4 loin pork chops, cut ½-inch thick
1 medium-size onion, chopped (½ cup)
1 or 2 cloves garlic, mashed

3 teaspoons vegetable oil
1 can (5½ ounces) tomato juice (¾ cup)
1 teaspoon Italian seasoning

1. Trim bone and fat from each chop. Cut meat into ⅛-inch slices. Pat dry on paper toweling.
2. Sauté onion and garlic in teaspoonful of the oil in a large skillet until soft. Remove but keep warm.
3. Add remaining 2 teaspoons oil to skillet; cook and stir pork over medium-high heat about 5 minutes.
4. Stir in tomato juice, Italian seasoning, reserved onion and garlic. Cook 5 to 8 minutes more to blend flavors. Taste; add salt and pepper if needed.

SAUTÉED ZUCCHINI
Makes 4 servings

2 medium-size zucchini (about 20 ounces)
1 egg, lightly beaten

⅔ cup seasoned bread crumbs
2 tablespoons grated Parmesan cheese
6 tablespoons oil

Cut the zucchini into ¼-inch slices. Dip in egg, then in crumbs mixed with cheese. Heat oil in a large skillet and fry slices until browned on both sides.

BEET AND SOUR CREAM SALAD
Makes 4 serving

1 cup dairy sour cream
1 teaspoon dry mustard
¼ teaspoon salt
1 tablespoon wine vinegar

1 can (1 pound) tiny whole beets, drained
Lettuce leaves

Combine the sour cream, mustard, salt and wine vinegar. Add beets and toss to coat; chill. Serve on shredded lettuce.

PEARS IN WINE
Makes 4 servings

1½ cups sugar
1½ cups dry red wine
¼ teaspoon cinnamon
⅛ teaspoon nutmeg

1 whole clove
4 Bosc or other firm pears (about 1½ pounds), pared with stems left on

1. In a straight-sided, nonaluminum saucepan combine the sugar, wine, cinnamon, nutmeg and clove. Heat, stirring until sugar is dissolved. Cut a slice from blossom end of pears so that they stand upright.
2. Place in syrup and add boiling water until pears are almost covered. Cover and cook gently until pears are tender when pierced with a toothpick.
3. Arrange pears in deep plate. Boil syrup until quantity is reduced to 2 cups. Pour over pears. Serve at room temperature or chilled with cream, if you wish.

MENU
Serves 6
* Inexpensive

BURGERS PLUS MENU

Cream of Broccoli Soup
Savory Beef Burgers • Green Chili, Cheese and Rice Bake
Mixed Salad
Chocolate Fondue or Fresh Pears and Cheese

TOTAL TIME

About 1 hour

A hearty menu and you'll find out burgers don't always have to be served between buns. The alternate accompaniment here is a real tasty, spicy cheese and hot chili pepper flavored casserole.

MARKET LIST

2 pounds ground beef round
1 cup light cream
1 pint dairy sour cream
4 ounces shredded sharp Cheddar
  cheese
1 cup heavy cream
6 ounces sliced Monterey Jack cheese
1 bunch fresh broccoli (1½ pounds)
1 potato
  Lemons
1 medium-size head Romaine
2 green onions
2 cans (13¾ ounces each) chicken broth

Seasoned salt
Bottled steak sauce
1 can (4 ounces) green chili peppers
2 cups long-grain rice
2 jars (6 ounces each) marinated
  artichoke hearts
1 jar (3¼ ounces) pitted black olives
2 bars (8 ounces each) milk chocolate
  candy
Brandy
Strawberries, seedless grapes,
  bananas, orange segments, pound
  cake, etc., for dippers

WORK PLAN

1. Start making the broccoli soup, steps 1 and 2. Preheat oven to 375°.
2. Cook rice for casserole. Prepare salad ingredients; refrigerate.
3. Finish off the green chili, cheese and rice bake and put in oven.
4. Complete soup and keep warm. Melt the chocolate for the fondue and line up dippers.
5. Shape and cook the burgers. Toss salad.

CREAM OF BROCCOLI SOUP
Makes 6 servings

1 bunch fresh broccoli (about 1½ pounds)	2 cans (13¾ ounces each) chicken broth
1 medium-size onion, chopped (½ cup)	½ teaspoon salt
	Dash cayenne pepper
2 tablespoons butter or margarine	1 cup light cream
1 potato, pared and diced (1 cup)	⅛ teaspoon ground nutmeg

1. Trim outer leaves and tough ends from broccoli. Separate stalks and cut into 2 or 3 shorter lengths. Parboil in boiling salted water in a large saucepan 5 minutes; drain well.
2. Sauté onion in butter in large saucepan until soft but not brown, 5 minutes. Add potato, chicken broth, salt and cayenne. Heat to boiling, lower heat and simmer 15 minutes. Add broccoli, reserving a few flowerettes for garnish. Simmer 5 minutes longer or until vegetables are tender.
3. Pour mixture half at a time into container of electric blender, cover and whirl until smooth. Return mixture to saucepan, add cream and nutmeg and bring to boiling. (If soup is too thick, add more cream or milk.) Taste and add more salt if needed. Garnish with flowerettes.

SAVORY BEEF BURGERS
Makes 6 servings
A simple deglazing of the skillet gives this hamburger its zesty flavor.

2 pounds ground beef round	¼ cup bottled steak sauce
2 teaspoons seasoned salt	2 tablespoons lemon juice
2 tablespoons butter or margarine	

1. Combine meat with seasoned salt. Shape into 6 patties, 3½ inches in diameter and ½ inch thick.
2. Melt butter or margarine in a large skillet. Brown beef patties, 3 to 4 minutes on each side for medium-rare or to desired doneness. Remove to serving platter.
3. Drain off all but 1 tablespoon of the drippings. Heat skillet; add steak sauce and lemon juice. Stir and scrape up the browned bits in the skillet to deglaze. Pour over beef patties. Sprinkle with chopped chives, if you wish.

GREEN CHILI, CHEESE AND RICE BAKE
Bake at 375° for 25 minutes
Makes 6 servings
This delicious meatless casserole never fails to become a favorite.

1 package (6 ounces) sliced Monterey
Jack cheese
2 cups (1 pint) dairy sour cream
1 can (4 ounces) green chili peppers,
seeded and chopped

6 cups cooked long-grain rice (about 2
cups uncooked)
⅛ teaspoon pepper
1 package (4 ounces) shredded
Cheddar cheese (1 cup)

1. Cut the Monterey Jack into ½-inch squares. Combine with sour cream, chilies, rice and pepper in a medium-size bowl.
2. Spoon rice mixture into 6 individual casseroles or 3 shallow 8-by-5-by-1-inch foil casseroles.
3. Bake at in a moderate oven (375°) for 25 minutes or until bubbly hot.

MIXED SALAD
Makes 6 servings

2 jars (6 ounces each) marinated
artichoke hearts
1 jar (4 ounces) pimientos
1 can (3¼ ounces) pitted black olives
(⅔ cup)
1 medium-size head escarole or
romaine

3 tablespoons sliced green onions
3 tablespoons lemon juice
½ teaspoon salt
¼ teaspoon pepper

1. Remove artichokes from jar with fork, leaving marinade. Halve the hearts lengthwise, if large, and place in bottom of salad bowl.
2. Pat pimientos dry between paper toweling. Cut into slivers and place in bowl. Drain olives and place in bowl.
3. Tear lettuce into bite-size pieces, place in bowl and cover with plastic wrap.
4. Add green onions, lemon juice, salt and pepper to marinade in jar; cover. Refrigerate with salad. Shake dressing well and toss with salad when ready to serve.

CHOCOLATE FONDUE
Makes 2½ cups
Candy bars are the basic ingredient.

2 bars (8 ounces each) milk chocolate
  candy
¾ to 1 cup heavy cream
3 tablespoons brandy

For dipping: strawberries, pear and
apple slices, seedless grapes, banana
chunks, tangerine and orange
sections, pound cake squares, angel
food cake squares

1. Combine chocolate candy and ¾ cup heavy cream in a heavy saucepan.
   Cook over low heat, stirring constantly, until chocolate is melted. Add
   brandy. Remove from heat.
2. Pour into small fondue pot; surround by fruit and cake. Spear pieces of
   fruit or cake on fondue forks and twirl in sauce. Provide small plates to
   catch drippings. If mixture becomes too thick, stir in additional cream.

Note: Fondue can be made ahead and reheated over hot (not boiling)
water in a double boiler.

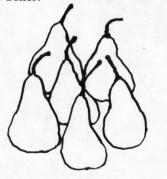

MENU
Serves 6
* *Inexpensive*

AFTER A LEAF-RAKING SESSION

Beef Roll Mozzarella
Eggplant and Tomato Casserole
Butter-Braised Onions
Tossed Green Salad with Bottled Dressing
Zabaglione or Fresh Fruit

TOTAL TIME
1¼ hours

MARKET LIST

1½ pounds lean ground beef
9 eggs
1½ cups shredded mozzarella (6
 ounces)
2 tablespoons grated Parmesan
1 medium-size eggplant
1 small green pepper
1 medium-size zucchini
3 ripe tomatoes
 Lemon
2 dozen small white onions

10 to 12 cups salad greens
1½ cups packaged bread crumbs
1 cup (4 ounces) mushroom stems
 and pieces
1 can (15 ounces) tomato sauce with
 tomato bits
2 tablespoons dry vermouth
 Seasoned pepper
 Bottled dressing
⅔ cup Marsala

WORK PLAN

1. Early in the day or 1¼ hours before serving prepare the Beef Roll through step 2, cover and refrigerate. Put the Eggplant and Tomato Casserole together and refrigerate.
2. About 1 hour before dinner is to be served preheat the oven to 375°.
3. Finish the Beef Roll and bake. Place eggplant casserole in oven to bake.
4. Wash the salad greens, dry and refrigerate.
5. About 25 minutes before Beef Roll is due to be ready prepare the onions.
6. Make zabaglione just before serving.

BEEF ROLL MOZZARELLA
Bake at 375° for 45 minutes
Makes 6 servings

1½ pounds lean ground beef
1 teaspoon salt
¼ teaspoon pepper
1 teaspoon dehydrated onion flakes
1 egg, lightly beaten
½ cup packaged bread crumbs
1 can (4 ounces) mushroom stems
 and pieces

1½ cups shredded mozzarella (6
 ounces)
1 can (15 ounces) tomato sauce with
 tomato bits
2 tablespoons dry vermouth

1. Combine meat, salt, pepper, onion, egg, and bread crumbs in a large bowl. Drain mushrooms; reserve. Add enough water to mushroom liquid to make ½ cup; add to meat mixture. Mix lightly, just until well combined.
2. Press mixture into a 14-by-10-inch rectangle on a piece of wax paper. Sprinkle surface with mozzarella, leaving a ½-inch border. Roll up, jelly-roll fashion starting with one of the short sides. Place, seam side down, in a 13-by-9-by-2-inch baking dish.
3. Combine tomato sauce with vermouth. Spread half the sauce over the roll.
4. Bake in a moderate oven (375°) for 45 minutes.
5. Combine remaining sauce with reserved mushrooms, spread over roll and bake 10 minutes longer. Lift onto heated platter with 2 wide spatulas.

EGGPLANT AND TOMATO CASSEROLE
Bake at 375° for 35 minutes
Makes 6 servings
Make early in the day and bake quickly for dinner.

1 medium-size eggplant	3 ripe tomatoes (medium-size), skinned and chopped
2 eggs, beaten	
1 cup packaged bread crumbs	1 teaspoon salt
¾ cup vegetable oil for frying	¼ teaspoon seasoned pepper
½ cup chopped onion	1 teaspoon leaf basil, crumbled or 1 tablespoon fresh basil, chopped
½ cup chopped green pepper	
1 medium-size zucchini, chopped	2 tablespoons grated Parmesan cheese
1 clove garlic, crushed	

1. Pare eggplant and cut into ½-inch slices. Dip in beaten egg, then lightly in crumbs. Cook in ½ cup hot oil in skillet until browned and tender. Set aside.
2. Sauté onion, green pepper, zucchini and garlic in remaining ¼ cup oil until tender. Add tomatoes, salt, pepper and basil; cook until liquid evaporates.
3. Layer eggplant and tomato mixture in shallow casserole. Sprinkle with Parmesan cheese.
4. Bake in a moderate oven (375°) about 35 minutes, or until bubbly and cheese is melted.

BUTTER-BRAISED ONIONS
Makes 6 servings
These disappear fast, and they look pretty arranged around the beef roll.

2 dozen small white onions (1½
  pounds)

2 tablespoons butter or margarine
1 teaspoon sugar

1. Peel onions, cook in boiling salted water 15 minutes and drain.
2. Heat butter or margarine in large saucepan just until it starts to brown. Add onions and sprinkle with sugar. Cook, stirring often, until golden and slightly glazed. Keep warm until serving.

ZABAGLIONE
Makes 6 servings

6 egg yolks
⅔ cup sugar

⅔ cup Marsala
½ teaspoon grated lemon rind

In the top of a double broiler set over, but not touching, boiling water, beat the yolks and gradually add the sugar beating until mixture is thick and pale. Continue beating while adding the wine and lemon rind. When custard foams up in the pan and thickens slightly pour into parfait or flat champagne glasses and serve at once.

MENU
Serves 6

A MENU FOR ENTERTAINING

Vegetable Tempura Appetizer
Chicken Curry • Green Onion Rice
Crème Caramel or Apples and Cheese

TOTAL TIME
About 1¼ hours ahead, plus about 30 minutes cooking before serving and 1 hour 10 minutes reheating

If you have a small electric deep fat fryer the vegetable tempura can be cooked to order during the cocktail hour at a party. The curry and rice can be made ahead and popped into the oven for reheating while the host and hostess are enjoying the guests.

MARKET LIST

4 pounds chicken breasts or parts
5 eggs
2 cups milk
1 cup heavy cream
2 medium-size zucchini
¼ head cauliflower
½ pound green beans
3 large onions
½ pound medium-size mushrooms
1 bunch green onions
Lemon
Banana

Radishes
Soy sauce (optional)
Hot mustard (optional)
Vegetable oil for frying
5 envelopes instant chicken broth
Ground coriander
Peanuts
Coconut
Raisins
Rice
Brandy (optional)
⅓ cup toasted almonds

WORK PLAN

1. A day ahead or early on the day make curry.
2. Make dessert and chill. Prepare green onion rice while curry is cooking.
3. Fix tempura and serve as soon as it is cooked. Reheat curry and rice in 350° oven. Set out curry condiments.
4. Fold whipped cream into dessert.

VEGETABLE TEMPURA APPETIZER
Makes 6 appetizer or side-dish servings

---

2 cups sifted all-purpose flour
1 teaspoon salt
⅛ teaspoon baking soda
1 egg yolk
2 cups ice water
Vegetable oil for frying
2 medium-size zucchini, thinly sliced
1 cup cauliflower flowerettes, parboiled for 3 minutes

½ pound whole green beans, parboiled for 3 minutes
2 large onions, sliced in rings and separated
½ pound medium-size mushrooms, sliced
Soy sauce and hot mustard for dipping (optional)

1. Combine flour, salt and baking soda in a medium-size bowl. Beat egg yolk and water in a small bowl until blended, pour into dry ingredients and beat until batter is smooth. Cover and let stand 10 minutes.
2. Pour oil into a large skillet or saucepan to ⅔ full. Heat to 375°.
3. Dip vegetables in batter, letting excess drip off. Fry in hot oil, a few at a time, until golden brown. Drain on paper toweling. Keep vegetables warm in a very slow oven (250°) until all are cooked.

CHICKEN CURRY
Makes 6 servings

To make ahead: Prepare curry early in the day, or the day before and refrigerate. 1½ hours before serving, reheat the curry (see note) and cook the rice in the oven at the same time. Prepare condiments (except bananas) and refrigerate.

4 pounds chicken breasts or broiler-fryers, cut up
3 cups water
3 envelopes or teaspoons instant chicken broth
2 tablespoons butter or margarine
1 large onion, diced (1 cup)
2 cloves garlic, minced
¼ cup flour
1 to 1½ tablespoons curry powder
2 teaspoons ground coriander
1½ teaspoons salt
½ teaspoon pepper
1 large lemon
Green Onion Rice (recipe follows)
Condiments: peanuts, shredded coconut, sliced bananas, sliced radishes, raisins, chopped hard-cooked egg, French-fried onion rings

1. Simmer chicken in water and broth in large saucepan 30 minutes for parts or 20 minutes if using breasts, or until tender. Reserve cooking liquid, skim off fat and measure. Return to saucepan and boil until reduced to 3 cups. Discard skin from chicken, remove meat from bones and cut into bite-size pieces.
2. Melt butter in large saucepan. Sauté onions and garlic until tender, about 5 minutes. Remove from heat.
3. Combine flour, curry powder, coriander, salt and pepper. Sprinkle over onions, stirring to coat. Gradually stir in the 3 cups reserved chicken broth until mixture is smooth. Return to heat. Bring to boiling, lower heat, cover and simmer 15 minutes, stirring often.
4. Grate 1 tablespoon rind from lemon. Squeeze 2 tablespoons juice. Stir into curry and heat thoroughly. Serve over Green Onion Rice and with choice of condiments.

Note: To reheat, place curry in a shallow 2-quart oven-proof casserole. Cover with aluminum foil and refrigerate. 1½ hours before serving remove from refrigerator, uncover and stir thoroughly. Recover. Place in a moderate oven (350°) for 1 hour and 10 minutes or until bubbly hot.

GREEN ONION RICE
Bake at 350° for 1 hour
Makes 6 servings
There's no need to watch when you bake the rice in the oven as the curry is reheating.

2 cups long grain rice
2 envelopes or teaspoons instant
  chicken broth

2 tablespoons butter or margarine
5 cups water
½ cup chopped green onion

1. Combine rice, broth, butter and water in a 2-quart baking dish; cover.
2. Bake in a moderate oven (350°) for 1 hour or until rice is tender and water is absorbed. Add onion and fluff rice with a fork.

CRÈME CARAMEL
Makes 6 servings
The caramel is in the crème, rather than being the usual topping.

½ cup sugar
2 cups hot milk
4 egg yolks
3 tablespoons cornstarch

1 to 2 tablespoons brandy (optional)
1 cup heavy cream, whipped
⅓ cup chopped toasted almonds or
  hazelnuts

1. Heat sugar over medium heat in a large heavy saucepan until golden and bubbly. (Do not brown or scorch.) Remove pan from heat and stir in milk. (Mixture will become lumpy but the lumps will dissolve.) If necessary, return pan to low heat and stir until sugar has dissolved.
2. Beat egg yolks slightly in medium-size bowl. Stir in cornstarch; then slowly stir in hot caramel mixture. Return to saucepan and cook, stirring constantly, until mixture thickens and bubbles 1 minute. Remove from heat and pour into bowl; cool. Stir in brandy and chill.
3. Fold in whipped cream. Spoon into a glass serving dish or individual dessert dishes. Sprinkle with nuts.

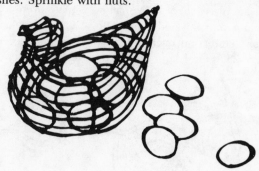

MENU
Serves 6
* *Inexpensive*

FRIENDS-FOR-DINNER SPECIAL

Breast of Chicken, Neapolitan Style
Rice (see page 137)
Green Beans with Bacon
Quick Blender Chocolate Mousse

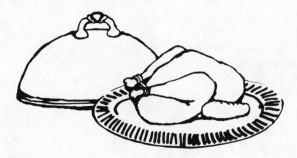

TOTAL TIME
About 1 hour

Great menu for the busy single cook—it can be put together in about an hour and it looks as though you have been slaving over a hot stove all day.

MARKET LIST

3 whole chicken breasts (about 12 ounces each)
6 slices bacon
4 eggs
12 small white onions
½ pound mushrooms
Parsley
1 can condensed tomato bisque

¾ dry red wine
8 pitted ripe olives, sliced
2 cups long-grain rice
2 packages (9 ounces each) whole frozen green beans
1 package (6 ounces) semisweet chocolate pieces
2 tablespoons golden rum (optional)

WORK PLAN

1. Preheat the oven to 350°, fix rice casserole and bake.
2. Prepare chocolate mousse and set to chill.
3. Prepare chicken dish.
4. While chicken dish is cooking, cook the green beans.

BREAST OF CHICKEN, NEAPOLITAN STYLE
Makes 6 servings

3 whole chicken breasts (about 12 ounces each)	1 clove garlic, minced
2 teaspoons salt	1 can condensed tomato bisque
½ teaspoon pepper	¾ cup dry red wine
4 tablespoons olive oil	¾ teaspoon leaf oregano, crumbled
12 small white onions	¾ teaspoon leaf basil, crumbled
½ pound mushrooms, quartered	4 tablespoons minced parsley
	8 pitted ripe olives, sliced

1. Cut chicken breasts in half through the breast bones, sprinkle with salt and pepper and let stand 5 minutes.
2. Sauté chicken, skin side down, in hot oil in a large skillet 5 minutes; turn. Add onions, mushrooms and garlic and cook 5 minutes.
3. Combine soup, wine, oregano and basil in a 2-cup measure; pour over chicken. Bring to boiling, lower heat and cover. Cook 15 minutes or until chicken is tender. Stir in parsley and olives.

GREEN BEANS WITH BACON
Makes about 6 servings

6 slices bacon	2 packages (9 ounces each) whole frozen green beans

1. Cook bacon in a small skillet until crisp. Drain on paper toweling; crumble. Reserve fat.
2. Cook green beans in a large saucepan, following label directions; drain. Heat 2 tablespoons of the bacon fat in same large saucepan. Return beans and stir gently to coat. Stir in crumbled bacon and serve at once or keep warm over low heat.

QUICK BLENDER CHOCOLATE MOUSSE
Makes 6 to 8 servings
Here is a real easy one—10 minutes to make, 1 hour to chill—and so delicious!

4 eggs, separated (whites should be at room temperature)	5 tablespoons boiling water or coffee
1 package (6 ounces) semisweet chocolate pieces	2 tablespoons golden rum or 3 teaspoons vanilla

1. Beat egg whites in a small bowl with electric mixer until stiff but not dry.
2. Place chocolate pieces in container of electric blender. Whirl to break up pieces. Add boiling water and whirl until smooth.
3. Add egg yolks and rum or vanilla. Whirl 1 minute until thoroughly blended. Pour chocolate mixture slowly over egg whites, and fold in gently until no white shows. Spoon into individual soufflé dishes, sherbet glasses or a 1-quart serving dish. Refrigerate about 1 hour or until firm and well-chilled. Garnish with whipped cream, if you wish.

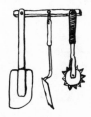

MENU
Serves 6
* Inexpensive

A MEXICAN MEDLEY

Tortilla Soup • Guacamole Salad
Green Chili-Mushroom Enchiladas
Refried Beans
Caramel Coconut Flan or Papayas with Lime

TOTAL TIME
About 1½ hours ahead if making flan, plus 30 minutes before serving

Mexican cooking is famous for its spicy flavor and low cost and here is a good example along vegetarian lines.

MARKET LIST

1 pint dairy sour cream
8 eggs
3 cups shredded Cheddar cheese
1 bunch green onions
5 to 6 medium-size tomatoes
4 large ripe avocados
 Lemon
 Lettuce
¾ pound mushrooms
1 package (10 ounces) corn chips

4 quarts chicken or beef stock
2 cans (4 ounces each) green chili peppers
 Ground cumin (optional)
12 canned or frozen tortillas
2 tall cans (13 ounces each) evaporated milk
½ cup flaked coconut
2 cans refried beans
 Vegetable shortening or lard

WORK PLAN

1. Night before or early in the day make the flan; cool and refrigerate.
2. About 30 minutes before serving prepare guacamole; refrigerate. Pre-heat oven to 400°.
3. Prepare enchiladas and bake.
4. Make soup. Unmold flan; refrigerate. Heat beans in shortening or lard.
5. Serve soup with guacamole.
6. Serve enchiladas with refried beans.

TORTILLA SOUP
Makes 6 servings

---

1 package (10 ounces) corn chips
1 bunch green onions, finely chopped
1½ cups shredded Cheddar cheese
4 quarts chicken or beef stock or 4 cans (13¾ ounces each) chicken broth

1 can (4 ounces) green chili peppers, seeded and cut into strips
1 teaspoon salt
½ teaspoon pepper
½ teaspoon ground cumin (optional)
Guacamole (recipe follows)

Divide corn chips among 6 individual soup bowls. Sprinkle onions, then cheese, over corn chips. Heat broth to boiling, add green chilies, then salt, pepper and cumin. Pour broth into bowls. Serve piping hot with guacamole salad.

GUACAMOLE (AVOCADO SALAD)
Makes 6 servings

---

2 medium-size tomatoes
4 large ripe avocados
2 tablespoons lemon juice
1 small onion, finely chopped (¼ cup)
1 clove garlic, minced
2 tablespoons olive oil or 1 tablespoon mayonnaise

1 teaspoon liquid red pepper seasoning
1 teaspoon salt
¼ teaspoon white pepper
Corn chips or lettuce

1. Dip tomatoes in boiling water for 15 seconds; peel off skins. Cut each in half and squeeze out as much of the juice and seeds as possible and discard; chop pulp.
2. Halve avocados, remove pit and peel. Sprinkle avocado halves with lemon juice in a medium-size bowl; mash coarsely with a fork, leaving some small chunks.
3. Add tomatoes, onion, garlic, oil, pepper seasoning, salt and pepper; mix well. Chill before serving. Serve as a dip with corn chips, or as a salad on lettuce.

GREEN CHILI-MUSHROOM ENCHILADAS
Makes 6 servings
This hearty, satisfying dish can be made almost entirely in advance—only the tortillas should be fried at the last minute.

4 large onions, finely chopped (2½ cups)
6 cloves garlic, mashed or finely chopped
⅓ cup vegetable oil
2 cups tomatoes, coarsely chopped
1 can (4 ounces) green chili peppers, seeded and finely chopped
¾ pound mushrooms, sliced
2 tablespoons leaf basil, crumbled
2 teaspoons leaf thyme, crumbled
2 teaspoons salt
½ teaspoon pepper
1 pint (2 cups) dairy sour cream
12 canned or frozen tortillas
Vegetable oil for frying
1½ cups shredded Cheddar cheese

1. Sauté 2 cups of the onions and the garlic in oil in a large skillet until tender, but not brown. Add ¾ cup of the tomatoes and the chili peppers; simmer 5 minutes. Add mushrooms and simmer until tender. Stir in basil, thyme, salt and pepper; simmer 2 minutes longer. Stir in sour cream; remove sauce from heat.
2. Combine remaining onion and tomato in a small bowl to use as filling.
3. Dip tortillas, one at a time, in hot oil in a skillet for 5 to 8 seconds on each side, or until softened. Drain on paper toweling.
4. Oil a baking dish large enough to hold 4 tortillas. On each tortilla, spread ¼ of the filling, a generous portion of sauce, another tortilla, rest of sauce, and top with cheese.
5. Bake in a hot oven (400°) about 10 minutes or until sauce is bubbling and enchilada is heated through.

CARAMEL COCONUT FLAN
Bake at 350° for 1 hour
Makes 6 to 8 servings
A very popular dessert, not only in Mexico but in many other parts of the world too.

1½ cups sugar
  8 large eggs
  2 tall cans (13 ounces each)
    evaporated milk, undiluted

⅛ teaspoon salt
½ cup flaked coconut

1. Place a 6-cup mold in a large shallow baking pan filled with 1 inch of hot water. Place in a moderate oven (350°) for 10 minutes to warm.
2. While mold is warming, heat 1 cup of the sugar in a small saucepan, stirring constantly until melted and golden. Remove mold from water with pot holder. Pour melted sugar into mold and swirl to coat bottom and sides with the caramel. Cool slightly.
3. Beat eggs until foamy in a large bowl. Beat in remaining sugar, milk and salt until blended. Stir in coconut. Pour mixture into caramel-lined mold. Replace mold in water bath.
4. Bake in a moderate oven (350°) for 1 hour or until knife inserted 1 inch from edge comes out clean. (Center will still be soft.) Remove from water bath and cool on wire rack 10 minutes.
5. Refrigerate until cold. To serve, loosen flan around edge with knife. Place rimmed serving dish upside down over mold. Holding mold and dish, turn dish upright and lift off mold. Caramel will flow out to form sauce. Garnish with toasted coconut, if you wish.

MENU
Serves 6
* *Inexpensive*

VEGETARIAN'S DELIGHT

Open-face Zucchini Omelet
Carrots with Caraway Seeds • Sliced Tomato Salad
Marinated Fruit

TOTAL TIME
About 50 minutes

Mixing the foods of different cultures is a fun thing to try, providing some thought is given to each component's contribution. Take care not to overcook the omelet or it will be dry. Sprinkle the tomato slices with a little chopped basil for extra pleasure.

MARKET LIST

9 eggs
1½ tablespoons cream
  Parmesan cheese
3 medium-size zucchini
2 small green peppers
4 large tomatoes
  Fresh or dried basil

1 medium-size pineapple or 1 can (1
  pound, 4 ounces) pineapple chunks
  in juice
4 navel oranges
2 pears
8 carrots
4 ribs celery
⅔ cup dry vermouth or orange juice

WORK PLAN

1. Skin and slice tomatoes, season according to recipe and refrigerate.
2. Prepare the fruit in the marinade and refrigerate.
3. Cook the carrots with caraway.
4. Cook the omelet.

OPEN-FACE ZUCCHINI OMELET
Makes 6 servings
This type of omelet, called frittata, is popular in both Spain and Italy. It can also be served cold, cut into cubes, as part of the antipasto table.

9 eggs
1½ tablespoons cream
1½ tablespoons butter, softened
3 tablespoons grated Parmesan
   cheese
3 drops liquid red pepper seasoning
1½ teaspoons salt

¼ teaspoon freshly ground pepper
3 medium-size zucchini, finely
   chopped (2 cups)
2 small green peppers, seeded and
   chopped
3 tablespoons olive or vegetable oil

1. Combine eggs, cream, butter, Parmesan, red pepper seasoning, salt and pepper in a large bowl. Whisk or beat with a rotary beater until well-blended.
2. Heat oven to moderate (350°).
3. Sauté the zucchini and pepper in oil in a large ovenproof skillet until very soft, about 5 minutes.
4. Add the beaten egg mixture. Stir gently and cook for 2 minutes or until the eggs are just set on bottom.
5. Place skillet in preheated oven for 6 to 8 minutes until top of eggs are set. Cut into wedges to serve.

CARROTS WITH CARAWAY SEEDS
Makes 6 servings

8 carrots, diced
1 cup diced celery
1 small onion, finely chopped
2 tablespoons butter
½ teaspoon salt

⅛ teaspoon pepper
1 teaspoon caraway seeds
1 tablespoon flour
1 tablespoon light brown sugar

1. Place the carrots in a medium-size saucepan, half cover with boiling salted water. Cover, bring to boiling and simmer until carrots are crisp-tender, about 10 minutes.
2. Sauté the celery and onion in the butter until wilted. Add to carrots.
3. Add salt, pepper, caraway seeds, flour and brown sugar and cook, stirring until mixture thickens. If there is too much sauce continue to boil rapidly while stirring to evaporate the excess.

SLICED TOMATO SALAD
Makes 6 servings

4 large tomatoes, skinned and sliced	2 tablespoons olive or vegetable oil
½ teaspoon salt	1 tablespoon wine vinegar
¼ teaspoon freshly ground black pepper	1 tablespoon chopped fresh basil or 1 teaspoon dried basil

Arrange the tomato slices on a serving platter. Sprinkle with salt and pepper. Sprinkle with oil and vinegar and basil. Cover and refrigerate.

MARINATED FRUIT
Makes 6 servings

⅔ cup dry vermouth or orange juice	1 medium-size pineapple or 1 can (1 pound, 4 ounces) pineapple chunks in juice
5 tablespoons sugar	4 navel oranges
½ teaspoon ground cinnamon	2 pears

1. Combine vermouth, sugar and cinnamon in a large bowl. (If using orange juice, reduce sugar to 2 tablespoons.)
2. With a sharp long-bladed knife, cut pineapple right through the frond into quarters. Remove pineapple, in one piece, from shells. Cut core from pineapple and discard. Cut pineapple into chunks and add to vermouth mixture.
3. Pare oranges with a sharp knife, cutting away white membrane and holding over bowl to collect juice; section into bowl. Cut pears in half, remove core and cut into lengthwise strips. Then cut each strip in half into bowl. Toss fruit gently to coat with vermouth mixture. Refrigerate for flavors to mellow, tossing occasionally.

MENU
Serves 8

AN ENTERTAINING EXTRAVAGANZA

Golden Chicken Casserole
Ratatouille
Rice (see page 137)
Spinach and Mushroom Salad
Poached Pears in Sherry

TOTAL TIME
1 hour, 20 minutes

This is a menu that could tempt the timid cook to entertain. You're free to sit and relax once you're down to step 4 in the work plan with the table ready and the ingredients for last minute fixings lined up.

MARKET LIST

2 broiler-fryers (about 2½ to 3 pounds each), cut up
½ pound frozen, uncooked, peeled and deveined shrimp (optional)
8 slices bacon
2 eggs
6 cloves garlic
2 large ribs celery
2 small green peppers
1 pound mushrooms
2 ripe tomatoes
2 zucchini
1 medium-size eggplant
Parsley (optional)

2 pounds fresh bulk spinach or 2 10-ounce bags
1 orange
Lemon
8 large pears
1 can (1 pound, 1 ounce) Italian plum tomatoes
1 cup dry white wine
Tomato paste
1 cup tomato juice
¼ cup prepared Italian salad dressing
2 cups long-grain rice
⅓ cup apricot, apple or pineapple jelly
⅔ cup cream sherry

WORK PLAN

1. Preheat oven to 350°. Prepare the chicken casserole and place in oven.
2. Fix pears and bake with chicken.
3. Make the ratatouille. Hard-cook eggs for salad.
4. Wash spinach, dry and refrigerate. Prepare dressing and line up other ingredients.
5. Remove pears from oven and cool to room temperature. Add shrimp to casserole if using. Prepare rice.
6. Toss salad.

GOLDEN CHICKEN CASSEROLE
Bake at 350° for 45 minutes
Makes 8 servings

2 broiler-fryers (about 2½ to 3 pounds each), cut up
½ cup all-purpose flour
1 tablespooon salt
1 teaspoon pepper
½ cup vegetable oil
2 cloves garlic, minced
1 large onion, diced (1 cup)
1 cup sliced celery
1 small green pepper, halved, seeded and cut into strips
½ pound mushrooms, sliced
1 teaspoon leaf thyme, crumbled
¼ teaspoon cayenne pepper
1 bay leaf
1 can (1 pound, 1 ounce) Italian plum tomatoes
1 cup dry white wine
2 tablespoons tomato paste
½ pound frozen, uncooked, peeled and deveined shrimp (optional)

1. Shake chicken pieces, a few at a time, in a plastic bag with flour, 1½ teaspoons of the salt and ½ teaspoon of the pepper. Reserve remaining seasoned flour mixture.
2. Brown chicken, a few pieces at a time, in oil in a large skillet. Place browned chicken in a 10-cup casserole.
3. Remove all but 2 tablespoons of the oil from skillet. Sauté garlic and onion until soft. Add celery, green pepper and mushrooms. Sauté just until crisp-tender.
4. Add remaining 1½ teaspoons salt, ½ teaspoon pepper, 2 tablespoons of the reserved seasoned flour mixture, thyme, cayenne and bay leaf. Toss to coat vegetables.
5. Add plum tomatoes with can liquid, wine and tomato paste and stir just to mix. Bring to boiling. Pour over chicken in casserole and cover.
6. Bake in a moderate oven (350°) for 25 minutes. Uncover and add shrimp, pushing shrimp down into liquid. Cover again and bake an additional 20 minutes until chicken and shrimp are tender. Uncover; gently stir to mix ingredients. Serve over rice. Garnish with chopped parsley, if you wish.

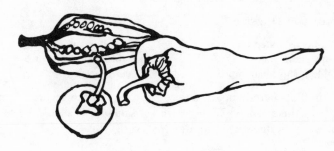

RATATOUILLE
Makes 8 servings

2 tablespoons olive oil	½ teaspoon leaf basil, crumbled
1 large onion, chopped (1 cup)	1½ teaspoons leaf oregano, crumbled
2 cloves garlic, chopped	1 cup tomato juice
1 green pepper, halved, seeded and chopped	¼ cup prepared Italian salad dressing
2 ripe tomatoes, chopped	2 teaspoons salt
2 zucchini, trimmed and chopped	½ teaspoon pepper
1 medium-size unpeeled eggplant, chopped	Chopped parsley (optional)

Heat oil in a large saucepan or Dutch oven. Sauté onion, garlic and green pepper until soft, about 5 minutes. Stir in tomato, zucchini, eggplant, basil, oregano, tomato juice, salad dressing, salt and pepper. Simmer, stirring occasionally, until mixture is thick and vegetables are soft, about 20 minutes. Cool. Serve warm or at room temperature sprinkled with parsley, if you wish.

SPINACH AND MUSHROOM SALAD
Makes 8 servings

2 pounds fresh bulk spinach or 2 bags (11 ounces each) fresh spinach	8 slices bacon, cooked and crumbled or real bacon bits
4 hard-cooked eggs, finely chopped	Orange Soy Dressing (recipe follows)
½ pound medium-sized mushrooms, sliced	

1. Wash spinach thoroughly, remove tough stems and bruised leaves and dry on paper toweling. Tear leaves into bite-size pieces and place in a salad bowl.
2. Add eggs, mushrooms and bacon. Cover bowl with plastic wrap; refrigerate.
3. Prepare Orange Soy Dressing.

Orange Soy Dressing

4 teaspoons grated orange rind	¾ cup olive oil
1⅓ cups orange juice	4 tablespoons soy sauce
2 tablespoons lemon juice	4 cloves garlic

Combine all ingredients in a screw-top jar. Shake vigorously until well blended. Makes about 2½ cups. (Each salad for 8 should be tossed with ¼ to ⅓ cup of dressing at time it is served.)

POACHED PEARS IN SHERRY
Bake at 350° for 30 minutes
Makes 8 servings

8 large ripe pears (about 3 pounds) ⅓ cup apricot, apple or pineapple jelly
3 tablespoons lemon juice ⅔ cup cream sherry

1. Peel pears (do not remove stems); remove core from the bottom. Place in a shallow 3-quart baking dish and brush with lemon juice.
2. Combine jelly and sherry and pour over pears. Cover with aluminum foil.
3. Bake in a moderate oven (350°) for 30 minutes or until pears are tender, basting once or twice. Cool while eating main dish and serve lukewarm. Serve with a dab of sour cream mixed with a pinch of mace.

MENU
Serves 8

HEARTY FARE

Stuffed Pork Chops with Carrots and Broccoli
Home-fried Potatoes
Celery Top and Olive Salad
Tortoni

TOTAL TIME
About 25 minutes ahead plus 40 minutes before serving

This menu includes cooking instructions for the vegetables right along with the meat . . . coordinated cooking which will give you a pretty, colorful platter to serve family or friends.

MARKET LIST

8 center loin pork chops (cut 1 inch
  thick) with a pocket cut in each for
  stuffing
2 egg whites
1 cup heavy cream
2 bunches carrots
2 bunches broccoli
2 green onions
2 pounds potatoes
  Parsley

1 head celery
1 cup unflavored dry bread crumbs
2 cups chicken broth
½ cup white wine
4 tablespoons tomato paste
4 cups pitted green or ripe olives,
  chopped
¼ cup chopped almonds
¼ cup sweet sherry or Marsala

WORK PLAN

1. Night before or early in the day make the tortoni and freeze. Cook potatoes for home fries.
2. Forty minutes before serving prepare and start cooking pork chops.
3. Continue with step 2 home fries.
4. Prepare salad. Remove tortoni from freezer to soften while eating main
   course.

STUFFED PORK CHOPS
Makes 8 servings

---

2 green onions, cleaned and finely
  chopped
1 cup dry bread crumbs
2 tablespoons chopped fresh parsley
½ teaspoon salt
  Dash pepper
½ teaspoon leaf rosemary, crumbled
6 tablespoons butter, melted
2 bunches carrots, scraped and cut
  into 4-inch lengths

8 center loin pork chops (1 inch thick),
  well-trimmed of fat with a pocket
  cut in each
6 tablespoons oil
2 bunches broccoli, trimmed and cut
  into flowerettes and washed
2 cups chicken broth
½ cup white wine
¼ cup tomato paste

1. Place green onions, bread crumbs, parsley, salt, pepper and rosemary
   in a small bowl. Add butter and mix.
2. Place carrots in saucepan; add ¾ cup water and ½ teaspoon salt. Bring
   to boiling; cover and simmer 20 minutes or until crisp-tender. Drain.
3. Fill pockets in chops with bread crumb mixture and close with tooth-
   picks.

4. Heat 6 tablespoons oil in a large heavy skillet. Add chops and sauté about 5 minutes on each side or until golden. Remove chops and discard fat from pan. Keep glaze in pan.
5. Steam broccoli over salted water 8 minutes or until crisp-tender.
6. Add chicken broth, wine and tomato paste to browned-on glaze in skillet, scraping to loosen bits. Bring to boiling, stirring.
7. Return chops to skillet. Simmer, partially covered, 10 minutes longer or until chops are cooked through.
8. Arrange chops on platter, and drained carrots and broccoli on either end. Turn up heat under sauce in skillet and boil until there's about ½ cup. Pour over chops. Garnish with chopped parsley, if you wish.

HOME-FRIED POTATOES
Makes 8 servings

2 pounds potatoes	¾ teaspoon salt
6 tablespoons (¾ stick) butter or margarine	2 tablespoons hot water

1. Cook potatoes in their skins in boiling salted water in a large saucepan until tender, preferably a day ahead. Cool potatoes; peel and shred or cut into thin julienne strips.
2. Heat butter in a large heavy skillet. Add potatoes and sprinkle with salt. Smooth top with the back of a spoon or wide spatula to make a flat cake. Sprinkle the hot water over potatoes. Cover and cook over medium heat until a golden crust is formed on the bottom, about 15 to 20 minutes. (Shake skillet frequently to prevent sticking.)
3. Turn out onto heated serving platter, crusty side up. Garnish with parsley, if you wish, and serve immediately.

CELERY TOP AND OLIVE SALAD
Makes 8 servings

4 cups pitted green or ripe olives, chopped	4 tablespoons wine vinegar
4 cups coarsely chopped celery tops	1 teaspoon salt
2 medium onions, chopped (1 cup)	½ teaspoon freshly ground pepper
½ cup olive or vegetable oil	4 cloves garlic, crushed

Combine ingredients in a salad bowl; toss to coat vegetables well with oil and vinegar. Let stand at room temperature before serving to improve flavors.

TORTONI
Makes 8 servings

¼ cup chopped almonds	½ cup sugar
2 egg whites	¼ cup sweet sherry or Marsala
Pinch salt	1 cup heavy cream, whipped

1. Place almonds in small skillet and toast slowly over low heat, shaking frequently, until toasted. Cool.
2. Beat egg whites and salt until foamy and gradually beat in the sugar until mixture forms a stiff meringue.
3. Stir in sherry or Marsala.
4. Fold cream in meringue. Spoon into 8 demitasse cups or 8 paper soufflé cups. Freeze about 4 hours.

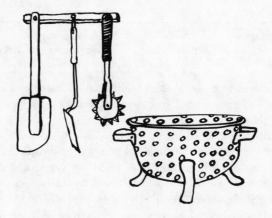

MENU
Serves 8
* Inexpensive

A SATURDAY NIGHT REPAST

Indonesian Lamb Roast
Rice (see page 137) • Green Beans Indian Style
Cucumber Salad
Ambrosia

TOTAL TIME
10 minutes ahead, plus 1 hour before serving

Cooking times are shortened when you broil and stir-fry so have all the ingredients together by the stove before you begin. A sumptuous meal to serve 8 in an hour!

MARKET LIST

8 thick rib or shoulder lamb chops or a
rack of lamb, trimmed of fat
1 rib celery
Lemons
2 pounds fresh green beans
6 small carrots
3 cucumbers
1 bunch green onions
1 large pineapple or 2 cans (1 pound,
4 ounces each) pineapple chunks in
juice
8 navel oranges

Parsley
2 cups fresh grated coconut or 2 cans
(4 ounces each) shredded coconut
½ cup prepared mustard
Curry powder
Honey
Bottled meat sauce
2 cups long-grain rice
2 teaspoons mustard seeds
Ground coriander
Dijon-style mustard
Leaf tarragon

WORK PLAN

1. Early in the day prepare the marinade and pour over chops; refrigerate.
2. Sixty minutes before serving prepare the cucumber salad according to recipe; refrigerate.
3. Make the ambrosia; refrigerate.
4. Start cooking the rice. Begin cooking the green beans.
5. Broil the lamb chops as suggested in the recipe.

INDONESIAN LAMB ROAST
Makes 8 servings

⅓ cup finely chopped celery
⅓ cup finely chopped onion
1 clove garlic, minced
½ cup vegetable oil
¼ cup vinegar
½ cup prepared mustard
3 tablespoons curry powder
1 teaspoon leaf oregano, crumbled
2 bay leaves

3 tablespoons honey
2 teaspoons grated lemon rind
3 tablespoons lemon juice
2 teaspoons bottled meat sauce
2 dashes liquid hot red-pepper
seasoning
8 thick rib or shoulder lamb chops, or
a rack of lamb, trimmed of fat

1. Sauté celery, onion and garlic in oil in a medium-size saucepan until onion is transparent. Stir in all remaining ingredients except meat, simmer a few minutes, cool and chill briefly.
2. Arrange chops in a shallow glass dish; pour marinade over. Let stand 3 to 8 hours, turning several times if practical.
3. Drain chops; wrap ends of rib chop bones with foil to keep them from charring when boiling. Arrange chops on rack in broiler pan; brush with marinade.
4. Broil, with tops 4 to 5 inches from heat, 4 minutes. Turn; brush again with marinade. Broil 4 minutes longer, or until meat is done as you like. (Do not overcook—lamb is delicious and juicy when cooked to the pink stage.)
5. Pour off any excess oil from marinade, then heat remainder to serve as a sauce for chops and rice.

GREEN BEANS INDIAN STYLE
Makes 8 servings
Spicy and delicious with poultry or lamb.

2 pounds fresh green beans	6 small carrots, thinly sliced (1½ cups)
4 tablespoons butter or margarine	
4 tablespoons vegetable oil	2½ teaspoons salt
2 teaspoons mustard seeds	2 teaspoons ground coriander
2 medium-size onions, chopped (1 cup)	¼ teaspoon ground ginger
	2 tablespoons lemon juice

1. Wash beans; trim ends with a sharp knife. Slice diagonally into 1-inch long bias slices.
2. Heat butter and oil in large skillet. Add mustard seeds and sauté 30 seconds or until seeds start to "pop." Stir in onion, carrots and beans. Cook 5 minutes, stirring constantly.
3. Stir in salt, coriander and ginger. Lower heat, cover and cook, stirring often, 8 to 10 minutes or until crisply tender. Stir in lemon juice.

CUCUMBER SALAD
Makes 8 servings
Herbs and mustard make the dressing for this salad extra special without adding too many calories.

3 cucumbers, each about 8 inches long
3 tablespoons lemon juice
1½ tablespoons vegetable oil
¾ teaspoon salt
¼ teaspoon freshly ground pepper

1½ teaspoons prepared Dijon-style mustard
3 tablespoons chopped parsley
1¼ teaspoons leaf tarragon, crumbled
7 green onions, minced

1. Wash cucumbers; pare thinly and cut in half, crosswise. Remove seeds by piercing core or cucumber all the way through with a sharp paring knife. Using dull side of blade, twist within the core until all seeds are removed. Slice cucumbers thinly.
2. Combine lemon juice, oil, salt, pepper, mustard, parsley, tarragon and green onion in a small bowl. Whip with fork until well blended. Pour dressing over cucumbers. Marinate at least an hour in refrigerator.

AMBROSIA
Makes about 8 servings

1 large pineapple or 2 cans (1 pound, 4 ounces each) pineapple chunks in juice

8 navel oranges
2 cups fresh grated coconut or 1 can (4 ounces) shredded coconut

1. Pare and core the fresh pineapple, and cut the fruit into chunks into a large bowl, saving as much juice as possible. (For canned pineapple, use all the juice.)
2. Remove rind from oranges with a sharp knife, holding fruit over bowl to catch juice and cutting through and removing the white part as well. Slice oranges, removing any seeds, if necessary.
3. Layer pineapple, part of the coconut and oranges in a serving bowl. Sprinkle top with remaining coconut. Cover; chill at least 4 hours before serving.

Winter

MENU
Serves 2

DIFFERENT AND DELICIOUS

Fillets of Sole in Cucumber Sauce
Butternut Squash • Buttered Spinach
Bean Sprout Salad
Pear Pancake

TOTAL TIME
About 1 hour

Fillets of sole are always good broiled, poached, baked or fried but once you've fixed them with a special cucumber sauce it will be your favorite, too. You can make the pancake with apples or plums, if you wish.

MARKET LIST

12 to 16 ounces fillets of sole, fresh or
  frozen
½ cup heavy cream
1 cup milk
3 eggs
1 large cucumber
  Lemon
  Parsley
1 small butternut squash (about 1
  pound)

1 pound fresh bean sprouts
  Lettuce leaves
2 pears
  Dijon-style mustard
  Soy sauce
  Dry sherry
1 package (10 ounces) frozen chopped
  spinach

WORK PLAN

1. Preheat oven to 350°. Make and bake the pear pancake and keep warm if necessary. It is best if you put it in the oven 35 minutes before you plan to serve it. Then it will have 5 minutes to stand.
2. Make the sauce for the fish; keep warm.
3. Cook the squash. Cook the spinach according to package directions. Drain well and add 1 tablespoon butter and dash nutmeg.
4. Prepare the salad plates.
5. Cook the fish and serve.

FILLETS OF SOLE IN CUCUMBER SAUCE
Makes 2 servings
This unusual sauce is also excellent served with baked whole fish.

1 large cucumber (¾ pound)	12 ounces fillet of sole, fresh or frozen,
2 tablespoons (¼ stick) butter	thawed
½ cup heavy cream	¼ teaspoon salt
¼ teaspoon salt	Pinch freshly ground pepper
Pinch pepper	Flour
1 tablespoon lemon juice	1 tablespoon minced parsley

1. Pare cucumber; halve lengthwise and scoop out seeds with tip of tea-spoon. Cut crosswise into ¼-inch slices.
2. Sauté cucumber in 1 tablespoon of the butter in a large skillet until lightly browned, about 2 minutes. Stir in the cream, ⅛ teaspoon salt, pinch pepper and lemon juice. Cook mixture, stirring constantly, until it is reduced and coats the spoon heavily.
3. Sprinkle the fish with the remaining salt and pepper. Dredge lightly in flour, shaking off the excess.
4. Heat remaining butter in a large skillet. Sauté fish 2 to 3 minutes on each side, turning carefully with a large spatula. Transfer fish to a warm serving platter.
5. Reheat cucumber sauce. Spoon sauce over fish; garnish with parsley.

BUTTERNUT SQUASH
Makes 2 servings

1 small butternut squash (about 1 pound)	Salt and freshly ground black pepper to taste
2 tablespoons butter	⅛ teaspoon nutmeg

Halve squash and remove seeds. Peel and cut into chunks. Cook in boiling salted water to cover until tender, about 20 minutes. Drain and mash. Add remaining ingredients and beat until mixed and smooth.

BEAN SPROUT SALAD
Makes 2 servings

⅓ cup red wine vinegar
2 tablespoons dry sherry
1 tablespoon sugar
3 tablespoons soy sauce
1 teaspoon salt

1½ teaspoons Dijon-style mustard
¼ cup oil
1 pound fresh bean sprouts
Lettuce leaves

1. Combine the vinegar, sherry, sugar, soy sauce, salt and mustard in a small bowl. Gradually beat in the oil.
2. Place bean sprouts in a medium-size bowl and pour over the dressing. Toss to coat and serve on lettuce leaves.

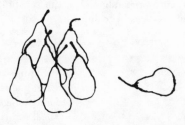

PEAR PANCAKE
Bake at 350° for 30 minutes
Makes 2 servings

1½ cups peeled pear slices (about 2 pears)
⅛ teaspoon cinnamon
2 tablespoons sugar
1 cup milk

3 eggs
½ cup flour
1 tablespoon sugar
1 teaspoon vanilla

1. Place the pear slices in a buttered 10-inch pie plate. Sprinkle with the 2 tablespoons sugar and cinnamon.
2. Put all the remaining ingredients in an electric blender and whirl until smooth. Pour over the pears and bake in a moderate oven (350°) for about 30 minutes or until puffed and brown. Serve warm with heavy cream or ice cream, if you wish.

MENU
Serves 2
* Inexpensive

BETTER AND CHEAPER THAN
THE COLONEL'S

Fried Chicken
Mashed Potatoes • Creamed Spinach
Sliced Onion and Orange Salad
Broiled Grapefruit

TOTAL TIME

About 10 minutes ahead plus 40 minutes before serving

Fried chicken for two is a breeze compared with doing it for a family picnic and
the recipe below has the added advantage of a tangy marinade plus the fact that it
is better to bread the pieces early in the day and let it set before frying. Cuts
down on the last minute preparation. You can substitute chicken breasts for the
legs and the cooking time would be less but the cost would rise.

MARKET LIST

2 chicken drumsticks	3 medium-size potatoes
2 chicken thighs	1 large grapefruit
2 eggs	1 large orange
½ cup half-and-half	½ small red onion
¼ cup sour cream	½ cup dry white wine
1 tablespoon chives	Packaged bread crumbs
1 pound loose spinach or 1 10-ounce	Light brown sugar
bag	Bottled dressing

WORK PLAN

1. Night before or early on day marinate chicken.
2. Early in day or 1 hour or longer before cooking, drain chicken and
   bread. Refrigerate.
3. Start chicken cooking. Put potatoes on to cook. Hard cook 1 egg.
4. Prepare salad; refrigerate.
5. Prepare grapefruit and set aside.
6. Fix spinach. Mash potatoes. Make sauce for chicken.
7. Broil grapefruit just before serving.

FRIED CHICKEN
Makes 2 servings

½ cup dry white wine
1 clove garlic, crushed
¼ teaspoon thyme
2 chicken drumsticks
2 chicken thighs
Flour
1 egg, lightly beaten

½ cup dry bread crumbs
½ teaspoon salt
¼ teaspoon pepper
½ teaspoon paprika
2 tablespoons oil
1 tablespoon oil

1. In a small bowl combine the wine, garlic and thyme. Add the chicken parts. Cover and marinate in the refrigerator overnight.
2. Early in the day remove chicken pieces, pat dry, remove garlic and reserve marinade. Dip chicken pieces in flour, then in egg and then in the bread crumbs mixed with the salt, pepper and paprika. Set on a plate, cover and refrigerate.
3. Heat the oil and butter in a small skillet. Add chicken pieces so that they do not touch and brown on all sides slowly. Cover and cook until done, about 10 minutes longer. Remove chicken to platter and pour off all but 1 tablespoon fat. Add marinade and cook, stirring to remove browned-on bits. Cook until reduced to about ¼ cup; pour over chicken.

MASHED POTATOES
Makes 2 servings

3 medium-size potatoes
Boiling salted water
1 tablespoon butter or margarine
¼ teaspoon salt

¼ cup sour cream
1 tablespoon chopped chives
⅛ teaspoon pepper

1. Skin potatoes and cut into chunks. Place in a small saucepan with boiling salted water to cover. Partially cover and simmer until tender, about 15 minutes. Drain.
2. Mash with a potato masher or electric beater. Beat in remaining ingredients until smooth.

CREAMED SPINACH
Makes 2 servings

1 pound loose spinach or 1 10-ounce bag spinach	Pinch salt
	Pinch pepper
1 tablespoon butter or margarine	Pinch nutmeg
1 tablespoon flour	Pinch paprika
½ cup half-and-half	1 hard-cooked egg, chopped

1. Wash and trim spinach and place in a large saucepan with just the water clinging to it. Cover tightly and cook until wilted, about 5 minutes. Drain and chop.
2. Meanwhile melt the butter in a small saucepan and stir in the flour. Gradually stir in the half-and-half. Bring to boiling, stirring and cook 1 minute. Add salt, pepper, nutmeg and paprika.
3. Stir spinach into sauce and season to taste with more salt, pepper and nutmeg, if you wish. Sprinkle with egg.

SLICED ONION AND ORANGE SALAD
Makes 2 servings

1 large navel orange, peeled and thinly sliced	¼ teaspoon salt
	⅛ teaspoon pepper
½ red onion, thinly sliced	Bottled dressing

Combine the orange, onion, salt, pepper and enough dressing to moisten in a small bowl. Toss and refrigerate.

BROILED GRAPEFRUIT
Makes 2 servings

1 large grapefruit	3 tablespoons light brown sugar

Halve the grapefruit, loosen the segments and remove pith, if you wish. Sprinkle halves with brown sugar and broil until sugar melts and bubbles. Do not allow to burn.

MENU
Serves 2

STEAK DINNER FOR TWO

White Beans and Tuna Appetizer
Broiled Flank Steak with Tomato Halves
Spinach and Bacon Salad
Individual Ice Cream Bombes

TOTAL TIME
10 minutes ahead plus 25 minutes before serving

In general, casseroles are not for twosomes. They take time to put together and smaller quantities do not cook well and waste energy (unless you are using a toaster oven). Grilled meats and fish are faster. Flank steak happens to be one of the few that has no waste and costs less than fancier cuts. Marinate it overnight to make it tender.

MARKET LIST

1 small, well-trimmed flank steak
  (about 1¼ pounds)
2 tablespoons real bacon bits or 2
  strips bacon
  Parmesan cheese
  Lemon
  Parsley
1 large tomato
½ pound loose spinach or half a 10-
  ounce bag
2 ounces mushrooms

2 green onions
½ can (1 pound, 4 ounces) cannelini
  beans
1 can (3½ ounces) tuna
  Red wine
1 slice soft bread
  Bottled Italian dressing
6 to 8 lady fingers
  Dark rum
½ pint butter pecan or rum ice cream
  Chocolate syrup

WORK PLAN

1. Night before or early in the day marinate the flank steak. Cover and re-frigerate.
2. 25 minutes before serving make the desserts; freeze. Wash the spinach; drain and refrigerate.
3. Prepare appetizer plates; refrigerate.
4. Fix tomato halves and broil with flank steak.

WHITE BEANS AND TUNA APPETIZER
Makes 2 servings

½ can (1 pound, 4 ounces) cannelini white beans, drained and rinsed (see note)

2 green onions, finely chopped

1 small can (3½ ounces) chunk white tuna

Lemon

Salt and pepper to taste

1 tablespoon chopped parsley

Combine beans and green onions and arrange on small plates. Divide tuna between plates and season with lemon, salt, pepper, parsley.

Note: Use leftover beans in soup or casserole.

BROILED FLANK STEAK WITH TOMATO HALVES
Makes 2 servings

¼ cup red wine

½ bay leaf, crumbled

½ teaspoon salt

¼ teaspoon pepper

¼ cup oil

1 tablespoon soy sauce

1 clove garlic, crushed

1 small flank steak, well-trimmed (about 1¼ pounds)

1 tablespoon butter

¼ cup soft bread crumbs

1 tablespoon grated Parmesan cheese

¼ teaspoon oregano

Salt and pepper to taste

1 large tomato

1. Combine the wine, bay leaf, salt, pepper, oil, soy and garlic in a shallow glass or ceramic dish. Coat the flank steak with the mixture on both sides. Cover and let marinate 2 hours or overnight.
2. Drain and broil or grill three minutes to the side for rare, 5 minutes for medium-rare. Cut into the thickest part to test.
3. Melt the butter, add bread crumbs, cheese, oregano, salt and pepper and cook, stirring, 3 minutes. Halve the tomato. Top the halves with crumb mixture and broil or grill until hot and bubbly.

SPINACH AND BACON SALAD
Makes 2 servings

½ pound loose spinach or ½ a 10-
ounce bag
2 ounces mushrooms, sliced
2 tablespoons real bacon bits or 2
strips bacon, cooked, drained and
crumbled

Freshly ground black pepper
Bottled Italian-style dressing

Combine spinach, mushrooms and bacon bits in a bowl. Season with pepper and toss with dressing just before serving.

INDIVIDUAL ICE CREAM BOMBES
Makes 2 servings

6 to 8 lady fingers
2 tablespoons dark rum

½ pint butter pecan or rum ice cream
Chocolate syrup

Sprinkle the lady fingers with rum. Cut in half crosswise and use to line two custard cups using extra pieces to fill in bottom. Soften ice cream slightly and spoon into lined custard cups. Freeze. Unmold and serve with chocolate syrup.

MENU
Serves 2
* *Inexpensive*

FROM THE DEEP BLUE SEA

Baked Fish Steaks
Sautéed Cherry Tomatoes • Broccoli
Lettuce Wedges with Blue Cheese Dressing
Chocolate Cream Dessert

TOTAL TIME
About 45 minutes if using frozen fish, 35 minutes if using fresh or thawed frozen

Two colorful vegetables counteract the pale look of the fish and make an appetizing as well as nutritious blue plate special for two people in a hurry to move along to leisure time activities.

MARKET LIST

2 fish steaks (halibut, bass or cod),
  about 6 ounces each or 1 package (12
  ounces) frozen fish
1 egg
½ cup heavy cream
½ pint cherry tomatoes
  Green onion or parsley
  Lemon
½ bunch broccoli or 1 package (10
  ounces) frozen broccoli

½ small head iceberg lettuce
⅓ cup dry white wine
2 squares (2 ounces) unsweetened
  chocolate
2 tablespoons dark rum
2 tablespoons coffee liqueur
  Bottled Blue Cheese Dressing

WORK PLAN

1. Preheat the oven to 375°. Prepare the chocolate dessert and chill.
2. Prepare fish and bake. Fix the cherry tomatoes.
3. Cook the broccoli until crisp-tender in a small amount boiling salted water or, if frozen, according to package directions. Leftover broccoli will make a quick soup in the blender or go into a salad bowl.
4. Cut and serve lettuce.

BAKED FISH STEAKS
Bake at 375° for 15 minutes for fresh fish; 30 minutes for frozen fish
Makes 2 servings

---

2 cod, halibut or bass steaks (6 ounces
  each) or 1 package (12 ounces)
  frozen fish
  Butter
½ teaspoon salt

¼ teaspoon pepper
1 tablespoon lemon juice
¼ teaspoon oregano
⅓ cup dry white wine

Place steaks in a buttered shallow baking dish. Dot with butter, sprinkle with salt, pepper, lemon juice and oregano. Pour wine into bottom of dish. Bake in a preheated oven (375°) for 15 minutes if using fresh or thawed frozen fish and 30 minutes if starting with frozen fish or until fish flakes with a fork.

SAUTÉED CHERRY TOMATOES
Makes 2 servings

½ pint cherry tomatoes
1 tablespoon butter
¼ teaspoon salt

⅛ teaspoon pepper
1 tablespoon chopped chives, green
  onions or parsley

Dip tomatoes briefly in boiling water and then into ice water. Skin. Heat the butter in a small skillet. Toss the tomatoes in the butter until warmed through. Sprinkle with the salt, pepper, chives or green onions or parsley.

CHOCOLATE CREAM DESSERT
Makes 2 servings

2 squares (2 ounces) unsweetened chocolate
1 tablespoon water
1 large egg, separated

2 tablespoons dark rum
2 tablespoons coffee liqueur
½ cup heavy cream, whipped

In the top of a double boiler melt the chocolate with the water, stirring constantly. Stir in the egg yolk, rum and liqueur. Remove from the heat. Beat the egg white until stiff but not dry. Fold the cream and then beaten egg white into chocolate mixture. Spoon into dessert dishes. Chill.

MENU
Serves 2
* Inexpensive

AFTER WORK QUICKIE

Quick Meatballs and Spaghetti
Herbed Mushroom Salad • Crusty Bread
Apple Squares with Whipped Cream

TOTAL TIME
About 40 minutes

A few extra moments putting the apple square ingredients together in a saucepan are well spent as you will agree when your dinner companion praises your baking skill and the moist, spicy dessert you turned out so effortlessly. Tuck the extra ones away in the freezer for a surprise later.

MARKET LIST

½ pound ground chuck
2 eggs
2 tablespoons milk
¼ cup heavy cream (optional)
1 small apple
¼ pound mushrooms

Lettuce
Lemon
1 jar (about 15 ounces) spaghetti sauce
½ cup chopped walnuts
Loaf Italian bread
1 slice bread

WORK PLAN

1. Preheat the oven to 350°.
2. Prepare and bake the apple squares.
3. Set mushrooms marinating for salad. Make the meatballs.
4. Cook the spaghetti. Slice and butter bread; wrap in foil if heating in oven for last 15 minutes of apple squares' baking. Serve salad.
5. Serve apple squares warm with whipped cream, if you wish.

QUICK MEATBALLS AND SPAGHETTI
Makes 2 servings

½ pound ground chuck
1 egg, lightly beaten
½ cup soft bread crumbs (about 1 slice)
2 tablespoons milk
1 tablespoon grated onion
¼ teaspoon salt
⅛ teaspoon pepper

¼ teaspoon oregano
1 tablespoon butter
1 tablespoon oil
1 jar (about 15 ounces) spaghetti sauce
½ pound spaghetti, cooked al dente and drained

1. In a medium-size bowl combine the chuck, egg, bread crumbs, milk, onion, salt, pepper and oregano. Mix lightly. Shape into 8 to 10 meat balls.
2. Heat the butter and oil in a skillet and brown the meatballs on all sides. Remove meatballs to a bowl with a slotted spoon.
3. Discard any fat remaining in the skillet, add spaghetti sauce and bring to boiling. Return meatballs and simmer 5 minutes. Serve over spaghetti.

HERBED MUSHROOM SALAD
Makes 2 servings

¼ pound mushrooms, sliced
3 tablespoons salad oil
1 tablespoon lemon juice
¼ teaspoon salt
¼ teaspoon marjoram

¼ teaspoon basil
½ teaspoon Worcestershire sauce
1 teaspoon soy sauce
Lettuce

Place the mushrooms in a small bowl. Combine the oil, lemon juice, salt, marjoram, basil, Worcestershire and soy and shake or beat to mix. Pour over mushrooms and let marinate 15 minutes. Arrange shredded lettuce in 2 salad bowls and top with mushrooms.

APPLE SQUARES
Bake at 350° for 30 minutes
Makes 16 squares
Turn these into blueberry squares by substituting fresh or frozen berries for apple.

1 cup sifted all-purpose flour	½ cup granulated sugar
1 teaspoon baking powder	1 egg
¼ teaspoon salt	1 teaspoon vanilla
¼ teaspoon ground cinnamon	½ cup chopped pared cooking apple
¼ cup (½ stick) butter or margarine	½ cup finely chopped walnuts
½ cup firmly packed light brown sugar	Cinnamon Sugar (recipe follows)

1. Sift flour, baking powder, salt and cinnamon onto wax paper.
2. Melt butter in a medium-size saucepan over moderate heat. Remove from heat. Beat in sugars, egg and vanilla with a wooden spoon until smooth.
3. Stir in flour mixture, apple and walnuts until thoroughly combined. Spread into a greased 8-by-8-by-2-inch pan. Sprinkle with 1 tablespoon of the cinnamon-sugar mixture.
4. Bake in a moderate oven (350°) for 30 minutes, or until top springs back when lightly pressed with fingertip. Cool completely in pan on wire rack. Cut into squares.

Cinnamon Sugar

½ cup granulated sugar	1½ teaspoons ground cinnamon

Combine sugar and cinnamon in a small jar with a screw-top lid. Cover and shake thoroughly. Store remainder for future use (French toast, pancakes, fruit-topped desserts).

MENU
Serves 4
* Inexpensive

WITH CREOLE ACCENTS

Creole-style Ham and Rice
Collard or Turnip Greens
Fresh Apple Salad
Strawberry Melba

TOTAL TIME
About 45 minutes

If you've ever been to New Orleans or in Louisiana Cajun country I'm sure that you have pleasant memories of many culinary delights. This meal is not meant to reproduce any of those dishes accurately but rather to give you a whiff of the Creole kitchen in less than 45 minutes.

MARKET LIST

6 slices cooked ham
2 ounces salt pork
¼ cup crumbled blue cheese
1 medium-size green pepper
1 lemon
1 large or 2 small Bibb or Boston lettuce
3 stalks celery
3 medium-size eating apples
1 quart strawberries or 1 package (1 pound) frozen unsweetened strawberries

1½ cups regular long-grain rice
1 can (1 pound) peeled whole tomatoes
1 can (13¾ ounces) chicken broth
1 package (10 ounces) frozen collard, mustard or turnip greens
½ cup broken walnuts
¼ cup raisins
1 package (10 ounces) frozen raspberries
1 pint vanilla ice cream

WORK PLAN

1. Hull and wash strawberries or thaw frozen strawberries.
2. Make the dressing for the salad; chill. Prepare remaining salad ingredients; chill.
3. Dice the salt pork finely and cook along with the greens according to package directions cooking 10 minutes longer than suggested for Southern style.
4. Prepare the Creole-style Ham and Rice. While it is cooking puree the partially thawed raspberries in an electric blender.

5. Pour dressing over salad. Drain greens.
6. To serve dessert, spoon vanilla ice cream into four dessert dishes, top with strawberries and pour pureed raspberries over.

CREOLE-STYLE HAM AND RICE
Makes 4 servings
A quick and easy skillet meal of ham and rice flavored with tomatoes and green peppers.

2 tablespoons bacon drippings or vegetable oil
6 slices cooked ham (about 3 by 4 inches)
1 medium-size onion, chopped (½ cup)
1 medium-size green pepper, halved, seeded and cut into strips
1 clove garlic, minced

1½ cups regular long-grain rice
1 can (1 pound) peeled whole tomatoes
1 can (13¾ ounces) chicken broth
1 bay leaf
½ teaspoon salt
½ teaspoon leaf thyme, crumbled
4 drops liquid hot pepper seasoning

1. Heat drippings in a large skillet. Add ham; cook until lightly browned. Remove to plate. Add onion, green pepper, garlic and rice to drippings left in pan. Sauté, stirring often, until vegetables are just wilted.
2. Stir in tomatoes, with their liquid, broth, bay leaf, salt, thyme and hot pepper seasoning, breaking up tomatoes with spoon. Bring to boiling, lower heat and cover. Simmer 15 minutes. Uncover and arrange ham on top of rice. Cover and continue to cook until rice is tender and liquid is absorbed.

FRESH APPLE SALAD
Makes 4 servings

¼ cup olive or vegetable oil
2 tablespoons cider vinegar
2 tablespoons lemon juice
½ teaspoon sugar
¼ teaspoon salt
½ teaspoon Worcestershire sauce

¼ cup crumbled blue cheese
2 cups broken Boston or Bibb lettuce
1 cup sliced celery
½ cup broken walnuts
¼ cup raisins
3 medium-size eating apples

1. Combine oil, vinegar, lemon juice, sugar, salt, Worcestershire sauce and blue cheese in jar with tight-fitting cover. Shake well to blend; chill.
2. Place lettuce in large bowl with celery, walnuts and raisins. Cover and place in refrigerator to keep chilled until serving time.
3. Wash, quarter and core apples, cut into bite-size chunks (about 3 cups) and add to salad bowl.
4. Pour blue cheese dressing over salad. Toss lightly to mix.

MENU
Serves 4

PLEASANT FAMILY-STYLE EATING

Sausage and Apple Skillet
Carrot Cornbread • Green Bean and Mushroom Salad
Bavarian Cream with Raspberry Sauce

TOTAL TIME
About 15 minutes ahead, plus about 45 minutes before serving

A main dish that cooks in less than 30 minutes suggests that there is time to add something extra that can be baking, such as carrot cornbread. Because it calls for crushed ice for quick chilling, the Bavarian cream can be made at the last moment.

MARKET LIST

1 package (1 pound) pork sausage
   links
6 eggs
1 cup buttermilk
½ cup milk
1 cup heavy cream
1 cup dairy sour cream
2 large onions
2 medium-size carrots
1 bunch green onions

½ pound mushrooms
1 pound green beans
1 can (1 pound, 4 ounces)
   unsweetened apple slices
1 cup cornmeal
2 envelopes unflavored gelatin
1½ cups crushed ice
1 package (10 ounces) frozen
   raspberries

WORK PLAN

1. The night before or early on the day make the green bean and mushroom salad; chill.
2. 45 minutes before serving, preheat oven to 425°. Make carrot cornbread.
3. Make Bavarian Cream. Puree raspberries and chill.
4. Prepare Sausage and Apple Skillet.

SAUSAGE AND APPLE SKILLET
Makes 4 servings
Here's a simple and popular combination for a quick main dish.

---

1 package (1 pound) pork sausage links	1 can (1 pound, 4 ounces) unsweetened
2 large onions, sliced	apple slices, undrained

1. Place sausages in large skillet and cook over low heat until lightly browned, about 10 minutes or until no pink shows in center. Remove sausages to a plate. Pour off all but 2 tablespoons fat from skillet.
2. Add onion slices. Sauté until tender and light brown. Stir in apples and sausages. Cook, stirring often, over low heat for 5 minutes.

CARROT CORNBREAD
Bake at 425° for 20 minutes
Makes 12 squares

---

1 cup sifted all-purpose flour	¼ cup (½ stick) butter or margarine,
1 cup cornmeal	softened
¼ cup sugar	1 egg
3 teaspoons baking powder	1 cup buttermilk
1 teaspoon salt	2 medium-size carrots, shredded

1. Sift flour, cornmeal, sugar, baking powder and salt into a large mixing bowl. Cut in butter with a pastry blender until mixture forms little balls the size of peas.
2. Beat egg in small bowl until frothy. Stir in buttermilk and carrots. Pour mixture into dry ingredients and stir until well-mixed. Pour into a greased 9-by-9-by-2-inch pan.
3. Bake in a hot oven (425°) for 20 minutes, or until center springs back when lightly pressed with fingertip. Cool in pan on wire rack; cut into large squares.

Note: Leftover is delicious toasted.

GREEN BEAN AND MUSHROOM SALAD
Makes 4 servings
Serve as an appetizer or as an accompaniment to meats.

1 tablespoon wine vinegar
3 tablespoons olive or vegetable oil
½ cup minced green onions
1 teaspoon Dijon-style mustard
½ teaspoon salt

⅛ teaspoon freshly ground pepper
½ pound fresh mushrooms
1 pound green beans
1 cup dairy sour cream

1. Combine vinegar, oil, green onions, mustard, salt and pepper in a screw-top jar. Shake until well-blended.
2. Quarter or slice the mushrooms into a large bowl. Pour the dressing over. Toss lightly and let stand.
3. Trim beans and snap to 1-inch lengths. Cook in boiling salted water in a large saucepan 8 minutes or until barely tender. Drain and run under cold water to stop further cooking.
4. Combine beans and sour cream with marinated mushrooms and toss lightly. Refrigerate, but remove salad from refrigerator about 20 minutes before serving. Taste; add additional seasoning, if necessary. Garnish with cherry tomatoes, if you wish.

BAVARIAN CREAM WITH RASPBERRY SAUCE
Makes 4 servings

2 envelopes unflavored gelatin
2 tablespoons water
1 tablespoon vanilla
½ cup hot milk
½ cup sugar

3 egg yolks
1 cup heavy cream
1½ cups crushed ice
1 package (10 ounces) partially
thawed frozen raspberries

1. Place the gelatin, water, vanilla and hot milk in container of electric blender. Cover and whirl for 20 seconds; add sugar and yolks and whirl 10 seconds longer.
2. Add cream and ice. Blend 20 seconds stopping if necessary to push down the ice with a spatula. Pour into a 1-quart mold or serving bowl. Chill briefly.
3. Puree the raspberries in the electric blender and serve as a sauce with the cream. Unmold, if you wish.

MENU
Serves 4

A ONE-POT MAIN COURSE

Chicken and Yellow Rice, Cuban Style
Waldorf Salad with Peanuts
Ice Cream and Double-Chocolate Walnut Brownies

TOTAL TIME
About 1 hour

My original recipe for the fabulous Double-Chocolate Brownies made only one dozen in my 8-inch square pan but I have found that they disappear so fast that there were more requests than I could fill. They keep beautifully and it really doesn't take any longer to make a double quantity. Variations on the chicken and rice combination are favorites in many of the world's cuisines.

MARKET LIST

1 broiler-fryer (2 pounds)
1 pint vanilla or chocolate ice cream
3 eggs
2 sticks butter or margarine
1 small green pepper
 Parsley
2 tart apples
2 stalks celery
1 red-skinned apple
 Lemon
 Lettuce leaves

1 can (16 ounces) whole tomatoes
 Achiote (optional)
2 cups long-grain rice
2 envelopes instant chicken broth
1 package (10 ounces) frozen peas
⅓ cup roasted dry peanuts
 Mayonnaise
4 squares unsweetened chocolate
1½ cups coarsely chopped walnuts
1 package (6 ounces) semisweet
 chocolate pieces

WORK PLAN

1. Preheat the oven to 350°. Make the brownies and set to bake.
2. Prepare the chicken and rice dish and put it in the same oven with the brownies. Each will come out at a different time.
3. Fix the salad.

CHICKEN AND YELLOW RICE, CUBAN STYLE
Bake at 350° for 30 minutes
Makes 4 servings
*The Cubans who came to Florida in the early 19th century to start the
cigar industry brought with them this dish they call arroz con pollo.*

¼ cup flour
½ teaspoon salt
¼ teaspoon pepper
1 broiler-fryer (2 pounds), cut up
¼ cup vegetable oil
½ teaspoon achiote, optional (see
note)
1 medium-size onion, chopped (½
cup)
½ cup chopped green pepper
1 clove garlic, minced

1 cup uncooked long-grain rice
1 can (16 ounces) whole tomatoes
½ bay leaf
⅛ teaspoon liquid hot pepper
seasoning
1¼ cups water
1½ envelopes or teaspoons instant
chicken broth
1 package (10 ounces) frozen peas
Parsley sprigs

1. Combine flour, salt and pepper in a paper or plastic bag. Add chicken,
   shake to coat evenly. Heat half of the oil in a large heavy skillet. Add
   achiote, brown for 5 minutes and discard achiote. Add chicken and
   brown on all sides. Place in 3-quart baking dish.
2. Add remaining oil to skillet. Sauté onion, green pepper and garlic until
   soft. Add rice and cook, stirring frequently, for 5 minutes. Add tomatoes, bay leaf, hot pepper seasoning, water and chicken broth. Bring to
   boiling. Stir in peas, pour mixture over chicken in casserole and cover.
3. Bake in a moderate oven (350°) for 30 minutes or until rice is tender.
   Garnish with parsley sprigs.

Note: Achiote is found in Puerto Rican or Cuban sections of some supermarkets.

WALDORF SALAD WITH PEANUTS
Makes 4 servings

2 tart apples, cored and coarsely
chopped
2 stalks celery, chopped
⅓ cup roasted dry peanuts, chopped

⅓ cup mayonnaise
1 red-skinned apple, cored and sliced
Lemon juice
Lettuce leaves

Combine the chopped apple, celery, peanuts and mayonnaise. Mix well
and chill. Dip apple slices in lemon juice to prevent browning. Pile salad
into lettuce cups and garnish with apple slices.

DOUBLE-CHOCOLATE WALNUT BROWNIES

Bake at 350° for 35 minutes
Makes about 2 dozen
*The real fudgy kind with chocolate chips and walnuts pressed onto the top
for a baked-on crunchy topping.*

1 cup (2 sticks) butter or margarine
4 squares unsweetened chocolate
2 cups sugar
3 eggs
1 teaspoon vanilla

1 cup sifted all-purpose flour
1½ cups coarsely chopped walnuts
1 package (6 ounces) semisweet
    chocolate pieces

1. Melt butter and chocolate in a medium-size saucepan over moderate
   heat. Remove from heat.
2. Beat in sugar gradually with a wooden spoon until thoroughly combined. Add eggs, one at a time, beating well after each addition; stir in
   vanilla. Stir in flour until thoroughly combined. Stir in 1 cup of the
   walnuts. Spread into a greased 13-by-9-by-2-inch pan. Combine remaining ½ cup walnuts with chocolate pieces and sprinkle over top of
   cooky mixture, pressing down lightly.
3. Bake in a moderate oven (350°) for 35 minutes, or until top springs
   back when lightly pressed with fingertip. Cool completely in pan on
   wire rack. Cut into bars.

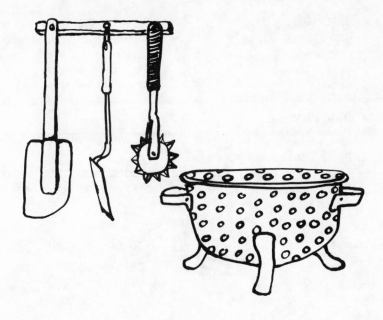

MENU
Serves 4
* *Inexpensive*

ENERGY-SAVING, NO-OVEN MEAL

Hungarian Beef and Noodles
Herbed Carrots • Avocado-Papaya Salad
No-Bake Cookies and Sherbet

TOTAL TIME
About 40 minutes

Here is a chopped meat dish with a difference . . . mustard, tomato paste and sour cream give it an elegant, continental flavor which goes so well with dill and parsley sprinkled carrots. Add an exotic touch with the papaya and avocado salad and no one will believe it took so little time to put together and the menu is not expensive either.

MARKET LIST

1 pound ground round
1 cup diary sour cream
1 pint sherbet
6 medium-size carrots
  Parsley
  Fresh dill weed
1 large firm ripe avocado
2 medium-size ripe papayas
  Chicory leaves
  Lemon

½ cup canned beef broth
1 tablespoon tomato paste
2 squares semisweet chocolate
½ cup ground almonds
¾ cup unsweetened coconut (available in health food stores)
½ cup toasted slivered almonds
  Honey
¼ cup wheat germ
1 pound fine noodles

WORK PLAN

1. Prepare the fruits for the salad and toss with dressing chill.
2. Fix the carrots and put on to cook.
3. Make the no-bake cookies. If the shaping starts to get tedious switch to fixing the noodles. Start the beef dish 15 minutes before serving time.
4. Finish cookies and serve salad over chicory.

HUNGARIAN BEEF AND NOODLES
Makes 4 servings

1 pound ground chuck
1 small onion, chopped
½ cup canned beef broth
2 teaspoons prepared mustard

1 tablespoon tomato paste
1 cup diary sour cream
1 pound fine noodles, cooked al
  dente, drained

1. Brown meat in a large skillet. Stir in onion; cook until soft.
2. Stir in broth, mustard and tomato paste. Cover and simmer 5 minutes to blend flavors.
3. Stir in sour cream very slowly, to prevent curdling, and heat, but do not allow to boil. Serve over hot, cooked noodles.

AVOCADO-PAPAYA SALAD
Makes 4 servings

1 large firm, ripe avocado
2 medium-size ripe papayas
¼ cup oil
1 tablespoon lemon juice

½ teaspoon salt
¼ teaspoon pepper
Chicory leaves

Pit, peel and dice avocado. Peel, seed and cube papayas and combine with avocado. Beat together the oil, lemon juice, salt and pepper and pour over the fruits. Toss and serve on chicory leaves.

HERBED CARROTS
Makes 4 servings

6 medium-size carrots, scraped and
  thinly sliced
3 tablespoons butter or margarine
⅓ cup water
½ teaspoon salt

¼ teaspoon freshly ground black
  pepper
2 tablespoons chopped parsley
2 tablespoons snipped fresh dill weed
2 teaspoons lemon juice

Place carrots, butter, water, salt and pepper in a medium-size saucepan. Cover tightly and cook over low heat until carrots are crisp-tender, about 15 minutes. Remove cover and evaporate extra liquid by boiling. Sprinkle with remaining ingredients.

NO-BAKE COOKIES
Makes about 15 cookies

¼ cup (½ stick) butter
2 squares (2 ounces) semisweet
  chocolate
½ teaspoon vanilla
½ cup finely ground almonds
½ cup toasted slivered almonds

¾ cup unsweetened coconut
  (available in health food stores)
1½ tablespoons honey
Pinch salt
¼ cup wheat germ

1. Melt the butter and chocolate over hot water. Stir in vanilla.
2. In a bowl combine the almonds, ½ cup coconut, honey, salt and wheat
   germ. Stir in butter mixture. Chill until firm enough to mold.
3. Form into tiny 1-inch balls, roll in remaining coconut and chill.

MENU
Serves 4
* Inexpensive

KIDS' SPECIAL

Italian Sausage Sauce with Spaghetti
Mixed Salad • Crusty Bread
Creamy Cottage Cheese Dessert

TOTAL TIME
About 15 minutes ahead, plus 45 minutes before serving

No time to fiddle at the last moment? Then this is the menu for you. Fix the
cheese dessert the evening before—it only takes 10 minutes and everything else
goes together in 45 minutes.

MARKET LIST

1 pound sweet Italian sausage or ½
pound each sweet and hot
1 container (1 pound) creamed cottage
cheese
1 package (3 ounces) cream cheese
½ cup heavy cream
1 green pepper
Lemon
Fresh fruit for garnish
1 small head Romaine or Boston
lettuce

½ cup sliced radishes
½ cup diced, peeled cucumber (¼
cucumber)
½ cup grated carrot (1 carrot)
1 pound spaghetti
1 jar (21 ounces) Italian cooking sauce
Loaf Italian bread
1 cup confectioners' sugar
Bottled Italian Salad Dressing

WORK PLAN

1. Night before prepare dessert through step 3. Chill.
2. 45 minutes before serving prepare the sausage sauce.
3. While sauce is cooking prepare salad ingredients. Chill.
4. Slice and butter bread. Wrap in aluminum foil and heat 10 minutes in a
   400° oven, if you wish.
5. Cook spaghetti. Arrange dessert and fruit.

ITALIAN SAUSAGE SAUCE WITH SPAGHETTI
Makes 4½ cups sauce

1 pound sweet Italian suasage or ½
pound each sweet and hot sausage
1 small onion, chopped
1 green pepper, seeded and chopped

1 jar (21 ounces) Italian cooking sauce
1 pound spaghetti, cooked al dente,
drained

1. Remove casing from sausage and cut into 1-inch pieces. Cook in large
   skillet until browned, about 15 minutes. Stir in onion and pepper; cook
   until soft.
2. Add sauce, bring to boiling, lower heat and cover. Simmer 25 minutes,
   stirring once or twice.
3. Serve over 1 pound hot cooked spaghetti. Sprinkle with Parmesan
   cheese, if you wish. Garlic bread and green salad complete the meal.

CREAMY COTTAGE CHEESE DESSERT
Makes 4 servings

1 container (1 pound) creamed cottage cheese	1½ tablespoons lemon juice
1 package (3 ounces) cream cheese, softened	½ teaspoon vanilla
1 cup confectioners' sugar	½ cup heavy cream
	Fresh fruit in season

1. Press cottage cheese through a sieve or food mill into a large bowl. Add cream cheese, confectioners' sugar, lemon juice and vanilla; beat with wire whisk or electric mixer until thoroughly blended.
2. Beat cream in a small bowl until soft peaks form; fold into cottage cheese mixture.
3. Line a heart-shaped basket or medium-size sieve about 6 inches wide with two layers of damp cheesecloth. Spoon mixture into basket. Level mixture by giving basket a firm tap over the bowl. Fold the overhanging ends of cloth over the mixture. Place basket over bowl to catch liquid that drains off. Refrigerate 24 hours.
4. When ready to serve, carefully peel back the cheesecloth and invert the cream cheese dessert gently over serving plate. Surround with strawberries, grapes, peaches or fruit of your choice.

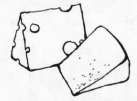

MENU
Serves 4

WHEN CALORIES DON'T COUNT

Pork Chops with Beer
Buttered Baked Potatoes
Lima Beans with Bacon
Grated Zucchini and Green Pepper Salad
Apple Crisp

TOTAL TIME
About one hour

On a cold wintry day the family will be looking for a stick-to-the ribs dinner even though you may not be able to spend all day cooking over a hot stove. You can have this good tasting meal on the table in less than an hour if you work fast.

MARKET LIST

4 rib pork chops, about 1 inch thick (2 pounds)
4 slices bacon
Parmesan cheese
6 apples, as tart as possible
1 cucumber
Parsley
Chopped chives
12 to 16 white new potatoes or 4 small Idaho potatoes
2 medium-size zucchini
2 medium-size green peppers

Lettuce leaves
Lemon
1 cup light beer
1 cup beef broth
Packaged bread crumbs
1 package (10 ounces) frozen lima beans
Bottled Italian salad dressing
1 small can (6 ounces) frozen orange juice concentrate
Crushed ice

WORK PLAN

1. Prepare the pork chops through step 5. Preheat oven to 400°. Fix the potatoes and start baking. Prepare the apple crisp and put in the oven with the potatoes.
2. Prepare the salad ingredients; chill.
3. When potatoes have been in the oven for 25 minutes sprinkle with bread crumbs and Parmesan cheese. Continue cooking.
4. Sauté the bacon. Add lima beans according to recipe.
5. Toss salad.

PORK CHOPS WITH BEER
Makes 4 servings

4 rib pork chops, about 1 inch thick (2 pounds)
3 cloves garlic, minced
½ teaspoon caraway seeds
½ teaspoon salt
¼ teaspoon pepper

2 tablespoons flour
2 tablespoons vegetable oil
1 cup light beer
1 tablespoon prepared mustard
1 cup canned beef broth or brown stock

1. Rub each pork chop on both sides with garlic, caraway seeds, salt and pepper. Dredge in flour.
2. Brown chops on both sides in oil in a large skillet. Remove; keep warm.
3. Drain off all fat in skillet, leaving brown bits in pan. Add beer and bring to boil over high heat, strring and scraping skillet to loosen brown bits. Simmer liquid until reduced to ½ cup.
4. Stir in mustard and beef broth; simmer to reduce to 1 cup.

5. Arrange browned pork chops in skillet. Cover and simmer for 45 minutes, turning once.
6. Serve with sauce in individual casseroles or serving platter. Garnish with chopped parsley, if you wish.

BUTTERED BAKED POTATOES
Bake at 400° for 35 to 40 minutes
Makes 4 servings
Small baking potatoes are good for size and shape, new potatoes for texture, so take your choice.

---

12 to 16 large new potatoes or 4 small
   Idaho potatoes
¼ cup (½ stick) butter, melted
1 teaspoon salt

¼ teaspoon pepper
2 tablespoons packaged bread crumbs
Freshly grated Parmesan cheese

1. Pare potatoes. With a sharp knife, score them in slices a little less than ¼-inch wide, cutting about ⅔ the way down, but not through to bottom. Drop each potato in cold water as it is scored.
2. Remove potatoes from water. Dry well on paper toweling. Pour melted butter into an oven-proof casserole that will hold the potatoes without cramming. Put potatoes in casserole and baste well with the butter; sprinkle with salt and pepper.
3. Bake in a hot oven (400°) for 25 minutes. Baste again with butter. Sprinkle with bread crumbs and a little Parmesan cheese and continue baking until potatoes are crisply roasted and tender, about 10 minutes.

LIMA BEANS WITH BACON
Makes 4 servings

---

4 slices bacon, chopped
1 package (10 ounces) frozen lima
   beans
½ cup water

¼ teaspoon salt
⅛ teaspoon pepper
⅛ teaspoon crushed rosemary
Chopped parsley

1. Sauté the bacon in a small saucepan until fat has been rendered.
2. Add frozen lima beans, water, salt, pepper and rosemary. Bring to boiling. Cover and cook 8 minutes or until beans are tender.
3. Remove cover and cook over high heat, shaking frequently until almost all the liquid has evaporated. Sprinkle with chopped parsley.

GRATED ZUCCHINI AND GREEN PEPPER SALAD
Makes 4 servings

2 medium-size zucchini, coarsely shredded
2 medium-size green peppers, cored and diced
1 medium-size cucumber, pared, halved, seeded and sliced

Bottled Italian salad dressing
Chopped chives
Chopped parsley
¼ teaspoon salt
⅛ teaspoon pepper
Lettuce leaves

1. Combine the shredded zucchini, green pepper and cucumber in a bowl. Add enough dressing to moisten.
2. Add chives, parsley, salt and pepper, toss and refrigerate. Serve in lettuce cups.

APPLE CRISP
Bake at 400° for 35 minutes
Makes 4 servings
This is the old-fashioned dessert that grandmother used to make.

6 tart apples, peeled, cored and sliced
1¼ cups light brown sugar
½ teaspoon cinnamon
¼ teaspoon nutmeg

2 teaspoons lemon juice
¾ cup flour
⅛ teaspoon salt
6 tablespoons butter or margarine

1. Place the apples, ½ of the sugar, cinnamon, nutmeg and lemon juice in a buttered 1½-quart casserole.
2. Place the flour and salt in a bowl and with the fingertips, or a pastry blender, work in the butter until mixture is crumbly.
3. Add the remaining sugar and mix well. Sprinkle over apples and bake in a hot oven (400°) for about 35 minutes or until browned and bubbly.

MENU
Serves 6

GOOD EATING, COUNTRY-STYLE

Chicken-fried Steak with Pan Gravy
Puree of Green Beans • Skillet Cornbread
Tossed Green Salad
Orange Baked Apples

TOTAL TIME
About 1 hour and 10 minutes

Chicken-fried Steak has nothing to do with chicken but it is the way that Texans like to fix their round steak. The gravy is great over the cornbread, too. The baked apples are different because they are stuffed with an orange-flavored almond mixture.

MARKET LIST

1¾ pounds round steak, sliced ½-inch thick or 6 cube steaks (about 1¾ pounds)
3 eggs
3⅓ cups milk (approximately)
½ cup heavy cream
1 cup dairy sour cream
2 pounds green beans
6 large baking apples
1 large head Romaine or about 8 cups
mixed salad greens
1 large navel orange
Bottled salad dressing
¼ cup ground almonds
2 to 3 tablespoons orange-flavored liqueur such as Grand Marnier
1 package (12 ounces) corn muffin mix
Cornmeal

WORK PLAN

1. Preheat the oven to 350°. Prepare apples and bake.
2. Fix salad greens; chill.
3. Prepare the chicken-fried steak.
4. Trim and cook the beans.
5. When apples are baked turn up oven heat to 400° and just prior to that make up the cornbread. Bake.
6. Finish off the puree of green beans.
7. Make the gravy for the fried steak. Toss salad.

CHICKEN-FRIED STEAK WITH PAN GRAVY
Makes 6 servings
Sometimes called "country-fried" but always called good eating.

1¾ pound round steak, sliced ½-inch thick or 6 cube steaks (about 1¾ pounds)	⅓ cup cornmeal
	1 teaspoon salt
	½ teaspoon pepper
2 eggs	Flour
2 tablespoons water	4 to 6 tablespoons vegetable oil
⅓ cup flour	

Pan Gravy

3 tablespoons pan drippings	½ teaspoon salt
2 tablespoons flour	⅛ teaspoon pepper
1½ cups milk (about)	

1. Pound steak to ¼-inch thick, or ask butcher to tenderize. Cut into 6 pieces.
2. Beat egg and water together in pie plate. Mix flour, cornmeal, salt and pepper in wax paper. Dip steaks first in plain flour, then in egg mixture. Dip in seasoned flour mixture to coat well.
3. Brown meat, 3 pieces at a time, in hot oil on both sides in a large heavy skillet. Return all meat to skillet, lower heat and cover. Cook 20 minutes or until tender. Remove steaks to heated platter.
4. To make the pan gravy: Pour off all but 3 tablespoons of the pan drippings; blend in flour. Stir in milk, salt and pepper. Continue cooking and stirring until gravy thickens and bubbles 1 minute. If gravy is too thick add more milk.

PUREE OF GREEN BEANS
Makes 6 servings
When you have more green beans than you know what to do with, try this delicious variation. It's different in both taste and texture.

2 pounds green beans	1 cup dairy sour cream
½ cup heavy cream	½ teaspoon salt
3 tablespoons butter	⅛ teaspoon freshly ground pepper
3 tablespoons flour	

1. Trim beans and snap to 1-inch lengths. Cook in boiling salted water in a large saucepan 10 minutes or until very tender. Drain.
2. Puree part at a time in container of electric blender, adding the heavy cream as needed. Transfer puree to saucepan.
3. Heat butter in a small skillet. Add flour and cook, stirring constantly, until mixture turns a hazelnut brown. Stir mixture into bean puree.
4. Add sour cream, salt and pepper. Reheat over low heat, stirring constantly.

Note: Puree can be kept hot in top of double boiler over hot water.

SKILLET CORNBREAD
Bake at 400° for 15 minutes
Makes 1 round loaf

1 package (12 ounces) corn muffin mix	1 egg
⅔ cup milk	⅓ to ⅔ cup additional milk

1. Preheat oven to 400°. Butter an 8-inch heavy skillet with ovenproof handle. Place in oven to heat.
2. Prepare corn muffin mix with the ⅔ cup milk and 1 egg, or follow package directions for ingredients. Add additional ⅓ to ⅔ cup milk (the smaller amount of milk will make a more or less usual cornbread while larger amount will create more pockets in bread). Mix just to moisten ingredients. Pour batter into hot skillet.
3. Bake in a hot oven (400°) for 15 minutes or until done. Cut into wedges to serve.

ORANGE BAKED APPLES
Bake at 350° for 50 minutes
Makes 6 servings
Something a little different inside baked apples—oranges and almonds.

6 large baking apples	¼ cup ground almonds
¾ cup water	1 large navel orange
¾ cup sugar	2 to 3 tablespoons Grand Marnier
4 tablespoons butter or margarine	

1. Wash apples and remove core from blossom end without cutting all the way through. Pare apples ⅓ from top. Save parings. Put apples in shallow baking dish that will hold apples snugly.
2. Place apple parings, water and ¼ cup of the sugar in small saucepan. Bring to boiling, lower heat and simmer 10 minutes. Strain.
3. Beat remaining ½ cup sugar, butter and almonds until well-blended. Grate enough rind from orange to make 1½ tablespoons; add to butter mixture. Fill apple centers, dividing mixture evenly.
4. Pare orange with small sharp knife (remove white part also). Dice orange coarsely; add to strained syrup. Pour syrup over apples.
5. Bake in a moderate oven (350°), basting often, for 50 minutes or until apples are tender. Arrange apples on serving dish or in individual serving dishes. Add Grand Marnier to syrup in baking dish; spoon over apples. Serve hot, warm or cold with cream to pour over.

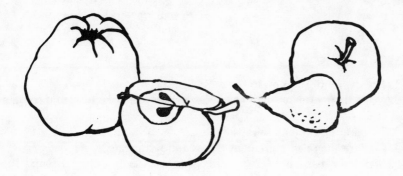

MENU
Serves 6
* Inexpensive

A MENU THAT WILL HOLD FOR LATECOMERS

Hot Sausage and Cheese Puffs
Greek Lentil Soup
Apple, Raisin and Nut Salad with Blue Cheese Dressing
Win Schuler's Caramel Ice Cream Pie

TOTAL TIME
1 hour

A hearty soup with nibbles, an interesting salad that tastes, as well as looks, good and a calorie-laden, luscious dessert make a good change of pace to spark jaded winter appetites.

MARKET LIST

¼ pound hot or sweet Italian sausage
¼ pound sharp Cheddar cheese
¼ cup light cream
1 egg
Romaine lettuce
Apples
1 pound lentils
¾ cup biscuit baking mix

1 can (1 pound, 12 ounces) Italian
plum tomatoes
Walnuts
Raisins
1 quart coffee ice cream
1 quart vanilla ice cream
½ cup firmly packed brown sugar
Bottled blue cheese dressing

WORK PLAN

1. Put the lentil soup on to cook. Preheat oven to 400°.
2. Make the meringue shell for the ice cream pie. Bake, cool and refrigerate.
3. Prepare the caramel sauce for the pie.
4. Prepare the salad ingredients. Toss and refrigerate.
5. Make and bake the hot sausage puffs and serve with the soup. Toss salad and dressing. Finish the pie just before serving and keep leftovers covered with transparent wrap in the freezer for another occasion.

HOT SAUSAGE AND CHEESE PUFFS
Bake at 400° for 12 to 15 minutes
Makes 6 servings

¼ pound hot or sweet Italian sausage
¼ pound sharp Cheddar cheese, shredded

¾ cup biscuit baking mix
3 to 4 tablespooons water

1. Remove sausage from casings. Cook in large skillet, breaking up the meat with a fork, until no longer pink, about 5 minutes. Drain off fat. Spoon sausage into large bowl and cool completely. Add cheese, biscuit mix and water. Mix with a fork just until blended.
2. Roll into 1-inch balls; place on large cooky sheets 2 inches apart.
3. Bake in a hot oven (400°) for 12 to 15 minutes or until puffed and browned. Remove from cooky sheets. Cool completely on wire racks.

To freeze ahead: Freeze in single layer on jelly-roll pans or cooky sheets. Place on plastic bag when frozen. **To reheat:** Arrange in single layer on large cooky sheet. Bake at 375° for 10 minutes.

GREEK LENTIL SOUP
Makes 6 servings
The Greeks have several famous soups, including "Faki," or Lentil Soup. In this particular recipe, we added tomato sauce for American tastes. Traditionally, the diner adds his own lemon juice or wine vinegar.

1 pound lentils
2 quarts cold water
1 medium-size onion, chopped (½ cup)
2 cloves garlic, crushed
2 teaspoons salt

¼ teaspoon pepper
¼ cup vegetable oil
1 can (1 pound, 12 ounces) Italian plum tomatoes
2 bay leaves

1. Wash lentils and drain well. Combine with water, onion, garlic, salt, pepper and oil in a large kettle. Bring to boiling. Add tomatoes and bay leaves.
2. Lower heat; cover and simmer for 45 minutes or until lentils are tender.
3. Serve with lemon juice or wine vinegar, if you wish.

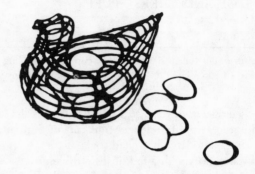

WIN SCHULER'S CARAMEL ICE CREAM PIE
Bake at 400° for 10 minutes
Makes 6 to 8 servings

---

1 egg white	1 quart coffee ice cream
¼ teaspoon salt	1 quart vanilla ice cream
¼ cup sugar	Caramel Sauce (recipe follows)
1½ cups chopped walnuts	

1. Beat egg white with salt in a small bowl until stiff but not dry. Beat in sugar, 1 tablespoon at a time, until meringue forms stiff peaks. Gently fold in walnuts.
2. Butter a 9-inch pie plate; spoon in meringue. With a wet spoon or spatula, spread mixture evenly over bottom and side, and slightly onto rim.
3. Bake in a hot oven (400°) for 10 minutes. Cool and refrigerate. To serve: Fill with scoops of coffee and vanilla ice cream. Spoon over Caramel Sauce. (Meringue shell can be filled with ice cream, covered with plastic wrap and stored in freezer until serving time.)

Caramel Sauce

Melt 2 tablespoons butter in a small saucepan. Add ½ cup firmly packed brown sugar; remove from heat. Very slowly stir in ¼ cup light cream. Return to heat for 1 minute, stirring constantly. Pour mixture into a small bowl; stir in 2 tablespoons chopped walnuts and ½ teaspoon vanilla. Spoon over pie, either warm or cold.

MENU
Serves 6

A FRUIT-FILLED MENU

Ham Steak with Glazed Apple Rings
Curried Orange Rice • Gingered Butternut Squash
Nutted Endive Salad
Tropical Pineapple Chiffon Dessert

TOTAL TIME
About 50 minutes

This is a menu that will appeal to all ages and please family or friends. Besides the apples with the ham and pineapple in the dessert there's orange juice in the curried rice for lots of flavor and sound nutrition.

MARKET LIST

1 fully cooked ham steak (about 1½ pounds), cut ½-inch thick
¾ cup heavy cream
4 eggs
1 apple
1 butternut squash (about 2 pounds)
4 Belgian endive
Lettuce leaves
Lemon
1 envelope unflavored gelatin
1 can (1 pound, 4 ounces) crushed pineapple

½ cup chopped walnuts
Maple syrup
2 tablespoons chopped crystallized ginger
Rice
1 cup orange juice
1 cup chicken broth
½ cup seedless raisins
¼ cup apple cider

WORK PLAN

1. Make the pineapple dessert and chill.
2. Start cooking the squash. Begin cooking rice.
3. Fix the salad and dressing; chill separately. Cook ham steak. Drain, beat and season squash.

HAM STEAK WITH GLAZED APPLE RINGS
Makes 6 servings

¼ cup (½ stick) butter or margarine
1 fully cooked ham steak (about 1½ pounds), cut ½-inch thick
1 teaspoon sugar

¼ teaspoon ground cinnamon
1 apple, cored and cut into 6 rings
¼ cup apple cider

---

1. Melt 2 tablespoons of butter in a large skillet. Brown ham steak 2 to 3 minutes on each side. Remove to serving platter; cover with foil and keep warm. Drain off fat.
2. Add remaining 2 tablespoons butter, sugar and cinnamon. When bubbly, add apple rings and cook 1 or 2 minutes on each side just to soften. Place on top of ham slice.
3. Add apple cider to skillet and bring to boiling, scraping up any browned bits in pan. Pour over ham and apples. Garnish platter with watercress, if you wish.

CURRIED ORANGE RICE
Makes 6 servings
The classic combination of fruits and curry makes rice into a fancy party dish.

¼ cup (½ stick) butter or margarine
1 medium-size onion, thinly sliced
2 teaspoons curry powder
1 cup uncooked rice
1 cup orange juice

1 cup chicken broth
1 teaspoon salt
½ cup seedless raisins
1 bay leaf

---

1. Melt butter in a heavy saucepan or flameproof casserole. Sauté onion until soft and golden, but not brown. Stir in curry and rice; cook 2 minutes longer, stirring constantly.
2. Add remaining ingredients; stir with fork. Bring to boiling. Lower heat, cover and simmer 15 to 20 minutes or until rice is tender and liquid has been absorbed. Remove bay leaf before serving.

GINGERED BUTTERNUT SQUASH
Makes 6 servings
Squash and spices go together. Here the squash is spiked with bits of crystallized ginger.

1 butternut squash (about 2 pounds)
2 tablespoons butter or margarine
1 tablespoon maple syrup
2 tablespoons finely chopped
  crystalized ginger

½ teaspoon salt
Pinch pepper
⅛ teaspoon ground nutmeg
¼ cup heavy cream

1. Split squash in half and scoop out seeds and membranes. Pare and cut into chunks. Cook in boiling salted water to cover 30 minutes or until tender. Drain.
2. Return saucepan to low heat a few minutes, shaking occasionally, to dry vegetables. Add butter, syrup, ginger, salt, pepper and nutmeg. Beat with a portable electric mixer until it is smooth. Gradually beat in heavy cream.
3. Spoon into heated serving dish; deep warm. Garnish with additional ginger, if you wish.

NUTTED ENDIVE SALAD
Makes 6 servings

⅓ cup oil
2 tablespoons lemon juice
1 teaspoon Dijon-style mustard
1 teaspoon salt
¼ teaspoon freshly ground black
  pepper

½ cup chopped walnuts
4 Belgian endive, coarsely chopped
  Lettuce leaves

Beat together the oil, lemon juice, mustard, salt and pepper. Add nuts. Arrange endive on lettuce leaves on 6 salad plates and pour the dressing over.

TROPICAL PINEAPPLE CHIFFON DESSERT
Makes 6 servings

1 envelope unflavored gelatin
⅓ cup cugar
4 eggs, separated
1 medium-size lemon

1 can (1 pound, 4 ounces) crushed
  pineapple
½ cup heavy cream, whipped

1. Mix gelatin and 3 tablespoons of the sugar in medium-size heavy saucepan. Add egg yolks and beat with wooden spoon until well-blended. Grate rind from lemon; measure and reserve 2 teaspoons. Squeeze lemon; measure 2 tablespoons juice. Drain juice from pineapple, ½ to ¾ cup, add to gelatin mixture along with lemon juice; stir in.
2. Cook gelatin mixture over low to medium heat, stirring constantly, 8 to 10 minutes or until gelatin is completely dissolved and mixture thickens slightly and coats a spoon. Cool slightly. Stir in lemon rind and pineapple. (For a smoother dessert, puree pineapple in container of electric blender until smooth before adding to gelatin mixture.) Place pan in a bowl of ice and water to speed setting. Chill, stirring often, until mixture starts to thicken.
3. While pineapple mixture chills, beat egg whites in medium-size bowl until foamy white; gradually beat in remaining sugar until meringue stands in soft peaks.
4. Fold whipped cream and meringue into gelatin mixture until no streaks of white remain. Spoon into chilled parfait or dessert dishes. Garnish with additional cream, pineapple and toasted coconut, if you wish.

MENU
Serves 6

WHEN THE SNOW IS BLOWING

Flank Steak with Dill
Parslied Potatoes • Green Beans in Lemon Sauce
Bean Sprout Salad
Lemon Ice Cream or Sherbet

TOTAL TIME
About 15 minutes ahead, plus about 40 minutes before serving

Flank steak is one of the best buys in the meat section because it is all edible and, if cut across the grain, eminently chewable and flavorful. It is also one of the most versatile cuts lending itself to stuffing, broiling, braising and, as here, pan-frying. With an exotic dilled yogurt sauce it only needs a couple of simply prepared vegetables to make an outstanding meal.

MARKET LIST

2 pounds trimmed flank steak or skirt
  steak
1 container (8 ounces) plain whole
  milk yogurt
2 eggs
2 cups light cream
½ cup heavy cream
  Fresh dill weed
3 lemons

Parsley
1½ pounds green beans
  Watercress
2 grapefruits
3 oranges
2 cups fresh bean sprouts
2 pounds red-skinned potatoes
1½ cups frozen chopped onion
1 cup chicken broth

WORK PLAN

1. Night before, or early on the day, prepare the lemon ice cream. Freeze.
2. 40 minutes before serving prepare salad ingredients and chill.
3. Scrub the potatoes and cook in their skins in boiling salted water.
4. Cook the beans and prepare the lemon sauce.
5. Prepare the flank steak with dill. Drain potatoes and toss with butter and chopped parsley.
6. Spoon dressing over salad.

FLANK STEAK WITH DILL
Makes 6 servings

2 pounds trimmed flank steak or skirt
  steak
¼ cup (½ stick) butter or margarine
1½ cups frozen chopped onions
1 large clove garlic, minced
1 tablespoon flour

1 teaspoon salt
¼ teaspoon pepper
1 container (8 ounces) whole milk
  yogurt
¼ cup chopped fresh dill

1. Cut flank steak in half lengthwise and slice each half into $1/16$-inch-thick slices against the grain.
2. Melt 2 tablespoons of the butter in a large skillet. Add ½ the meat and cook just until meat loses its red color. Remove with slotted spoon to bowl. Add remaining meat to juices in skillet and cook just until meat loses its red color. Remove with spoon to bowl.
3. Add remaining 2 tablespoons butter to skillet with onions and garlic. Cook over high heat until liquid evaporates from onions, about 1 minute.
4. Return meat to skillet. Sprinkle with flour, salt and pepper. Add yogurt and dill, stirring thoroughly. Cover and simmer 10 minutes or until tender. Serve over rice. Garnish with dill, if you wish.

GREEN BEANS IN LEMON SAUCE
Makes 6 servings

You can keep these lemon-sauced beans warm in the top of a double boiler over hot water.

2 egg yolks
½ cup heavy cream
¼ cup lemon juice
1½ tablespoons flour
½ teaspoon salt

⅛ teaspoon freshly ground pepper
1 cup chicken broth
1½ pounds green beans
2 tablespoons minced parsley

1. Combine egg yolks, cream and lemon juice in a small bowl. Beat with rotary beater until smooth.
2. Heat butter in a medium-size saucepan. Stir in the flour, salt and pepper. Cook 2 minutes over low heat, stirring constantly. Stir in broth. Bring mixture to boiling. Lower heat and simmer until thickened and bubbly, about 3 minutes. Stir part of the hot mixture into the egg yolk mixture and add to saucepan. Simmer 2 minutes longer, stirring constantly. Keep warm.
3. Trim beans and snap to 1-inch lengths or leave whole. Cook in boiling salted water in a large saucepan for 10 minutes or until tender. Drain. Transfer to serving dish.
4. Pour sauce over beans and toss lightly. Sprinkle with parsley.

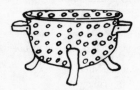

BEAN SPROUT SALAD
Makes 6 servings

½ cup oil
2 tablespoons lemon juice
¼ teaspoon dry mustard
    Salt and freshly ground black pepper
1 bunch watercress, washed and
    chilled

2 grapefruits, sectioned and coarsely
    chopped
3 oranges, sectioned
2 cups fresh bean sprouts

1. Combine the oil, lemon juice, mustard, salt and pepper. Chill.
2. Arrange watercress on six plates. Top with grapefruit and orange pieces and bean sprouts. Chill.
3. Just before serving spoon over the dressing.

LEMON ICE CREAM
Makes 6 servings

3 tablespoons lemon juice
2 teaspoons grated lemon rind
1 cup sugar
2 cups light cream

⅛ teaspoon salt
1 egg white (leftover from Green
Beans in Lemon Sauce recipe)

Combine juice, rind and sugar; mix well. Slowly stir in the cream and salt.
Pour into a freezer tray and freeze until solid round the edges and mushy
in the middle. Stir well with wooden spoon. Beat the egg white until stiff
but not dry and stir into lemon mixture. Refreeze.

MENU
Serves 6

A TASTE OF EASTERN EUROPE

Balkan Sausage Ragout
Carrot Salad in Lemon and Mustard Dressing
Pumpernickel Bread
Espresso Parfait Pie

TOTAL TIME
About 1 hour

Half of the time it takes to get this meal on the table will only require sitting back
and listening to the ragout simmering away unless you have something more excit-
ing to do like jogging around the block.

MARKET LIST

½ pound slab bacon
6 knockwurst
1 pint vanilla or coffee ice cream
3 eggs
1 cup dairy sour cream
1 lemon
2 green peppers
2 medium-size potatoes
3 tomatoes
2 medium-size zucchini
Parsley

4 green onions
Fresh dill weed, if available
8 carrots
12 to 14 chocolate chip cookies
2 envelopes unflavored gelatin
2 tablespoons instant espresso coffee
½ cup olive oil
1 can (4 ounces) finely sliced
pimientos
Caraway seeds
Pumpernickel bread

WORK PLAN

1. Prepare ragout through step 3.
2. Make the pie and chill quickly in the freezer, or make ahead if you wish.
3. Fix the carrot salad and chill.
4. 10 minutes before ragout is ready to be served, add the tomatoes and zucchini.

BALKAN SAUSAGE RAGOUT
Makes 6 servings

A sausage casserole can be made with simple frankfurters or a mixture of frankfurters and knockwurst. Here is a spicy version of the stew typical of all Balkan countries.

½ pound slab bacon, cut into 1-inch cubes

2 tablespoons olive oil

2 large onions, peeled and thinly sliced

2 large green peppers, seeded and thinly sliced

1 cup finely sliced pimientos (4-ounce can)

1½ teaspoons paprika

½ teaspoon crushed red pepper

1 teaspoon leaf marjoram, crumbled

½ teaspoon leaf oregano, crumbled

1 teaspoon caraway seeds

1 bay leaf

1½ teaspoons salt

½ teaspoon black pepper

6 knockwurst, sliced

2 medium-size potatoes, peeled and cubed

3 ripe tomatoes, cut into chunks

2 medium-size zucchini, cut into 1-inch cubes

2 tablespoons minced parsley

1. Cover bacon in water 5 minutes, drain and pat dry.
2. Cook bacon in oil until almost crisp. Remove and reserve.
3. Remove all but 2 tablespoons fat from skillet. Sauté onions and green peppers for 10 minutes or until very soft. Add pimientos, paprika, crushed pepper, marjoram, oregano, caraway, bay leaf, salt and pepper. Bring to boiling. Add knockwurst, potatoes and bacon. Cover skillet and simmer mixture 30 minutes.
4. Add tomatoes and zucchini. Simmer another 10 minutes or until vegetables are tender.
5. Taste; add additional seasoning, if you wish. Sprinkle with parsley and serve with sour cream, pumpernickel bread and beer.

CARROT SALAD IN LEMON AND MUSTARD DRESSING
Makes 6 servings
Tender young garden carrots make a delicious salad for a family picnic or as a side dish with cold meats.

¼ cup lemon juice
2 teaspoons Dijon-style mustard
2 teaspoons sugar
½ cup minced green onions
6 tablespoons olive or vegetable oil
½ teaspoon salt
⅛ teaspoon freshly ground pepper

2 tablespoons snipped fresh dill or 2 tablespoons dried dillweed
8 carrots, scraped and cut in julienne strips
3 cups water
Pinch of salt
1 teaspoon sugar

1. Combine lemon juice, mustard, the 2 teaspoons sugar, green onions, oil, the ½ teaspoon salt, pepper and dill in a screw-top jar. Shake until well-blended.
2. Combine carrots with water to cover in a large saucepan. Add remaining salt and sugar. Bring to boiling, lower heat and cover. Simmer 5 minutes or until tender. Don't overcook. Drain, then cool under cold running water. Drain again and transfer to a salad bowl.
3. Pour the dressing over and toss lightly to coat. Taste; add additional seasoning, if needed. Chill.

ESPRESSO PARFAIT PIE
Makes one 9-inch pie

12 to 14 chocolate chip cookies
2 tablespoons butter or margarine
1 pint vanilla or coffee ice cream
1 envelope plus 1 teaspoon unflavored gelatin

⅓ cup sugar
3 eggs, separated
2 tablespoons instant espresso coffee
¾ cup cold water
2 teaspoons grated lemon rind

1. Crush cookies in plastic bag with rolling pin (see note). You will have about 1¼ cups. Melt butter in medium-size heavy skillet, add cookie crumbs, and stir over medium heat 1 minute. Press crumb mixture against side and bottom of a 9-inch pie plate. Chill while preparing filling.
2. Remove ice cream from freezer to soften.
3. Mix gelatin and 3 tablespoons of the sugar in medium-size heavy saucepan. Beat in egg yolks until well-blended. Dissolve coffee in water and gradually stir into yolk mixture. Cook, stirring constantly, over low heat 8 to 10 minutes or until gelatin is completely dissolved and mixture is slightly thickened and coats a spoon. Remove from heat; stir in lemon rind.
4. Beat egg whites in medium-size bowl until foamy white. Gradually beat in remaining sugar until meringue stands in soft peaks.
5. Beat ice cream into hot gelatin mixture a few tablespoons at a time. (Ice cream should set gelatin just enough to fold in meringue.) Fold in meringue quickly until no streaks of white remain. Spoon into prepared pie crust. Chill 4 hours or until firm, or chill quickly in the freezer. Garnish with thin strips of lemon rind, if you wish.

Note: Cookies may be whirled in blender but the crumbs will be much finer and the crust different in texture.

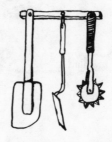

MENU
Serves 6
* Inexpensive

MEAT STRETCHER

Chili Meatball Stew
Corn Biscuits
Radish Salad
Quick Carrot Cake or Broiled Grapefruit

TOTAL TIME
About 1½ hours if making cake, about 1 hour without cake

1 pound of ground chuck serves six when it's stretched in this spicy stew. As it freezes well it is one of those dishes that you can make double or triple quantity and freeze the extras for quick dinners another day. If you go with the carrot cake, which is delicious, it can be made ahead. Leftovers are great for lunchboxes.

MARKET LIST

1 pound ground chuck
½ cup milk
1 cup heavy cream
4 eggs
1 green pepper
10 cups salad greens
2 bunches radishes
1 cup soft bread crumbs
2 envelopes instant onion soup (2 1-cup portions)

1 can (1 pound, 12 ounces) tomatoes
1 can (1 pound) red kidney beans
2½ cups biscuit mix
Yellow cornmeal
2 junior-size jars (7½ ounces each) baby food carrots
1 cup chopped walnuts
1 cup vegetable oil
Bottled garlic dressing
1 can (1¾ ounces) flat anchovy fillets

WORK PLAN

1. Preheat the oven to 325°.
2. Make the carrot cake; bake.
3. Prepare the stew.
4. Wash, dry and refrigerate salad greens. Trim, wash and slice radishes. Refrigerate.
5. As soon as carrot cake comes from the oven, turn up the oven heat to 400°.
6. Make the biscuits; bake.
7. Mix the greens and radishes in a salad bowl and toss with dressing.

CHILI MEATBALL STEW
Makes 6 servings
A perfect make-ahead—freezes well.

1 pound ground chuck
1 cup soft bread crumbs (2 slices)
2 envelopes instant onion soup (2 1-cup portions)
1 teaspoon parsley flakes
½ cup milk
2 tablespoons butter or margarine
3 medium-size onions, chopped (1½ cups)
1 clove garlic, minced
1 green pepper, seeded and diced (1 cup)
1½ to 2 tablespoons chili powder
1 can (1 pound, 12 ounces) tomatoes
1 teaspoon salt
¼ teaspoon cumin seeds, crushed
1 can (1 pound) red kidney beans, drained

1. Combine beef, bread crumbs, instant soup, parsley flakes and milk in medium-size bowl. Mix lightly but thoroughly with a fork. Shape mixture into 24 balls.
2. Heat butter or margarine in heavy Dutch oven. Add meatballs, about half at a time; sauté until evenly browned. Remove as they brown.
3. Stir onion and garlic into drippings. Sauté until soft, 5 minutes. Stir in pepper and chili and cook 1 minute. Add tomatoes, salt and cumin; bring to boiling. Return meatballs; cover. Simmer 30 minutes. Add beans and cook 5 to 10 minutes longer.

CORN BISCUITS
Bake at 400° for 12 minutes
Makes 12 to 15 biscuits

2½ cups biscuit mix
1 cup (½ pint) heavy cream
Yellow cornmeal

1. Put biscuit mix into a medium-size bowl.
2. Add all but 1 tablespoon heavy cream; mix to make a barely handleable dough. Handle it lightly, knead it half a dozen times, then roll it ½-inch thick on a lightly floured (use some of the biscuit mix) surface, and cut biscuits into 2-inch rounds.
3. Brush tops with the reserved 1 tablespoon cream and sprinkle generously with yellow cornmeal.
4. Bake at 400° for about 12 minutes or just until golden brown.

RADISH SALAD
Makes 6 servings

2 bunches radishes, sliced
10 cups salad greens (iceberg, Boston, Bibb, romaine, chicory), washed and dried

Bottled garlic dressing
1 can (1¾ ounces) flat anchovy fillets

Toss radishes and greens together and add dressing just before serving. Chop anchovies finely and sprinkle over salad.

QUICK CARROT CAKE
Bake at 325° for 1 hour
Makes 1 10-inch tube cake

3 cups sifted all-purpose flour
3 teaspoons baking powder
2 teaspoons baking soda
2½ teaspoons ground cinnamon
½ teaspoon salt
4 eggs

2 cups sugar
1 cup vegetable oil
2 junior-size jars (7½ ounces each) baby-food carrots
1 cup chopped walnuts

1. Sift flour, baking powder, baking soda, cinnamon and salt into a large bowl.
2. Beat eggs and sugar together in a medium-size bowl with an electric mixer until fluffy. Stir in oil and carrots; mix well. Pour into dry ingredients. Stir just until dry ingredients are moistened (do not overmix). Stir in nuts. Pour into a greased and floured 10-inch tube pan.
3. Bake in a slow oven (325°) for 1 hour, or until top springs back when lightly pressed with fingertip. Cool in pan on wire rack for 10 minutes. Loosen around edges with spatula, turn out of pan and cool completely.

MENU
Serves 8
* *Inexpensive*

EASY ON THE BUDGET

Braised Beef Rolls
Spaghettini • Maple-Butter Glazed Carrots
Tossed Green Salad with Bottled Dressing
Apricot-Almond Upside-Down Cake

TOTAL TIME
About 1¼ hours

There are only 3 ingredients in the main dish recipe . . . it goes together fast and while it's simmering there's time to make the upside-down cake or, if you prefer, the cake can be made ahead. This is hearty family fare which will become a favorite after you've served it once. If your family numbers four—make full quantity beef rolls, carrots and cake and freeze half for another time.

MARKET LIST

2 pounds beef round steak, cut about
    ½-inch thick or 2 pounds cubed
    steaks or beef for braciola
1 package (8 ounces) pork sausages
2 eggs
    Half-and-half
2 heads salad greens (iceberg,
    romaine, Boston)
2 pounds carrots

2 pounds spaghettini
1 jar (14 ounces) spaghetti sauce
    Bottled salad dressing
¼ cup maple syrup
½ cup light brown sugar
½ cup silvered blanched almonds
1 can (1 pound) apricot halves
1 cup cake flour

WORK PLAN

1. Prepare the beef rolls according to the recipe.
2. Preheat the oven to 350°.
3. Follow the recipe for the upside-down cake; bake.
4. Wash and dry and refrigerate salad greens. Place a very large kettle of hot salted water on to come to boiling. Add 1 tablespoon oil.
5. Prepare the carrots and keep warm.
6. 10 minutes before the beef rolls are cooked, add spaghettini to boiling salted water. Cook uncovered until barely tender, about 6 minutes. Drain and toss with 1 tablespoon oil. Serve spaghettini and carrots with beef rolls. Toss salad just before serving. Cake will still be warm to serve with cream, if you wish.

BRAISED BEEF ROLLS
Makes 8 servings
Sausage links make a savory filling for these beef roll-ups.

2 pounds beef round steak, cut about ½-inch thick or 2 pounds cubed steaks or beef for braciola

1 package (8 ounces) pork sausages
1 jar (14 ounces) spaghetti sauce

1. Trim all fat from steak; cut meat into 8 even-size pieces. Pound each slice of beef with a mallet or edge of saucer to ¼-inch thickness. (If using meat for braciola, omit this step.)
2. Brown sausages in a large skillet, following label directions. Drain on paper toweling. Leave drippings in skillet.
3. Roll each steak around a sausage; fasten with wooden picks.
4. Brown rolls, a few at a time, in the drippings. Drain on paper toweling. Pour off all fat from skillet.
5. Pour spaghetti sauce and ¾ cup water into skillet. Bring to boiling, scraping up browned bits, and lower heat. Add beef rolls; turn to coat with sauce. Cover and simmer 1 hour or until meat is tender. Remove wooden picks from the steak rolls before serving.

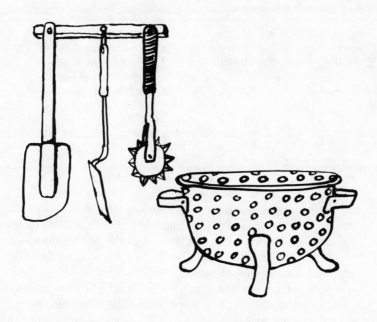

MAPLE-BUTTER GLAZED CARROTS
Makes 8 servings
The maple syrup gives carrots a great flavor.

1 cup water
1 teaspoon salt
2 pounds carrots, pared, cut in half
   crosswise
¼ cup maple syrup

¼ cup butter or margarine
1 teaspoon leaf marjoram, crumbled
1 teaspoon salt
¼ teaspoon pepper

1. Bring water and 1 teaspoon salt to boiling in a medium-size heavy saucepan. Add carrots, return to boiling and cover. Simmer 15 to 20 minutes or until carrots are just tender. Drain thoroughly.
2. Cook maple syrup, butter, marjoram, salt and pepper in a large skillet over low heat 2 or 3 minutes or until bubbly and caramel-like in consistency.
3. Add carrots. Toss gently to coat in the maple butter. Cook over high heat, tossing gently, until carrots are glazed and liquid is absorbed.

APRICOT-ALMOND UPSIDE-DOWN CAKE
Bake at 350° for 35 minutes
Makes 1 9-inch square cake

⅓ cup butter or margarine
½ cup finely packed light brown sugar
½ cup slivered blanched almonds
1 can (1 pound) apricot halves, drained
   (reserve juice)
2 eggs

⅔ cup sugar
1 teaspoon almond extract
1 cup sifted cake flour
½ teaspoon baking powder
¼ teaspoon salt

1. Melt butter in a small saucepan and stir in sugar. Pour mixture into a 9-by-9-by-2-inch baking pan. Arrange almonds and apricot halves over butter-sugar mixture.
2. Beat eggs in a medium-size bowl with electric mixer until thick and lemon colored, about 5 minutes. Gradually beat in sugar.
3. Add 6 tablespoons of the reserved apricot juice with the almond extract. Sift together cake flour, baking powder and salt. Add to egg mixture, beating until well-blended. Pour over the fruit in the saucepan.
4. Bake in a moderate oven (350°) for 35 minutes or until center springs back when lightly pressed with fingertip.
5. Invert pan on serving plate; leave in place for a few minutes to allow brown sugar mixture to run down over cake. Carefully lift off pan. Serve warm and include whipped cream or ice cream, if you wish. To double the recipe, divide between 2 pans.

CONVERSION TABLES
FOR WEIGHTS AND MEASURES

All conversions are approximate. They have been rounded off to the nearest useful measure. Weights and measures of specific ingredients may vary with altitude, humidity, and variations in method of preparation.

LIQUID MEASURE

American	British	Metric
1 teaspoon	1 teaspoon	5 milliliters
1 tablespoon = 3 teaspoons	1 dessertspoon	15 milliliters
1 cup = 16 tablespoons =		
8 fluid ounces	8¾ fluid ounces	250 milliliters = ¼ liter
1 quart = 4 cups	scant 1¾ pints	1 scant liter
1 gallon = 4 quarts	7 pints	3.7 liters

DRY MEASURE

American and British	Metric
1 ounce	28 grams
1 pound	450 grams
3½ ounces	100 grams
1 pound 1½ ounces	500 grams
2 pounds 3 ounces	1 kilogram = 1000 grams

OVEN TEMPERATURES

	Electricity °C	°F	British Gas Mark	French Setting
Very slow	110	225	¼	2
	120	250	½	3
Slow	140	275	1	3
	150	300	2	4
Moderate	160	325	3	4
	180	350	4	4
Moderately hot	190	375	5	5
	200	400	6	5
Hot	220	425	7	6
	230	450	8	6
Very hot	240	475	9	6

SELECTED MEASUREMENTS

	American	British	Metric
Baking powder	1 teaspoon	1 teaspoon	4 grams
Beans, dried	2 cups, scant	1 pound	450 grams
Bread crumbs	1 cup	2 ounces	60 grams
Butter	1 teaspoon	1 teaspoon	5 grams
	1 tablespoon	½ ounce	15 grams
	½ cup (1 stick)	4 ounces	115 grams
	1 cup (2 sticks)	8 ounces	225 grams
	2 cups (4 sticks)	1 pound	450 grams
Cheese, grated	1 cup	4 ounces	115 grams
Chocolate	1 square	1 ounce	30 grams

	American	British	Metric
Cocoa	1 cup	4 ounces	120 grams
Cornmeal	3 cups	1 pound	450 grams
Flour, all-purpose, unsifted	1 teaspoon	1 teaspoon	3 grams
	1 tablespoon	¼ ounce	9 grams
	1 cup	4 ounces	115 grams
	3⅔ cups	1 pound	450 grams
Lentils	2 cups	1 pound	450 grams
Macaroni, raw (1 cup raw = 2 cups cooked)	3 cups	1 pound	450 grams
Noodles (1 cup raw = 1½ cups cooked)			
Nuts, chopped	1 cup	4 ounces	115 grams
Oats, rolled (oatmeal)	1 cup, generous	4 ounces	115 grams
Onions, raw (sliced, chopped, or minced)	1 tablespoon	1 tablespoon	9 grams
	1 cup	4 ounces	115 grams
Peas, fresh	1 pound un-shelled = 1 cup shelled	1 pound, un-shelled	450 grams, unshelled
Rice (1 cup raw = 3–4 cups cooked)	1 cup	7 ounces	200 grams
Spinach, fresh, cooked	1¼ pounds raw = 1 cup cooked (squeezed dry, chopped)	1¼ pounds, raw	575 grams, raw
Sugar, regular granulated	1 teaspoon	1 teaspoon	5 grams
	1 tablespoon	½ ounce	15 grams
	1 cup	7 ounces	200 grams
Sugar, confectioners' (icing)	1 teaspoon	1 teaspoon	4 grams
	1 tablespoon	1 tablespoon	9 grams
	1 cup	4½ ounces	125 grams
Tomatoes, fresh	¾–1 pound, whole = 1 cup, peeled and seeded	¾–1 pound, whole	350–450 grams, whole
Vegetables, raw, chopped fine (such as carrots and celery)	1 cup	8 ounces	225 grams

INDEX